Inspire English International

Year 8 Teacher Guide

David Grant

Contents

Welcome to Inspire English International!

We hope that your students will find this book useful (and inspiring!) as they develop their skills and knowledge in written English. We believe this course will help all lower secondary students looking to make good progress in English.

The books have been written using a mix of real-world texts and purpose-written passages, designed to inspire discussion and help to maintain a focus on key curriculum objectives.

The programme explicitly supports learners following Pearson Edexcel's international curriculum (iLowerSecondary) **and** learners following the English National Curriculum. It provides specific preparation for International GCSE teaching in English Language and Literature, as well as for English Curriculum GCSEs in the same subjects.

Students may choose to sit the Year 9 examination in iLowerSecondary English, and details can be found on the Pearson Edexcel qualifications website. This provides an international benchmark for achievement and progress.

How Inspire English International supports learning

The course has four key principles:

- Explicitly curriculum driven
- Rigorous, challenging and supportive
- Structured preparation for later assessment (at GCSE or International GCSE)
- Focused, in-depth delivery of skills

Each unit is based around a theme and has an overarching outcome (either reading or writing) with a range of linked skills building recursive familiarity and development.

Each lesson of the course is clearly linked to curriculum objectives. Inspire English International follows Pearson's iLowerSecondary English curriculum, which meets all the requirements of the English National Curriculum (2013) but provides greater granularity and progression.

The course ensures students are not only given a structure to their learning, but also the chance to apply this learning to different contexts, preparing them fully to meet different challenges. Inspire English International supports the development of students 'learning to learn' through the growth of a range of 21st-century skills, such as critical thinking, creativity, collaboration and communication.

The use of the iLowerSecondary curriculum, and the design of the course, ensure that students are explicitly prepared to begin their next phase of education, whether they are taking Pearson Edexcel GCSEs or International GCSEs.

The use of a key focus throughout each unit, supported by secondary areas of focus, makes sure students can achieve mastery of key concepts and understand key ideas. This means that the foundations for future learning and success are secure.

Course Components

There are three core components to the course:

- Student Book
- Teacher Guide
- Workbook.

Student Book

- The Student Book provides a clear structure. Each unit is based around a theme and uses a range of engaging texts to help students focus on the mastery of key skills. These skills are set out at the start of each unit, along with a clear explanation of what students will be able to do by the end of that unit.
- Within each unit, the theme is broken down into sections designed to help students master those key skills in a clear learning progression.
- Activities and Boosts (covering skills, grammar, spelling and punctuation) all build towards students' learning.
- Two assessment sections per unit provide students with the tools and structure to enhance their assessment skills.
- A glossary at the end of the book contains the key terms identified across all years of the course, along with clear definitions.

Teacher Guide

- This Teacher Guide provides lesson-by-lesson planning, closely linked to the Student Book and Workbook.
- At the start of the book there is a comprehensive document mapping the iLowerSecondary curriculum to the English National Curriculum, which means you can be confident of all of the areas of curriculum coverage.
- A scheme of work outlines the coverage of each unit, including key skills, student outcomes, and the curriculum objectives covered in each section of the unit.
- The glossary from the Student Book is included at the end of the Teacher Guide for reference.

Workbook

- The Workbook gives students the chance to practise and embed the key skills introduced in the Student Book and through teaching.
- The Workbook helps deepen and broaden students' understanding of their learning, with clear links to the corresponding learning in the Student Book.
- Set extension activities within each section provide further practice of the key skills covered.
- Two Assessment sections per unit provide students with further opportunities to practise their assessment skills.

Pedagogy

Pedagogical structure and approach

Each unit of work in Inspire English International focuses students on the specific curriculum areas of either reading or writing. In the reading-focused units, in addition to responding to a range of extracts, students are frequently asked to write their own texts to deepen their understanding of the choices that writers make and the impact these can have on a reader. Similarly, in the writing-focused units, as well as crafting their own texts, students explore a range of extracts in depth in order to emulate the skills exemplified and so develop their own.

Each unit is also sharply focused on a specific text purpose: for example, Reading Information, Writing Description, Reading Narrative. The units are designed to support students in exploring and building the skills essential in either responding to, or achieving, that particular text purpose. Units are unified with an overarching theme, linking the reading extracts and writing tasks, and providing an accessible and familiar topic for students to work with, allowing them to concentrate their efforts more closely on developing skills than on familiarising themselves with, or generating, content.

Over the course of the three years' learning that Inspire English International is intended to support, each skill is visited and re-visited as appropriate, each visit building on the last. This recursive, skills-focused approach has been designed to foster and build a cumulative competence and confidence in the application of these essential skills throughout the broader English curriculum and, indeed, the whole school curriculum.

Pedagogical content

The text extract in each section of each unit has been written or selected to exemplify the skills on which that section focuses. Similarly, each activity in each section explicitly focuses on one specific aspect or skill found in, or prompted by, that text. An appropriate level of support is often provided in activities in order to facilitate and sharpen the skill focus: for example, sentence starts or sentence frames may be provided to support students in expressing their response to a text; relevant vocabulary may be provided to allow students to focus on crafting sentence structure, without being distracted by the need to select their own; likewise, appropriate information may be provided to support the skill of structuring an information text without students having to overcome the distraction of gathering that information beforehand.

The Skills Boosts that appear in each section have been designed to encourage students to explore and understand the mechanics of spelling, punctuation and grammar, rather than simply to provide rote practice. Embedded within the context of the broader skill focus, the intention is to make the Boosts both relevant and integral to the effective crafting of fluent and accurate responses, both in reading and writing.

At the end of each section, there is a supported, structured opportunity for students to demonstrate and further develop the skills they have built in the course of that section, and for teachers to evaluate their progress. The Teacher Guide frequently identifies opportunities for students to peer-assess their achievement in these final activities: an opportunity for readers to discuss and compare their personal response to a text, and for writers to discuss their work with readers.

At the end of each unit, an assessment provides a less supported, more formal opportunity for students to demonstrate their progress in reading and/or writing, and for teachers to assess that progress. Teachers can then make use of that assessment to identify opportunities, objectives and targets for the future learning and progression of individual students and the whole class.

About the Teacher Guide

Curriculum mapping from iLowerSecondary English to the National Curriculum

READING	
English National curriculum objective	**This matches the iLowerSecondary curriculum objective...**
reading a wide range of fiction and non-fiction, including in particular whole books, short stories, poems and plays with a wide coverage of genres, historical periods, forms and authors.	**R8.2D:** Make developed comparisons of writers' ideas and perspectives between two texts.
choosing and reading books independently for challenge, interest and enjoyment.	**R8.1F:** Choose age-appropriate texts, considering their genre, form and origin, and basing decisions on books already read.
re-reading books encountered earlier to increase familiarity with them and provide a basis for making comparisons.	**R8.1D:** Compare, contrast and/or combine key points of information within a text or in spoken language with a given focus.
learning new vocabulary, relating it explicitly to known vocabulary and understanding it with the help of context and dictionaries	**R8.1A (A):** Use a range of strategies to decode unfamiliar words. **R8.1A (B):** Read largely accurately and with understanding.
making inferences and referring to evidence in the text	**R8.1B:** Identify and retrieve a range of key information in a text or in spoken language. **R8.1E:** Make inferences from specific evidence found in a text or in spoken language, including specific vocabulary choices. **R8.2C:** Select relevant, focused evidence to support ideas.
knowing the purpose, audience for and context of the writing and drawing on this knowledge to support comprehension	**R8.1D:** Compare, contrast and/or combine key points of information within a text or in spoken language with a given focus. **R8.2A:** Explore a writer's or speaker's intention and viewpoint.
checking their understanding to make sure that what they have read makes sense.	**R8.1A (A):** Use a range of strategies to decode unfamiliar words. **R8.1A (B):** Read largely accurately and with understanding.
knowing how language, including figurative language, vocabulary choice, grammar, text structure and organisational features, presents meaning	**R8.1E:** Make inferences from specific evidence found in a text or in spoken language, including specific vocabulary choices. **R8.2B:** Express a critical response to a text through writing, discussion or presentation, by considering the text's features and their effects. **R8.3A:** Explore the impact of some of the writer's key structural or organisational choices. **R8.4A:** Explore the impact of some of a writer's or speaker's choices of grammatical features and sentence structure. **R8.4B:** Explore the impact of some of the writer's or speaker's significant vocabulary choices.
recognising a range of poetic conventions and understanding how these have been used	**R8.2B:** Express a critical response to a text through writing, discussion or presentation, by considering the text's features and their effects. **R8.3A:** Explore the impact of some of the writer's key structural or organisational choices.
studying setting, plot, and characterisation, and the effects of these	**R8.2B:** Express a critical response to a text through writing, discussion or presentation, by considering the text's features and their effects. **R8.3A:** Explore the impact of some of the writer's key structural or organisational choices.

The mapping at the start of the book demonstrates how the iLowerSecondary objectives relate to the English National Curriculum objectives.

Scheme of work

Year:	8
Unit:	1
Theme:	Heroes and Villains
Outcome:	Short story
Key skills:	Writing: Writing processes (W8.1); Writing: Whole text (W8.2); Writing: Language use (W8.3)
Lesser skills:	Reading: Text structure (R8.3); Reading: Language use (R8.4)
Minor skills:	Reading: Reading for meaning (R8.1); Reading: Responding to texts (R8.2)

By the end of the unit, students will be able to structure and craft a short story.
During the course of the unit, students will explore a range of narrative extracts linked by the theme of heroes and anti-heroes.

This unit focuses on engaging the reader in the characters, setting and action of a short narrative story.
Students will practise planning, structuring and crafting narrative writing.
Students will revise punctuation and sentence structure and develop language skills.

The scheme of work gives you an overview of each unit and the main focuses.

Section	Section summary	Curriculum reference	Boosts
1	Students read two extracts based on the same story and answer comprehension questions on each. They practise the skills of picking out key points, using active and passive voices, thinking about characters and comparing texts.	R8.1A/B/C/D, R2.A/B/D	R8.4A/W8.2B Active and passive voices
2	Students read an extract from a novel and answer comprehension questions. They practise the skills of inferring and responding to characters, revealing a villain, punctuating speech and building a villainous of their own.	R8.1B/E, R8.2A/B, R8.3A, R8.4B, W8.1A, W8.3G	W8.3I Speech punctuation
3	Students read an extract from a short story. They practise the skills of tracking key events, identifying elements of the story, using word classes, exploring vocabulary and writing an extract of their own.	R8.1B/E, R8.2A/B, R8.3A, R8.4B, W8.1A, W8.2C, W8.3G	W8.3J Word classes
4	Students read the opening of a short story. They practise the skills of reading between the lines, responding to the opening, choosing tense and person, choosing the first sentence and writing an opening.	R8.1B, R8.1E, R8.2A/B, R8.3A, W8.1A, W8.2C	W8.2B Choosing tense and person
5	Students complete an assessment by reading a fictional extract, then answering questions about what they have read and writing the opening to a story of their own.	R8.1B/D/E, R8.2B, R8.3A, R8.4B, W8.1A, W8.2C, W8.3G	–
6	Students read a summary of a short story. They practise the skills of using apostrophes, exploring ideas and intentions, and structuring and planning a story.	R8.1B, R8.2A, R8.3A, W8.1A, W8.2C	W8.3I Apostrophes
7	Students read synopses of three different stories. They practise the skills of identifying endings, responding to endings, using colons and semi-colons, exploring the writer's intention and writing an ending of their own.	R8.1B, R8.2A, R8.2B, R8.3A, W8.1A, W8.2C	W8.3I Colons and semi-colons
8	Students read an extract from a story and answer comprehension questions. They practise the skills of identifying and using different ways of telling stories, using identifier verbs and adverbs, and writing an extract from a story of their own.	R8.1B, R8.2A, R8.3A, R8.4B, W8.2C, W8.3A/G	W8.3G/W8.3J Identifier verbs and adverbs
9	Students read the opening of a short story. They practise the skills of exploring short sentences and longer sentences, building sentences, linking with adverbials and experimenting with structure.	R8.2A, R8.3A, R8.4A, W8.1A, W8.3B/C/D/E	W8.2D Linking with adverbials
10	Students practise the skills of identifying homophones, using irregular past tenses, proofreading, reviewing vocabulary, conjunctions and relationships, reviewing sentence structure and reviewing and proofreading writing.	W8.1B/C	W8.3H Homophones: W8.2D Conjunctions and relationships
11	Students complete an assessment by planning, writing, reviewing and revising a short story.	W8.1A/B, W8.2C, W8.3A/C/D/E/G/H/I	–

The teaching and learning progression is provided as an 'at-a-glance' overview for you here.

The main iLowerSecondary English curriculum objectives covered in each section are recorded here.

Any additional 'boosts' in the lessons are covered here.

About the Teacher Guide

The skills focus of a lesson can be found here.

Each individual lesson within a unit provides more detail to support your teaching.

Workbook and Student Book page references are clearly labelled.

The main and secondary objectives covered by a lesson are found here.

Support and Deepen activities help support differentiation and ensure content can be accessed at multiple levels.

The teaching itself is split into a clear and consistent structure and progression, with indicative timings – and clear notes where the teaching links to the Student Book.

This section summarises the extension, embedding and challenge opportunities in the Workbook that link to this lesson.

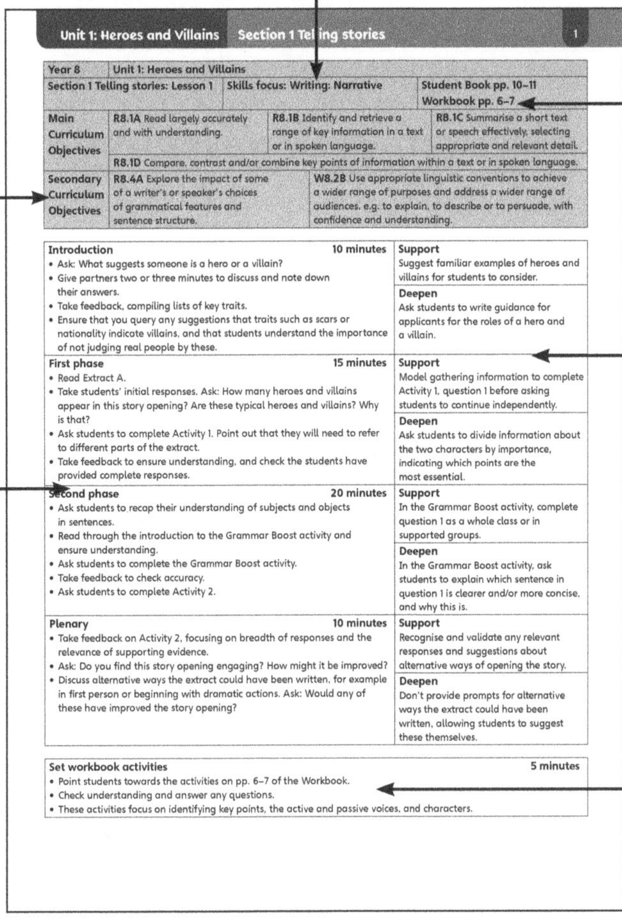
Unit 1: Heroes and Villains Section 1 Telling stories 1

Year 8	Unit 1: Heroes and Villains		
Section 1 Telling stories: Lesson 1	Skills focus: Writing: Narrative		Student Book pp. 10–11 Workbook pp. 6–7
Main Curriculum Objectives	**R8.1A** Read largely accurately and with understanding.	**R8.1B** Identify and retrieve a range of key information in a text or in spoken language.	**R8.1C** Summarise a short text or speech effectively, selecting appropriate and relevant detail.
	R8.1D Compare, contrast and/or combine key points of information within a text or in spoken language.		
Secondary Curriculum Objectives	**R8.4A** Explore the impact of some of a writer's or speaker's choices of grammatical features and sentence structure.	**W8.2B** Use appropriate linguistic conventions to achieve a wider range of purposes and address a wider range of audiences, e.g. to explain, to describe or to persuade, with confidence and understanding.	

Introduction **10 minutes** • Ask: What suggests someone is a hero or a villain? • Give partners two or three minutes to discuss and note down their answers. • Take feedback, compiling lists of key traits. • Ensure that you query any suggestions that traits such as scars or nationality indicate villains, and that students understand the importance of not judging real people by these.	**Support** Suggest familiar examples of heroes and villains for students to consider. **Deepen** Ask students to write guidance for applicants for the roles of a hero and a villain.
First phase **15 minutes** • Read Extract A. • Take students' initial responses. Ask: How many heroes and villains appear in this story opening? Are these typical heroes and villains? Why is that? • Ask students to complete Activity 1. Point out that they will need to refer to different parts of the extract. • Take feedback to ensure understanding, and check the students have provided complete responses.	**Support** Model gathering information to complete Activity 1, question 1 before asking students to continue independently. **Deepen** Ask students to divide information about the two characters by importance, indicating which points are the most essential.
Second phase **20 minutes** • Ask students to recap their understanding of subjects and objects in sentences. • Read through the introduction to the Grammar Boost activity and ensure understanding. • Ask students to complete the Grammar Boost activity. • Take feedback to check accuracy. • Ask students to complete Activity 2.	**Support** In the Grammar Boost activity, complete question 1 as a whole class or in supported groups. **Deepen** In the Grammar Boost activity, ask students to explain which sentence in question 1 is clearer and/or more concise, and why this is.
Plenary **10 minutes** • Take feedback on Activity 2, focusing on breadth of responses and the relevance of supporting evidence. • Ask: Do you find this story opening engaging? How might it be improved? • Discuss alternative ways the extract could have been written, for example in first person or beginning with dramatic actions. Ask: Would any of these have improved the story opening?	**Support** Recognise and validate any relevant responses and suggestions about alternative ways of opening the story. **Deepen** Don't provide prompts for alternative ways the extract could have been written, allowing students to suggest these themselves.

Set workbook activities **5 minutes**
- Point students towards the activities on pp. 6–7 of the Workbook.
- Check understanding and answer any questions.
- These activities focus on identifying key points, the active and passive voices, and characters.

The glossary at the end of the book contains the key terms identified across all years of the course, along with clear definitions.

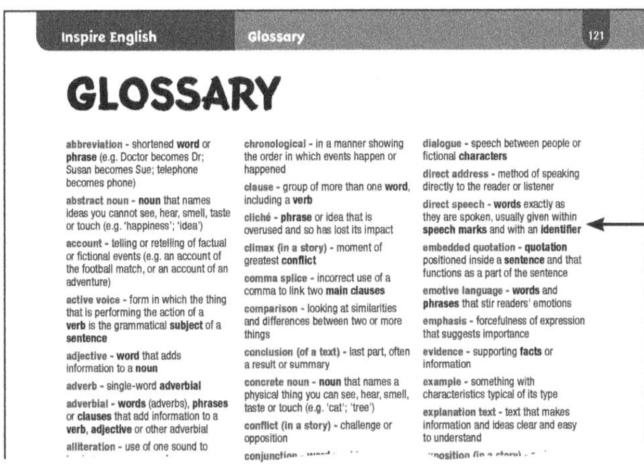
Inspire English Glossary 121

GLOSSARY

abbreviation - shortened **word** or **phrase** (e.g. Doctor becomes Dr; Susan becomes Sue; telephone becomes phone)

abstract noun - **noun** that names ideas you cannot see, hear, smell, taste or touch (e.g. 'happiness'; 'idea')

account - telling or retelling of factual or fictional events (e.g. an account of the football match, or an account of an adventure)

active voice - form in which the thing that is performing the action of a **verb** is the grammatical **subject** of a **sentence**

adjective - **word** that adds information to a **noun**

adverb - single-word **adverbial**

adverbial - **words** (adverbs), **phrases** or **clauses** that add information to a **verb**, **adjective** or other adverbial

alliteration - use of one sound to

chronological - in a manner showing the order in which events happen or happened

clause - group of more than one **word**, including a **verb**

cliché - **phrase** or idea that is overused and so has lost its impact

climax (in a story) - moment of greatest **conflict**

comma splice - incorrect use of a comma to link two **main clauses**

comparison - looking at similarities and differences between two or more things

conclusion (of a text) - last part, often a result or summary

concrete noun - **noun** that names a physical thing you can see, hear, smell, taste or touch (e.g. 'cat'; 'tree')

conflict (in a story) - challenge or opposition

conjunction -

dialogue - speech between people or fictional **characters**

direct address - method of speaking directly to the reader or listener

direct speech - **words** exactly as they are spoken, usually given within **speech marks** and with an **identifier**

embedded quotation - **quotation** positioned inside a **sentence** and that functions as a part of the sentence

emotive language - **words** and **phrases** that stir readers' emotions

emphasis - forcefulness of expression that suggests importance

evidence - supporting **facts** or information

example - something with characteristics typical of its type

explanation text - text that makes information and ideas clear and easy to understand

Curriculum mapping from iLowerSecondary English to the National Curriculum

READING	
English National curriculum objective	**This matches the iLowerSecondary curriculum objective...**
reading a wide range of fiction and non-fiction, including in particular whole books, short stories, poems and plays with a wide coverage of genres, historical periods, forms and authors.	**R8.2D:** Make developed comparisons of writers' ideas and perspectives between two texts.
choosing and reading books independently for challenge, interest and enjoyment.	**R8.1F:** Choose age-appropriate texts, considering their genre, form and origin, and basing decisions on books already read.
re-reading books encountered earlier to increase familiarity with them and provide a basis for making comparisons.	**R8.1D:** Compare, contrast and/or combine key points of information within a text or in spoken language with a given focus.
learning new vocabulary, relating it explicitly to known vocabulary and understanding it with the help of context and dictionaries	**R8.1A (A):** Use a range of strategies to decode unfamiliar words. **R8.1A (B):** Read largely accurately and with understanding.
making inferences and referring to evidence in the text	**R8.1B:** Identify and retrieve a range of key information in a text or in spoken language. **R8.1E:** Make inferences from specific evidence found in a text or in spoken language, including specific vocabulary choices. **R8.2C:** Select relevant, focused evidence to support ideas.
knowing the purpose, audience for and context of the writing and drawing on this knowledge to support comprehension	**R8.1D:** Compare, contrast and/or combine key points of information within a text or in spoken language with a given focus. **R8.2A:** Explore a writer's or speaker's intention and viewpoint.
checking their understanding to make sure that what they have read makes sense.	**R8.1A (A):** Use a range of strategies to decode unfamiliar words. **R8.1A (B):** Read largely accurately and with understanding.
knowing how language, including figurative language, vocabulary choice, grammar, text structure and organisational features, presents meaning	**R8.1E:** Make inferences from specific evidence found in a text or in spoken language, including specific vocabulary choices. **R8.2B:** Express a critical response to a text through writing, discussion or presentation, by considering the text's features and their effects. **R8.3A:** Explore the impact of some of the writer's key structural or organisational choices. **R8.4A:** Explore the impact of some of a writer's or speaker's choices of grammatical features and sentence structure. **R8.4B:** Explore the impact of some of the writer's or speaker's significant vocabulary choices.
recognising a range of poetic conventions and understanding how these have been used	**R8.2B:** Express a critical response to a text through writing, discussion or presentation, by considering the text's features and their effects. **R8.3A:** Explore the impact of some of the writer's key structural or organisational choices.
studying setting, plot, and characterisation, and the effects of these	**R8.2B:** Express a critical response to a text through writing, discussion or presentation, by considering the text's features and their effects. **R8.3A:** Explore the impact of some of the writer's key structural or organisational choices.

Curriculum mapping from iLowerSecondary English to the National Curriculum

READING	
English National curriculum objective	**This matches the iLowerSecondary curriculum objective...**
understanding how the work of dramatists is communicated effectively through performance and how alternative staging allows for different interpretations of a play	**R8.2B:** Express a critical response to a text through writing, discussion or presentation, by considering the text's features and their effects. **R8.3A:** Explore the impact of some of the writer's key structural or organisational choices.
making critical comparisons across texts	**R8.2D:** Make developed comparisons of writers' ideas and perspectives between two texts.
studying a range of authors, including at least two authors in depth each year	**R8.2D:** Make developed comparisons of writers' ideas and perspectives between two texts.

WRITING	
English National curriculum objective	**This matches the iLowerSecondary curriculum objective...**
writing for a wide range of purposes and audiences, including: well-structured formal expository and narrative essays; stories, scripts, poetry and other imaginative writing; notes and polished scripts for talks and presentations; a range of other narrative and non-narrative texts, including arguments, and personal and formal letters	**W8.2A:** Use the presentational conventions of a range of forms, for a range of purposes and audiences (e.g. academic essays, stories, scripts and notes for talks and presentations), with confidence and understanding. **W8.2B:** Use appropriate linguistic conventions to achieve a wider range of purposes and address a wider range of audiences, e.g. to explain, to describe or to persuade, with confidence and understanding. **W8.2C:** Use the organisational conventions of a range of forms, for a range of purposes and audiences, with confidence and understanding, including spoken-language forms such as presentations.
summarising and organising material, and supporting ideas and arguments with any necessary factual detail	**W8.1A:** Gather and structure a range of relevant ideas before writing.
applying their growing knowledge of vocabulary, grammar and text structure to their writing and selecting the appropriate form	**W8.2A:** Use the presentational conventions of a range of forms, for a range of purposes and audiences (e.g. academic essays, stories, scripts and notes for talks and presentations), with confidence and understanding. **W8.2C:** Use the organisational conventions of a range of forms, for a range of purposes and audiences, with confidence and understanding, including spoken-language forms such as presentations. **W8.2D:** Link paragraphs in text and spoken language using adverbials to signal the development of ideas. **W8.3B:** Divide text into paragraphs with accuracy and consistency. **W8.3C:** Use a balance of single-clause sentences, coordinate and subordinate clauses with confidence. **W8.3D:** Use a range of sentence openings in addition to subject-verb sentence openings, starting to develop variety. **W8.3E:** Make deliberate choices of sentence length to achieve clarity. **W8.3F:** Use determiners to achieve cohesion and clarity. **W8.3G:** Select vocabulary in text and spoken language with growing precision.

Curriculum mapping from iLowerSecondary English to the National Curriculum

WRITING	
English National curriculum objective	**This matches the iLowerSecondary curriculum objective...**
drawing on knowledge of literary and rhetorical devices from their reading and listening to enhance the impact of their writing	**W8.2B:** Use appropriate linguistic conventions to achieve a wider range of purposes and address a wider range of audiences, e.g. to explain, to describe or to persuade, with confidence and understanding. **W8.3B:** Divide text into paragraphs with accuracy and consistency. **W8.3C:** Use a balance of single-clause sentences, coordinate and subordinate clauses with confidence. **W8.3D:** Use a range of sentence openings in addition to subject-verb sentence openings, starting to develop variety. **W8.3E:** Make deliberate choices of sentence length to achieve clarity. **W8.3G:** Select vocabulary in text and spoken language with growing precision.
plan, draft, edit and proof-read through: considering how their writing reflects the audiences and purposes for which it was intended	**W8.1A:** Gather and structure a range of relevant ideas before writing. **W8.2A:** Use the presentational conventions of a range of forms, for a range of purposes and audiences (e.g. academic essays, stories, scripts and notes for talks and presentations), with confidence and understanding. **W8.2B:** Use appropriate linguistic conventions to achieve a wider range of purposes and address a wider range of audiences, e.g. to explain, to describe or to persuade, with confidence and understanding. **W8.2C:** Use the organisational conventions of a range of forms, for a range of purposes and audiences, with confidence and understanding, including spoken-language forms such as presentations.
plan, draft, edit and proof-read through: amending the vocabulary, grammar and structure of their writing to improve its coherence and overall effectiveness	**W8.1B:** Correct a range of errors in spelling, punctuation and grammar independently after writing, beginning to develop strategies for proofreading. **W8.1C:** Review and revise vocabulary choice after writing.
plan, draft, edit and proof-read through: paying attention to accurate grammar, punctuation and spelling; applying the spelling patterns and rules set out in English Appendix 1 to the key stage 1 and 2 programmes of study for English.	**W8.1B:** Correct a range of errors in spelling, punctuation and grammar independently after writing, beginning to develop strategies for proofreading. **W8.3B:** Divide text into paragraphs with accuracy and consistency. **W8.3C:** Use a balance of single-clause sentences, coordinate and subordinate clauses with confidence. **W8.3D:** Use a range of sentence openings in addition to subject-verb sentence openings, starting to develop variety. **W8.3E:** Make deliberate choices of sentence length to achieve clarity. **W8.3G:** Select vocabulary in text and spoken language with growing precision. **W8.3H:** Spell homophones, words with single/double letters and 'silent' letters with some accuracy.

Curriculum mapping from iLowerSecondary English to the National Curriculum

GRAMMAR AND VOCABULARY	
English National curriculum objective	**This matches the iLowerSecondary curriculum objective...**
extending and applying the grammatical knowledge set out in English Appendix 2 to the key stage 1 and 2 programmes of study to analyse more challenging texts	**W8.3B:** Divide text into paragraphs with accuracy and consistency. **W8.3C:** Use a balance of single-clause sentences, coordinate and subordinate clauses with confidence. **W8.3D:** Use a range of sentence openings in addition to subject-verb sentence openings, starting to develop variety. **W8.3E:** Make deliberate choices of sentence length to achieve clarity. **W8.3F:** Use determiners to achieve cohesion and clarity. **W8.3G:** Select vocabulary in text and spoken language with growing precision. **W8.3I:** Use upper-case letters, end punctuation, commas, speech marks and apostrophes correctly, with accuracy and consistency. **W8.3J:** Use grammatical terminology for parts of speech with some accuracy.
studying the effectiveness and impact of the grammatical features of the texts they read	**R8.4A:** Explore the impact of some of a writer's or speaker's choices of grammatical features and sentence structure.
drawing on new vocabulary and grammatical constructions from their reading and listening, and using these consciously in their writing and speech to achieve particular effects	**W8.3B:** Divide text into paragraphs with accuracy and consistency. **W8.3C:** Use a balance of single-clause sentences, coordinate and subordinate clauses with confidence. **W8.3D:** Use a range of sentence openings in addition to subject-verb sentence openings, starting to develop variety. **W8.3E:** Make deliberate choices of sentence length to achieve clarity. **W8.3F:** Use determiners to achieve cohesion and clarity. **W8.3G:** Select vocabulary in text and spoken language with growing precision. **W8.3I:** Use upper-case letters, end punctuation, commas, speech marks and apostrophes correctly, with accuracy and consistency.
knowing and understanding the differences between spoken and written language, including differences associated with formal and informal registers, and between Standard English and other varieties of English	**W8.3A:** Write in Standard English and a largely appropriate register.
using Standard English confidently in their own writing and speech	**W8.3A:** Write in Standard English and a largely appropriate register.
discussing reading, writing and spoken language with precise and confident use of linguistic and literary terminology	**W8.3B:** Divide text into paragraphs with accuracy and consistency. **W8.3C:** Use a balance of single-clause sentences, coordinate and subordinate clauses with confidence. **W8.3D:** Use a range of sentence openings in addition to subject-verb sentence openings, starting to develop variety. **W8.3E:** Make deliberate choices of sentence length to achieve clarity. **W8.3G:** Select vocabulary in text and spoken language with growing precision. **W8.3J:** Use grammatical terminology for parts of speech with some accuracy.

Scheme of work

Year:	8
Unit:	1
Theme:	Heroes and Villains
Outcome:	Short story
Key skills:	Writing: Writing processes (W8.1); Writing: Whole text (W8.2); Writing: Language use (W8.3)
Lesser skills:	Reading: Text structure (R8.3); Reading: Language use (R8.4)
Minor skills:	Reading: Reading for meaning (R8.1); Reading: Responding to texts (R8.2)

By the end of the unit, students will be able to structure and craft a short story.

During the course of the unit, students will explore a range of narrative extracts linked by the theme of heroes and anti-heroes.

This unit focuses on engaging the reader in the characters, setting and action of a short narrative story.

Students will practise planning, structuring and crafting narrative writing.

Students will revise punctuation and sentence structure and develop language skills.

Section	Section summary	Curriculum reference	Boosts
1	Students read two extracts based on the same story and answer comprehension questions on each. They practise the skills of picking out key points, using active and passive voices, thinking about characters and comparing texts.	R8.1A/B/C/D, R2.A/B/D	R8.4A/W8.2B Active and passive voices
2	Students read an extract from a novel and answer comprehension questions. They practise the skills of inferring and responding to characters, revealing a villain, punctuating speech and building a villainous character of their own.	R8.1B/E, R8.2A/B, R8.3A, R8.4B, W8.1A, W8.3G	W8.3I Speech punctuation
3	Students read an extract from a short story. They practise the skills of tracking key events, identifying elements of the story, using word classes, exploring vocabulary and writing an extract of their own.	R8.1B/E, R8.2A/B, R8.3A, R8.4B, W8.1A, W8.2C, W8.3G	W8.3J Word classes
4	Students read the opening of a short story. They practise the skills of reading between the lines, responding to the opening, choosing tense and person, choosing the first sentence and writing an opening.	R8.1B, R8.1E, R8.2A/B, R8.3A, W8.1A, W8.2C	W8.2B Choosing tense and person
5	Students complete an assessment by reading a fictional extract, then answering questions about what they have read and writing the opening to a story of their own.	R8.1B/D/E, R8.2B, R8.3A, R8.4B, W8.1A, W8.2C, W8.3G	–
6	Students read a summary of a short story. They practise the skills of using apostrophes, exploring ideas and intentions, and structuring and planning a story.	R8.1B, R8.2A, R8.3A, W8.1A, W8.2C	W8.3I Apostrophes
7	Students read synopses of three different stories. They practise the skills of identifying endings, responding to endings, using colons and semi-colons, exploring the writer's intention and writing an ending of their own.	R8.1B, R8.2A, R8.2B, R8.3A, W8.1A, W8.2C	W8.3I Colons and semi-colons
8	Students read an extract from a story and answer comprehension questions. They practise the skills of identifying and using different ways of telling stories, using identifier verbs and adverbs, and writing an extract from a story of their own.	R8.1B, R8.2A, R8.3A, R8.4B, W8.2C, W8.3A/G	W8.3G/W8.3J Identifiers and adverbs
9	Students read the opening of a short story. They practise the skills of exploring short sentences and longer sentences, building sentences, linking with adverbials and experimenting with structure.	R8.2A, R8.3A, R8.4A, W8.1A, W8.3B/C/D/E	W8.2D Linking with adverbials
10	Students practise the skills of identifying homophones, using irregular past tenses, proofreading, reviewing vocabulary, conjunctions and relationships, reviewing sentence structure and reviewing and proofreading writing.	W8.1B/C	W8.3H Homophones; W8.2D Conjunctions and relationships
11	Students complete an assessment by planning, writing, reviewing and revising a short story.	W8.1A/B, W8.2C, W8.3A/C/D/E/G/H/I	–

Scheme of work

Year:	8
Unit:	2
Theme:	Safe and Sound
Outcome:	Critical writing
Key skills:	Reading: Responding to texts (R8.2); Reading: Text structure (R8.3); Reading: Language use (R8.4)
Lesser skills:	Reading: Reading for meaning (R8.1); Writing: Language use (W8.3)
Minor skills:	Writing: Writing processes (W8.1)

By the end of the unit, students will be able to analyse and respond to a persuasive text, exploring the writer's choices and their impact on the reader.

During the course of the unit, students will explore a range of persuasive texts, focusing on keeping healthy and safe.

This unit focuses on critical analysis of the language and structure of persuasive texts, supported with relevant, focused evidence.

Students will practise reading persuasive texts, identifying the writer's intentions and analysing the writer's choices.

Students will revise punctuation, paragraph structure and sentence structure, and develop critical writing skills.

Section	Section summary	Curriculum reference	Boosts
1	Students read an informative poster and answer comprehension questions. They practise the skills of identifying, linking and comparing ideas, using imperative verbs, vocabulary choices, using parts of speech and writing persuasively.	R8.1B, R8.1D, R8.4B, W8.1A, W8.3G	W8.2C Imperative verbs; W8.3J Parts of speech
2	Students read an extract from a webpage and answer comprehension questions. They practise the skills of inferring key ideas, using connotations, using persuasive vocabulary and writing persuasively.	R8.1B, R8.1E, R8.4B, W8.1A, W8.3G	R8.4B Connotations
3	Students read an extract from a webpage. They practise the skills of identifying the message, the intention and the audience, punctuating and choosing quotations, exploring vocabulary choice and commenting on the writer's choices.	R8.1B, R8.2A, R8.2B, R8.2C, R8.4B	W8.3I Punctuating quotations
4	Students read an extract from a webpage. They practise the skills of identifying intentions, choosing the best evidence, structuring a paragraph of critical response, exploring emotive and dramatic vocabulary choices, and writing a response to a text.	R8.1B, R8.2A, R8.2B, R8.2C, R8.4B	W8.3B Structuring a paragraph of critical response
5	Students complete an assessment by reading a leaflet, then answering comprehension questions and writing a critical response to the leaflet.	R8.1B/D, R8.2A/B/C, R8.4B	–
6	Students answer questions based on a step-by-step reading of an extract. They practise the skills of reading the opening, exploring elements of persuasion, giving orders and conditions, using demonstrative pronouns and writing persuasive paragraphs.	R8.2A, R8.2B, R8.3A, W8.1A, W8.2C	W8.3F Demonstrative pronouns
7	Students read an extract from a webpage and answer comprehension questions. They practise the skills of exploring structure, using determiners, responding to the text and planning a text.	R8.1B, R8.2A, R8.2B, R8.3A, W8.1A, W8.2C	W8.3F Determiners
8	Students read an extract from a webpage. They practise the skills of identifying persuasive ideas, considering vocabulary effects, sentence types, readers' reactions to a text and developing a response.	R8.1B, R8.2A, R8.2B, R8.4A, R8.4B, W8.3C/E, W8.3G	W8.3C Sentence types
9	Students read a fact sheet about not smoking. They practise the skills of identifying persuasive ideas and rhetorical devices, commas in lists, and exploring and creating rhetorical devices.	R8.1B, R8.2A, R8.2B, R8.4A, R8.4B, W8.3C/E, W8.3G	W8.3I Commas in lists
10	Students read an extract from a webpage and answer comprehension questions. They practise the skills of looking at structure, vocabulary and intention, selecting vocabulary, looking at sentences structure, rhetorical devices and intention, and putting together a critical response.	R8.2A/B/C, R8.3A, R8.4A/B	W8.3G Selecting vocabulary in your response
11	Students complete an assessment by reading a newspaper article, then answering comprehension questions and writing a critical response to the article.	R8.1B, R8.2A/B/C, R8.3A, R8.4A/B	–

Scheme of work

Year:	8
Unit:	3
Theme:	A Perfect World
Outcome:	Article
Key skills:	Writing: Writing processes (W8.1); Writing: Whole text (W8.2); Writing: Language use (W8.3)
Lesser skills:	Reading: Reading for meaning (R8.1); Reading: Responding to texts (R8.2); Reading: Text structure (R8.3); Reading: Language use (R8.4)
Minor skills:	–

By the end of the unit, students will be able to construct an effectively structured article, expressing a clear and compelling point of view.

During the course of the unit, students will explore a range of fiction and non-fiction argument and advice texts, drawing on the writers' structural and language choices to develop their own ideas and writing choices.

This unit focuses on structuring an effective argument and selecting language for effect in an article exploring ways in which the world could be made a better place.

Students will practise planning, structuring and writing to express their point of view.

Students will revise sentence structure and verb agreement, and develop spelling and proofreading skills.

Section	Section summary	Curriculum reference	Boosts
1	Students read an extract from the first chapter of a novel and answer comprehension questions. They practise the skills of summarising and inferring ideas, responding to the writer's ideas, using subjects and verbs in standard English, and planning and writing a story opening.	R8.1B, R8.1C, R8.2A, R8.2B, R8.3A, W8.1A	W8.3A Subjects and verbs in Standard English
2	Students read a newspaper article. They practise the skills of identifying features and key ideas, exploring structure and planning an argument.	R8.1B, R8.1C, R8.1E, R8.2A, R8.3A, W8.1A	R8.1B Identifying features
3	Students read a webpage and answer comprehension questions. They practise the skills of inferring ideas, exploring nouns, using 'silent' consonants and arguing a point of view.	R8.1B, R8.1E, R8.4B, W8.3G	W8.3H 'Silent' consonants
4	Students read a webpage and answer comprehension questions. They practise the skills of selecting adjectives and adverbs, using 'silent' vowels, building noun phrases and adding impact to an argument.	R8.1B, R8.1E, R8.2A, R8.4B, W8.3G	W8.3H Unspoken or 'silent' vowels
5	Students complete an assessment by reading a webpage, then answering comprehension questions and writing an argument.	R8.1B/E, R8.2A, R8.4B, W8.1A, W8.2C, W8.3G	–
6	Students read a newspaper article. They practise the skills of identifying evidence, identifying and sequencing points, examples and comments, linking points with adverbials and building a paragraph.	R8.3A, W8.3B	W8.2D Linking points with adverbials
7	Students read an article. They practise the skills of identifying ideas and intentions, exploring and writing sentences, and using dashes and semi-colons.	R8.2A, R8.4A, W8.1A, W8.3C/D/E	W8.3I Dashes and semi-colons
8	Students read an introduction to a book and answer comprehension questions. They practise the skills of exploring and using rhetorical devices, using apostrophes and adding impact to their ideas.	R8.1B, R8.2A, R8.4B, W8.1A, W8.3G	W8.3I Using apostrophes
9	Students read extracts from two texts and answer comprehension questions on them. They practise the skills of exploring an introduction, engaging readers, exploring conclusions, writing in a formal register, and writing introductions and conclusions.	R8.2A, R8.2B, R8.3A, W8.1A, W8.2C, W8.3C/E/G	W8.2B/W8.3A Writing in a formal register
10	Students practise the skills of checking for key features, reviewing vocabulary and sentence structure, and looking for errors.	R8.3A, W8.1B, W8.1C, W8.2C	W8.3H/W8.3I Looking for careless errors
11	Students complete an assessment by planning, writing, and reviewing and revising an article.	W8.1A, W8.1C, W8.2C, W8.3A/B/C/E/G/H/I	–

Scheme of work

Year:	8
Unit:	4
Theme:	World of Sport
Outcome:	Critical writing
Key skills:	Reading: Reading for meaning (R8.1); Reading: Responding to texts (R8.2); Reading: Language use (R8.4)
Lesser skills:	Reading: Text structure (R8.3); Writing: Writing processes (W8.1); Writing: Whole text (W8.2); Writing: Language use (W8.3)
Minor skills:	–

By the end of the unit, students will be able to analyse an information text, exploring the writer's choices and their impact on the reader.

During the course of the unit, students will explore a range of information texts about sports from around the world, exploring how information is presented to engage the reader.

This unit focuses on critical analysis of information texts, exploring and comparing writers' selection of ideas and language, and its impact on the reader.

Students will practise reading and summarising information.

Students will revise sentence structures and develop critical writing skills.

Section	Section summary	Curriculum reference	Boosts
1	Students read an information text. They practise the skills of using word families, working out unfamiliar words, linking ideas and writing a summary.	R8.1A, R8.1B, R8.1C, R8.1D	R8.1A Word families
2	Students read an extract from an article and answer comprehension questions. They practise the skills of identifying types of information, informing and describing, identifying intentions and writing an information text.	R8.1B, R8.1E, R8.2A, R8.2B, R8.4B	R8.2A/W8.3G Identifying intentions
3	Students read an extract from an article and answer comprehension questions. They practise the skills of exploring vocabulary choice, using clauses, focusing on evidence and writing a response.	R8.1B, R8.1E, R8.2A, R8.2B, R8.2C, R8.4B	W8.3C Clauses
4	Students read an article and answer comprehension questions. They practise the skills of exploring intention and vocabulary choice, exploring register, selecting evidence, responding to vocabulary choice and writing about vocabulary choice.	R8.1B, R8.2A, R8.2B, R8.2C, R8.4B	R8.4B Exploring register
5	Students read an article and answer comprehension questions. They practise the skills of gathering evidence of intention, using sentence starts, considering paragraphs, making points and commenting.	R8. 2A, R8.2B, R8.2C, R8.4B, W8.1A, W8.3B	W8.3D Sentence starts
6	Students complete an assessment by reading an information text, then answering comprehension questions and writing a critical response.	R8.1B/C/D/E; R8.2A/B/C, R8.4B	–
7	Students read an extract from an information text and answer comprehension questions. They practise the skills of exploring intention and paragraph structure, using subheadings, and writing an information text.	R8.1A, R8.2A, R8.2B, R8.3A, W8.1A, W8.2C	W8.2A Using subheadings
8	Students read an article and answer comprehension questions. They practise the skills of exploring vocabulary choice and intention, using sentence types, exploring sentence structure and intention, and writing a response.	R8.2A, R8.2B, R8.4A, R8.4B, W8.1A, W8.2C	W8.3C Revising sentence types
9	Students read an extract from an article and answer comprehension questions. They practise the skills of looking at structure, vocabulary and sentence structure, gathering and organising ideas, and planning.	R8.1B, R8.2A, R8.2B, R8.2C, R8.3A, R8.4A, R8.4B, W8.1A, W8.2C	W8.1A Ways of gathering and organising your ideas
10	Students read two extracts and answer comprehension questions. They practise the skills of comparing key information, using adverbials for comparison, comparing intentions and viewpoints, and writing a comparison.	R8.1B, R8.2A/B/C/D, R8.4A/B, W8.1A, W8.2C	W8.2D Adverbials for comparison
11	Students complete an assessment by reading two extracts, then answering comprehension questions and writing a comparison of the extracts.	R8.1B, R8.2A/B/C/D, R8.4A/B, W8.1A, W8.2C, W8.3B	–

Scheme of work

Year:	8
Unit:	5
Theme:	A Moment in Time
Outcome:	Speech
Key skills:	Writing: Writing processes (W8.1); Writing: Whole text (W8.2); Writing: Language use (W8.3)
Lesser skills:	Reading: Responding to texts (R8.2); Reading: Language use (R8.4)
Minor skills:	Reading: Text structure (R8.3)

By the end of the unit, students will be able to write an article, evocatively describing and explaining a personal memorable event.

During the course of the unit, students will explore a range of explanation texts in which writers recount an experience and the impact it had on them, focusing on their structural and language choices to develop their own writing.

This unit focuses on crafting an engaging article in which an experience is vividly recounted.

Students will practise planning a text and making effective vocabulary choices.

Students will revise summary skills, sentence structure and apostrophes, and develop structuring and language skills.

Section	Section summary	Curriculum reference	Boosts
1	Students read an extract and answer comprehension questions. They practise the skills of pulling ideas together, identifying key points for a summary, responding to ideas and writing about a moment or two.	R8.1B/C/D, R8.2A, R8.2B, W8.1A	R8.2C Key points for summarising
2	Students read a newspaper article. They practise the skills of gathering impressions and inferring ideas, tracking their response, using first, second and third person, creating a response and structuring their writing.	R8.1E, R8.2A, R8.2B, R8.3A, W8.1A, W8.2C	W8.2B First, second and third person
3	Students read an extract and answer comprehension questions. They practise the skills of exploring narrative structures, exploring writer's intention, using chronological and non-chronological structures, and planning an article.	R8.1B, R8.2A, R8.3A, W8.1A, W8.2C	W8.2C Chronological and non-chronological structure
4	Students read a newspaper article and answer comprehension questions. They practise the skills of responding to vocabulary choice, using a thesaurus, exploring vocabulary choices, and writing text that explains and describes.	R8.2A, R8.2B, R8.4B, W8.1A, W8.2C, W8.3G	W8.3G Using a thesaurus
5	Students complete an assessment by reading a newspaper article, then answering comprehension questions and writing a descriptive text.	R8.2A, R8.2B, R8.3A, R8.4B, W8.1A, W8.2C, W8.3G	–
6	Students read an extract and answer comprehension questions. They practise the skills of responding to people and events, describing feelings, using direct and reported speech, and writing an account.	R8.1E, R8.2A, R8.2B, W8.1A, W8.2C, W8.3G	W8.3I Direct and reported speech
7	Students read an extract. They practise the skills of responding to the text, exploring structure and using, building and writing paragraphs.	R8.2A, R8.2B, R8.3A, W8.2C	W8.3B Paragraphing
8	Students read an article and answer comprehension questions. They practise the skills of structuring sentences for impact, restructuring sentences, structuring sentences for clarity and reviewing sentence structure.	R8.1B, R8.2A/B, R8.4A, W8.1A. W8.2C, W8.3C/E	W8.3C Restructuring sentences
9	Students read an extract from an article. They practise the skills of responding to ideas, exploring openings, guiding the reader with adverbials of time, and selecting and planning an opening.	R8.2A, R8.2B, R8.3A, W8.1A, W8.2C	W8.2D Guiding the reader with adverbials of time
10	Students read an extract and answer comprehension questions. They practise the skills of exploring endings, proofreading, and selecting and planning an ending.	R8.2A, R8.2B, R8.3A, W8.1A, W8.2C	W8.1B Polishing your proofreading skills
11	Students complete an assessment by planning, writing, reviewing and revising an article.	W8.1A, W8.2C, W8.3B/C/E/G	–

Scheme of work

Year:	8
Unit:	6
Theme:	Dramatic!
Outcome:	Critical writing
Key skills:	Reading: Reading for meaning (R8.1); Reading: Responding to texts (R8.2); Reading: Language use (R8.4)
Lesser skills:	Reading: Text structure (R8.3)
Minor skills:	Writing: Writing processes (W8.1); Writing: Whole text (W8.2)

By the end of the unit, students will be able to analyse a play extract, exploring the writer's choices and their intended impact on an audience.

During the course of the unit, students will explore a range of play extracts, from Shakespeare to contemporary drama.

This unit focuses on analysis of drama texts: close reading, critical response and analysis of language.

Students will practise selecting evidence and responding to texts.

Students will revise parts of speech, and develop spelling and critical writing skills.

Section	Section summary	Curriculum reference	Boosts
1	Students read an extract from the opening of a play. They practise the skills of reading between the lines, responding to characters and action, deciding where to begin, setting out a script and writing an opening scene.	R8.1B, R8.1E, R8.2A, R8.2B, R8.3A, W8.1A, W8.2C	W8.2A Setting out a script
2	Students read an extract from a play. They practise the skills of imagining performance, creating mood and character, spelling drama terminology, exploring the playwright's intentions and writing a scene.	R8.1B, R8.2A, R8.2B, R8.3A, W8.1A	W8.3H Drama terminology
3	Students read an extract from the opening of a play and the prose text from which it is adapted and answer comprehension questions. They practise the skills of comparing and responding to the script and the novel, and adapting a prose extract for the stage.	R8.1B, R8.1E, R8.2A, R8.2B, R8.3A, R8.4B, W8.1A, W8.2C, W8.3G	–
4	Students read an extract from the opening of a play and answer comprehension questions. They practise the skills of creating conflict, building a story, using word classes and planning conflict.	R8.1B, R8.2A, R8.2B, R8.2C, R8.3A, R8.4B, W8.2C	W8.3J Word classes
5	Students read an extract from the ending of a play. They practise the skills of exploring characters and language choices, referring back to previous ideas, writing a response to characters and building characters.	R8.1E, R8.2A, R8.2B, R8.2C, R8.4B, W8.1A	W8.3F Referring back
6	Students complete an assessment by reading an extract from a play, then answering comprehension questions and writing a critical response to the extract.	R8.1BE, R8.2A/B/C, R8.4B	–
7	Students read an extract from *King Lear* and answer comprehension questions. They practise the skills of responding to and exploring dialogue, using word families and writing a script.	R8.1A, R8.1E, R8.2A, R8.2B, R8.2C, R8.4A, R8.4B, W8.1A, W8.3C/E/G	W8.3H Word families
8	Students read an extract from *Hamlet* and answer comprehension questions. They practise the skills of reading Shakespeare's language, changing responses, reviewing vocabulary choices and writing a response.	R8.1A, R8.1E, R8.2A, R8.2B, R8.2C, W8.1A, W8.2C	R8.1A Shakespeare's language; W8.1C Reviewing vocabulary choices
9	Students read an extract from *Macbeth* and answer comprehension questions. They practise the skills of selecting evidence, exploring themes, reviewing sentence structures and writing a response.	R8.1A, R8.2A, R8.2B, R8.2C, R8.4B, W8.1A, W8.2C	W8.3E Reviewing sentence structures
10	Students read an extract from *Macbeth* and answer comprehension questions. They practise the skills of planning a response, writing an introduction, proofreading and writing a conclusion.	R8.1A, R8.2B, W8.1A, W8.2C	W8.1B Proofreading skills
11	Students complete an assessment by reading an extract from *Macbeth*, then answering comprehension questions and writing a critical response to the extract.	R8.1A, R8.2A/B/C, R8.4A/B, W8.1A, W8.2C	–

Year 8	Unit 1: Heroes and Villains		
Section 1 Telling stories: Lesson 1	Skills focus: Writing: Narrative		Student Book pp. 10–11 Workbook pp. 6–7
Main Curriculum Objectives	**R8.1A** Read largely accurately and with understanding.	**R8.1B** Identify and retrieve a range of key information in a text or in spoken language.	**R8.1C** Summarise a short text or speech effectively, selecting appropriate and relevant detail.
	R8.1D Compare, contrast and/or combine key points of information within a text or in spoken language.		
Secondary Curriculum Objectives	**R8.4A** Explore the impact of some of a writer's or speaker's choices of grammatical features and sentence structure.	**W8.2B** Use appropriate linguistic conventions to achieve a wider range of purposes and address a wider range of audiences, e.g. to explain, to describe or to persuade, with confidence and understanding.	

Introduction 10 minutes • Ask: What suggests someone is a hero or a villain? • Give partners two or three minutes to discuss and note down their answers. • Take feedback, compiling lists of key traits. • Ensure that you query any suggestions that traits such as scars or nationality indicate villains, and that students understand the importance of not judging real people by these.	**Support** Suggest familiar examples of heroes and villains for students to consider. **Deepen** Ask students to write guidance for applicants for the roles of a hero and a villain.
First phase 15 minutes • Read Extract A. • Take students' initial responses. Ask: How many heroes and villains appear in this story opening? Are these typical heroes and villains? Why is that? • Ask students to complete Activity 1. Point out that they will need to refer to different parts of the extract. • Take feedback to ensure understanding, and check the students have provided complete responses.	**Support** Model gathering information to complete Activity 1, question 1 before asking students to continue independently. **Deepen** Ask students to divide information about the two characters by importance, indicating which points are the most essential.
Second phase 20 minutes • Ask students to recap their understanding of subjects and objects in sentences. • Read through the introduction to the Grammar Boost activity and ensure understanding. • Ask students to complete the Grammar Boost activity. • Take feedback to check accuracy. • Ask students to complete Activity 2.	**Support** In the Grammar Boost activity, complete question 1 as a whole class or in supported groups. **Deepen** In the Grammar Boost activity, ask students to explain which sentence in question 1 is clearer and/or more concise, and why this is.
Plenary 10 minutes • Take feedback on Activity 2, focusing on breadth of responses and the relevance of supporting evidence. • Ask: Do you find this story opening engaging? How might it be improved? • Discuss alternative ways the extract could have been written, for example in first person or beginning with dramatic actions. Ask: Would any of these have improved the story opening?	**Support** Recognise and validate any relevant responses and suggestions about alternative ways of opening the story. **Deepen** Don't provide prompts for alternative ways the extract could have been written, allowing students to suggest these themselves.

Set workbook activities 5 minutes

- Point students towards the activities on pp. 6–7 of the Workbook.
- Check understanding and answer any questions.
- These activities focus on identifying key points, the active and passive voices, and characters.

Year 8	Unit 1: Heroes and Villains		
Section 1 Telling stories: Lesson 2	Skills focus: Writing: Narrative		Student Book pp. 12–13 Workbook pp. 8–9
Main Curriculum Objectives	**R8.2A** Explore a writer's or speaker's intention and viewpoint.	**R8.2B** Express a critical response to a text through writing, discussion or presentation, by considering the text's features and their effects.	**R8.2D** Make developed comparisons between two texts.
Secondary Curriculum Objectives			

Introduction 10 minutes • Ask students to suggest films, novels or short stories that begin in a way that engaged them from the very start. • Ask: What makes an effective opening? • Look for responses that recognise the power of vividly drawn characters and tense situations.	**Support** Suggest the openings of familiar films or books, and ask students to rank them in order of effectiveness. **Deepen** Ask volunteers to share opening sentences from creative writing they have completed in past lessons. Ask the class: Do you find this opening engaging? Why is that?
First phase 15 minutes • Read Extract B. • Take students' initial responses. Ask: Is this an effective opening? Do you find it more effective than Extract A? • Ensure students have access to their responses to Activity 1, from the previous lesson. • Ask students to complete Activity 3. • Take feedback to check understanding and compare responses. • Ask: Does the reader need to know all the key information in a story as soon as possible?	**Support** Complete Activity 3, question 2a as a whole class or in supported groups, referring closely to students' responses to Activity 1. **Deepen** Ask: Could any key information be withheld until the very end of the story, for effect? If helpful, prompt students to consider the information about Heracles' reward for completing the challenge.
Second phase 20 minutes • Explain to students that Activity 4 will focus on the reasons the two writers of the extracts made their choices of structure and style. • Ask students to complete Activity 4.	**Support** Take feedback after Activity 4, question 1 and after question 2, to check understanding and progress. **Deepen** Encourage students to respond as fully as possible, using evidence from the extracts wherever appropriate.
Plenary 10 minutes • Take feedback on Activity 4, gathering as wide a range of responses as possible. • Note that one extract was chronological and explanatory for clarity, and the other was non-chronological and descriptive to achieve impact. • Ask students to evaluate the two different approaches to writing a story opening.	**Support** Recognise and validate any relevant responses. **Deepen** Challenge students to write a short but powerful description of Cerberus, considering which of his features they could highlight to achieve maximum impact.

Set workbook activities 5 minutes

- Point students towards the activities on pp. 8–9 of the Workbook.
- Check understanding and answer any questions.
- These activities focus on comparing two texts.

Year 8	Unit 1: Heroes and Villains		
Section 2 Building a character: Lesson 3	Skills focus: Writing: Narrative		Student Book pp. 14–15 Workbook pp. 10–11
Main Curriculum Objectives	**R8.1B** Identify and retrieve a range of key information in a text or in spoken language.	**R8.1E** Make inferences from specific evidence found in a text or in spoken language, including specific vocabulary choices.	**R8.2B** Express a critical response to a text through writing, discussion or presentation, by considering the text's features and their effects.
Secondary Curriculum Objectives	**R8.2A** Explore a writer's or speaker's intention and viewpoint.	**R8.4B** Explore the impact of some of the writer's or speaker's significant vocabulary choices.	

Lesson	Support / Deepen
Introduction **10 minutes** • Ask students to name as many fictional villains as they can. • Ask students to recap the characteristics of a villain, looking for awareness of villains' opposition to heroes. • Note students' suggestions for reference to be used in the writing task at the end of Lesson 4.	**Support** Prompt students with locally familiar examples of villains. Ask: What do they have in common? **Deepen** Ask students to consider the positive purposes of villains in fiction, and how necessary they are in stories.
First phase **15 minutes** • Read the extract. • Take students' immediate responses to the extract, and to the villainous Count Fosco in particular. • Ask students to complete Activity 1, questions 1 and 2. • Take feedback to check students' inference skills. • Ask students to complete Activity 1, questions 3–6. • Take feedback to share and develop understanding.	**Support** Complete Activity 1, questions 1 and 2 as a whole class or in supported groups, to guide students' inference skills. **Deepen** Ask students to consider (with reference to other texts): Do we always learn about character in these ways? Are actions and speech always more significant than appearance? Can you think of any situation in which appearance would be more powerful?
Second phase **20 minutes** • Read through Activity 2. Remind students of the importance of using evidence to support their ideas. • Ask students to complete Activity 2. Encourage them to express their own honest, personal responses.	**Support** Discuss Activity 2, question 1 as a whole class or in supported groups. **Deepen** Ask students to select and explain two possible responses, exploring which they can make more compelling.
Plenary **10 minutes** • Take feedback on Activity 2, exploring as wide a range of responses, supporting evidence and explanations as possible. • Encourage debate, asking: How did the writer intend the reader to respond to this villain?	**Support** Recognise and validate any relevant responses. **Deepen** Ask students for their responses to the character of Mr Hartright.

Set workbook activities **5 minutes**
- Point students towards the activities on pp. 10–11 of the Workbook.
- Check understanding and answer any questions.
- These activities focus on inferring character.

Year 8	Unit 1: Heroes and Villains		
Section 2 Building a character: Lesson 4	Skills focus: Writing: Narrative		Student Book pp. 16–17 Workbook pp. 12–13
Main Curriculum Objectives	**R8.3A** Explore the impact of some of the writer's key structural or organisational choices.	**W8.1A** Gather and structure a range of relevant ideas before writing.	**W8.3I** Use upper-case letters, end punctuation, commas, speech marks and apostrophes correctly, with accuracy and consistency.
Secondary Curriculum Objectives	**W8.3G** Select vocabulary in text and spoken language with growing precision.		

Lesson	Support / Deepen
Introduction **10 minutes** • Display the following sentence. "*Will you please be quiet?" said the teacher.* • Ask students to suggest near-synonyms for 'said'. • Take feedback, displaying examples for reference. • Explain that phrases such as '... said the teacher' or '... the student answered' are referred to as 'identifiers': they identify the speaker.	**Support** Prompt students with examples of different identifier verbs, such as 'asked', 'shouted' and 'whispered'. **Deepen** Ask students to experiment with the effect created by each near-synonym, and what it implies about the teacher's mood.
First phase **15 minutes** • Briefly recap the content of the extract. • Ask students to complete Activity 3. • Take feedback to share and develop ideas. • Ask students to consider their responses to Activities 1 and 2 in the previous lesson, as well as to Activity 3. • Ask: Can you identify 'ingredients' that make a villain? Guide their answers to apply to generic villains rather than only Count Fosco. • Ask students to complete the Skills Boost activity. • Take feedback to check accuracy.	**Support** Complete Activity 3 in discussion, as a whole class or in supported groups. **Deepen** During Activity 3, ask students to consider the structure of how elements of Count Fosco's character are revealed.
Second phase **20 minutes** • Remind students of the villainous characteristics they have discussed. • Read through Activity 4 to check understanding. • Ask students to complete Activity 4. Emphasise that they are writing notes, not a complete text.	**Support** Refer students to examples of dialogue and description in the extract as models. **Deepen** Encourage students to choose identifier verbs that help build character.
Plenary **10 minutes** • Give students a minute or two to check that each element of characterisation they have noted contributes to their intention. • Take feedback. • Ask the class to identify the intention in each case, and how the writer has tried to achieve it.	**Support** Recognise and validate any effective elements in students' responses. **Deepen** Ask students to consider whether a villain's gender has an effect on responses to the character.

Set workbook activities **5 minutes**
- Point students towards the activities on pp. 12–13 of the Workbook.
- Check understanding and answer any questions.
- These activities focus on revealing and planning a villain.

Year 8	Unit 1: Heroes and Villains		
Section 3 Creating danger: Lesson 5	Skills focus: Writing: Narrative		Student Book pp. 18–19 Workbook pp. 14–15
Main Curriculum Objectives	**R8.1B** Identify and retrieve a range of key information in a text or in spoken language.	**R8.2B** Express a critical response to a text through writing, discussion or presentation, by considering the text's features and their effects.	**R8.3A** Explore the impact of some of the writer's key structural or organisational choices.
Secondary Curriculum Objectives	**R8.1E** Make inferences from specific evidence found in a text or in spoken language, including specific vocabulary choices.	**R8.2A** Explore a writer's or speaker's intention and viewpoint.	

Introduction 10 minutes • Ask students to describe favourite scenes of action, tension and danger in films or books. • Ask students to suggest some of the typical scenarios used, for example the hero's life being in danger, a meeting with a villain and a last-minute escape. • Explain that students will be planning and writing a short action sequence at the end of the next lesson.	**Support** Prompt students with examples of heroic characters or action stories. **Deepen** Ask students to imagine new heroes, some of the difficult situations in which they may find themselves, and daring escapes they could make.
First phase 15 minutes • Read the extract and check students' understanding of the setting. • Take students' initial responses. Ask: What do you think will happen next? • Ask students to complete Activity 1, questions 1–3. • Take feedback to check and share understanding. • Ask students to complete Activity 1, question 4. • Take feedback. Compare responses and encourage debate.	**Support** Model plotting the first two paragraphs on the graph in Activity 1, question 4, before asking students to complete the task independently. **Deepen** Ask students to comment on the writer's intention in alternating between danger and apparent safety.
Second phase 20 minutes • Read through Activity 2. Check students' understanding of the second element listed: describing a likely consequence of the current events. • Ask students to complete Activity 2. Explain that, in their response to question 1, they can use direct quotation or paraphrase the text.	**Support** Focus on the first paragraph as a whole class or in supported groups. Ask: Which elements are present? **Deepen** Ask students to find at least two examples of each element.
Plenary 10 minutes • Take feedback on Activity 2. • Guide discussion to conclude that the writer is focusing on describing events rather than senses, creating a focus on action.	**Support** Recognise and validate any relevant responses. **Deepen** Ask students to comment on the writer's intention in focusing on events.

Set workbook activities 5 minutes
- Point students towards the activities on pp. 14–15 of the Workbook.
- Check understanding and answer any questions.
- These activities focus on tracking danger through a story.

Year 8	Unit 1: Heroes and Villains		
Section 3 Creating danger: Lesson 6	Skills focus: Writing: Narrative		Student Book pp. 20–21 Workbook pp. 16–17
Main Curriculum Objectives	**R8.4B** Explore the impact of some of the writer's or speaker's significant vocabulary choices.	**W8.1A** Gather and structure a range of relevant ideas before writing.	**W8.3G** Select vocabulary in text and spoken language with growing precision.
	W8.3J Use grammatical terminology for parts of speech with some accuracy.		
Secondary Curriculum Objectives	**W8.2C** Use the organisational conventions of a range of forms, for a range of purposes and audiences, with confidence and understanding, including spoken-language forms such as presentations.		

Lesson	Support / Deepen
Introduction **10 minutes** • Display jumbled pairs of near-synonymous verbs, with one verb in each pair more dramatic than the other. For example: 'break' and 'destroy', 'fall' and 'plummet', 'run' and 'race', and 'worry' and 'panic'. • Give students two or three minutes to pair the verbs. • Take feedback. • Ask students to identify the more dramatic or emotive verb choice in each pair, and discuss the fact that their extremity makes these more dramatic.	**Support** Identify and discuss only one near-synonymous pair as a whole class or in supported groups. **Deepen** Ask students to suggest their own examples of paired near-synonymous verbs, ensuring one is more dramatic than the other.
First phase **15 minutes** • Read through the Skills Boost activity, checking understanding of the terms and definitions. • Ask students to complete the Skills Boost activity. • Take feedback, compiling lists of nouns, adjectives, verbs and adverbs to reinforce understanding. • Ask students to complete Activity 3. • Take feedback to share and develop understanding. • Ask: Can you identify other effective verb choices in the extract?	**Support** Work with the whole class or supported groups to identify relevant verbs for Activity 3, question 1. **Deepen** Encourage students to consider the limited use of adjectives and adverbs in the sentences given in Activity 3. Point out that the focus is on action, not description.
Second phase **20 minutes** • Read through Activity 4, ensuring students' understanding of the scenario. • Recap students' responses to Activity 2 in the previous lesson to support their responses. • Ask students to complete Activity 4, explaining that they do not need to plan a conclusion to the story.	**Support** Take feedback after each step in the writing process to ensure understanding and progression. **Deepen** Focus students' planning on the key threats: the villains, cliffs and sea.
Plenary **10 minutes** • Give students time to review and revise their verb choices, reminding them of the intention to create a dramatic sense of danger. • Ask partners to select the most effective sentences in their writing. • Ask partners to share their selection with the class.	**Support** Recognise and validate any effective structural or vocabulary choices. **Deepen** Encourage students to identify each verb in their writing, then gather, consider and select from a range of possible improvements.

Set workbook activities **5 minutes**
- Point students towards the activities on pp. 16–17 of the Workbook.
- Check understanding and answer any questions.
- These activities focus on vocabulary choices and tracking danger.

Year 8	Unit 1: Heroes and Villains		
Section 4 Openings: Lesson 7	Skills focus: Writing: Narrative		Student Book pp. 22–23 Workbook pp. 18–19
Main Curriculum Objectives	**R8.1B** Identify and retrieve a range of key information in a text or in spoken language.	**R8.1E** Make inferences from specific evidence found in a text or in spoken language, including specific vocabulary choices.	**R8.2B** Express a critical response to a text through writing, discussion or presentation, by considering the text's features and their effects.
Secondary Curriculum Objectives	**R8.2A** Explore a writer's or speaker's intention and viewpoint.		

Introduction 10 minutes • Explain that you are going to describe five different people very briefly, and ask students to picture each one. Ask them to explain what they can infer about each person based on your limited descriptions. • Ask the class to imagine, in turn: a crying person, a pale and unsteady person, someone with messy hair and clothes, a very neatly dressed person, and someone biting their nails and sweating. • Take feedback.	**Support** Use one example as a model, for example discussing that crying suggests someone is upset. **Deepen** Ask students to act out the physical signs of a feeling and invite the class to infer what they can from the actions.
First phase 15 minutes • Read the extract and take students' initial responses. Ask: Does this make you want to read on? • Ask students to complete Activity 1. • Take feedback, encouraging as wide a range of responses as possible. Make explicit reference to the skill of inference, which students are using to deduce their responses.	**Support** Ask students to summarise the story opening verbally first, to ensure understanding. **Deepen** Encourage students to give evidence to support their responses.
Second phase 20 minutes • Read through Activity 2. Emphasise the importance of engaging the reader from the very start of the story (as an engaging middle is wasted if the reader has already stopped reading). • Discuss which of the different techniques given in the activity the writer has used. • Ask students to complete Activity 2, making use of the sentence starts provided if necessary.	**Support** Model gathering evidence and ideas for a comment to support a response. **Deepen** Encourage students to develop their comments as fully as possible, considering what the writer has done, how they have done it, and why.
Plenary 10 minutes • Give students two minutes to check that their paragraphs give a response that is supported by evidence and explanation. • Ask volunteers to read or paraphrase their written responses. • Encourage the class to evaluate these responses. Ask: Is the response valid? Is the evidence relevant? Is the explanation clear and convincing?	**Support** Recognise and validate any relevant responses, choices of evidence and/or explanations. **Deepen** Ask students to summarise all the ways in which the writer of the story opening has tried to engage the reader.

Set workbook activities 5 minutes
- Point students towards the activities on pp. 18–19 of the Workbook.
- Check understanding and answer any questions.
- These activities focus on reading between the lines.

<table>
<tr><td>Year 8</td><td colspan="3">Unit 1: Heroes and Villains</td></tr>
<tr><td colspan="2">Section 4 Openings: Lesson 8</td><td>Skills focus: Writing: Narrative</td><td>Student Book pp. 24–25
Workbook pp. 20–21</td></tr>
<tr><td rowspan="2">Main Curriculum Objectives</td><td>R8.3A Explore the impact of some of the writer's key structural or organisational choices.</td><td>W8.1A Gather and structure a range of relevant ideas before writing.</td><td>W8.2B Use appropriate linguistic conventions to achieve a wider range of purposes and address a wider range of audiences, e.g. to explain, to describe or to persuade, with confidence and understanding.</td></tr>
<tr><td colspan="3">W8.2C Use the organisational conventions of a range of forms, for a range of purposes and audiences, with confidence and understanding, including spoken-language forms such as presentations.</td></tr>
<tr><td>Secondary Curriculum Objectives</td><td colspan="3"></td></tr>
</table>

<table>
<tr><td rowspan="2">Introduction — 10 minutes
• Ask students to write or tell the opening of a well-known folk tale in the first person, present tense. (For example: 'I am walking in the woods, and…')
• Ask students to write or tell the same opening in the third person, past tense. (For example: 'She was walking in the woods, and…')
• Take feedback to check students' familiarity with, and ability to use, the past and present tenses, and the first person and the third person.</td><td>Support
Display the opening of a folk tale, ask students to identify the relevant pronouns and verbs that indicate person and tense, before the activity.</td></tr>
<tr><td>Deepen
Ask students to name as many irregular past-tense verb forms as they can.</td></tr>
<tr><td rowspan="2">First phase — 15 minutes
• Ask students to complete the Skills Boost activity. Explain that they will use this skill in Activity 4.
• Take feedback to check accuracy.
• Read through the introduction to Activity 3. Do students agree that each of these sentences could be used as the story's opening sentence?
• Ask students to complete Activity 3.
• Take feedback. Make the point that effective storytelling is not simply recounting events.</td><td>Support
Encourage partners to check each other's use of past-tense verb forms in the Skills Boost activity.</td></tr>
<tr><td>Deepen
Encourage students to explore the writer's intention further in their responses to Activity 3, question 2.</td></tr>
<tr><td rowspan="2">Second phase — 20 minutes
• Explain that Activity 4 will support students in developing their storytelling skills.
• Read through Activity 4, checking understanding and noting parallels with the extract.
• Ask students to complete Activity 4.</td><td>Support
Take feedback after each step in the writing process.</td></tr>
<tr><td>Deepen
Encourage students to write as clearly and vividly as possible, giving careful thought to vocabulary choice.</td></tr>
<tr><td rowspan="2">Plenary — 10 minutes
• Ask volunteers to share their story openings and explain their choices of first sentence.
• Discuss the openings. Ask: Do you agree that the opening makes you want to read on and find out what happens next?</td><td>Support
Look again at the intentions outlined in Activity 2 in the previous lesson, as prompts for students' explanations.</td></tr>
<tr><td>Deepen
Ask students to rewrite their story openings in the present tense. Ask: What impact does this have?</td></tr>
</table>

Set workbook activities — **5 minutes**

- Point students towards the activities on pp. 20–21 of the Workbook.
- Check understanding and answer any questions.
- These activities focus on choosing tense and person, and writing an opening.

Year 8	Unit 1: Heroes and Villains		
Section 5 Assessment: Lesson 9		Skills focus: Writing: Narrative	Student Book pp. 26–27 Workbook pp. 22–23
Main Curriculum Objectives	**R8.1B** Identify and retrieve a range of key information in a text or in spoken language.	**R8.1E** Make inferences from specific evidence found in a text or in spoken language, including specific vocabulary choices.	**R8.2B** Express a critical response to a text through writing, discussion or presentation, by considering the text's features and their effects.
	R8.3A Explore the impact of some of the writer's key structural or organisational choices.	**R8.4B** Explore the impact of some of the writer's or speaker's significant vocabulary choices.	**W8.1A** Gather and structure a range of relevant ideas before writing.
	W8.2C Use the organisational conventions of a range of forms, for a range of purposes and audiences, with confidence and understanding, including spoken-language forms such as presentations.	**W8.3G** Select vocabulary in text and spoken language with growing precision.	
Secondary Curriculum Objectives			

Introduction **10 minutes**

- Ask students to read the extract. Check their understanding of any unfamiliar vocabulary and, in particular, the meaning of the word 'draconian' (strict).
- Explain to students that they will have 25 minutes to complete the reading section of the assessment, and a further 25 minutes to complete the writing section.

Assessment task **50 minutes**

- Ask students to complete the reading section of the assessment. Any students finishing sooner can begin the writing task.
- After 25 minutes, ask students to move on to complete the writing section of the assessment.
- Point out that they should plan their writing, and that you will assess their plans as well as their finished pieces of writing.
- You may wish to give students further guidance on how much they should write, and the amounts of time they should use for planning, writing and checking their responses.

Workbook assessment task

- Point students towards the extract and activities on pp. 22–23 of the Workbook.
- Give students the opportunity to read the extract. Briefly discuss it with them and answer any questions.
- Students should read the extract again carefully before answering the questions that follow it.
- Make clear your expectations of when this task will be completed. For example, it may be a homework, or students may be given time during an additional lesson.

Year 8	Unit 1: Heroes and Villains		
Section 6 Story structure: Lesson 10	Skills focus: Writing: Narrative		Student Book pp. 28–29 Workbook pp. 24–25
Main Curriculum Objectives	**R8.1B** Identify and retrieve a range of key information in a text or in spoken language.	**R8.2A** Explore a writer's or speaker's intention and viewpoint.	**W8.3I** Use upper-case letters, end punctuation, commas, speech marks and apostrophes correctly, with accuracy and consistency
Secondary Curriculum Objectives			

Lesson	Support / Deepen
Introduction **10 minutes** • Display the following question. *What are the ingredients of a good story?* • Give partners five minutes to discuss and note down their responses. • Take feedback to assess and refresh prior knowledge, highlighting references to story structure such as beginnings, surprises and endings.	**Support** Focus students' discussions on one or two familiar novels or films. **Deepen** Encourage students to organise their thoughts under headings such as 'structure', 'character' and 'setting'.
First phase **15 minutes** • Read the summary and take students' initial responses. Ask: Is this an example of a good story? Why or why not? Encourage students to justify their views. • Ask students to read the summary again, and to note down all the words containing apostrophes. • Read through the Punctuation Boost activity. • Ask students to categorise the words they noted from the summary as showing contraction or possession. • Ask students to complete the Punctuation Boost activity. • Take feedback. Ask: How many apostrophes did you add?	**Support** Provide additional examples to support those given in the Punctuation Boost activity. **Deepen** Ask students to write their own sentences summarising the end of the story, using more apostrophes.
Second phase **20 minutes** • Return students' attention to the key points in the story summary. • Ask students to complete Activity 1, emphasising that writers make purposeful and deliberate choices to create a satisfying story, and that responses should focus on why each choice is important. • Take feedback to check and discuss understanding.	**Support** Take feedback after Activity 1, question 1 to ensure focus on the relevance of these elements to later events in the story. **Deepen** Ask students to identify and comment on the intention of any other of the writer's choices.
Plenary **10 minutes** • Take feedback, again emphasising that all of the story's elements fit together to make the story 'work', like cogs in a machine. • Ask students to consider how the story would be affected if Marshall had a well-paid job and plenty of money. • Ask students to consider next how the story would be affected if Everard had not been married. Draw out that this element is more subtle: it acts only as a clue for the reader.	**Support** Recognise and validate any relevant responses, continually focusing students' attention back on how elements fit together. **Deepen** Ask students to consider the role of Everard's wife as a way the writer tries to mislead the reader.

Set workbook activities **5 minutes**
- Point students towards the activities on pp. 24–25 of the Workbook.
- Check understanding and answer any questions.
- These activities focus on apostrophes, and ideas and intentions.

Year 8	Unit 1: Heroes and Villains		
Section 6 Story structure: Lesson 11	Skills focus: Writing: Narrative		Student Book pp. 30–31 Workbook pp. 26–27
Main Curriculum Objectives	**R8.3A** Explore the impact of some of the writer's key structural or organisational choices.	**W8.1A** Gather and structure a range of relevant ideas before writing.	**W8.2C** Use the organisational conventions of a range of forms, for a range of purposes and audiences, with confidence and understanding, including spoken-language forms such as presentations.
Secondary Curriculum Objectives			

Lesson	Support / Deepen
Introduction **10 minutes** • Present students with the familiar concept of stories having a beginning, middle and end. • Ask: What does each of these elements do? Give partners three minutes to discuss and note down their ideas. • Take feedback, highlighting the purpose of each element, and giving some examples of content that could be part of each one (for example, an introduction to characters, a journey and a return).	**Support** Give students a three- or four-point synopsis of a familiar story for reference, as a model. **Deepen** Ask students to use the synopsis of *The Brazilian Cat* for reference.
First phase **15 minutes** • Explain to students that, in this lesson, they will be exploring a more-developed and detailed model of story structure. • Read through the introduction to Activity 2. • Ask students to complete Activity 2. • Take feedback, with regular reference to each of the story structure's four parts.	**Support** Complete Activity 2, question 1a as a whole class or in supported groups. **Deepen** Ask students to apply this structure to other stories.
Second phase **20 minutes** • Read through the introduction to Activity 3, question 1. • Ask: What are the purposes of the hero and the villain in stories? Look for responses that recognise villains' roles in creating conflict. • Ask students to complete Activity 3, assuring them that they should write only notes, not their whole story.	**Support** Take feedback after each of the first two or three steps in the planning process to ensure understanding and progression. **Deepen** Encourage students to create two different endings and select the most satisfying.
Plenary **10 minutes** • Ask partners to discuss their story plans. Ask: Does each of the elements achieve its given purpose? Do the elements work well together? Is the story likely to be engaging and entertaining? • Take feedback on Activity 3, question 2 from a range of volunteers. Invite the class to evaluate each plan, focusing on positive aspects. • Ask students to recall their learning about powerful opening lines, and about stories that are not told in chronological order. • Discuss the idea that the four story elements could be narrated in any order.	**Support** Recognise and validate any effective examples of each of the four elements of story structure. **Deepen** Ask students to choose between the two possible endings they have planned, and to write a justification of their choice.

Set workbook activities **5 minutes**
- Point students towards the activities on pp. 26–27 of the Workbook.
- Check understanding and answer any questions.
- These activities focus on story structure.

Year 8	Unit 1: Heroes and Villains		
Section 7 Endings: Lesson 12		Skills focus: Writing: Narrative	Student Book pp. 32–33 Workbook pp. 28–29
Main Curriculum Objectives	**R8.2A** Explore a writer's or speaker's intention and viewpoint.	**R8.2B** Express a critical response to a text through writing, discussion or presentation, by considering the text's features and their effects.	**R8.3A** Explore the impact of some of the writer's key structural or organisational choices.
Secondary Curriculum Objectives	**R8.1B** Identify and retrieve a range of key information in a text or in spoken language.		

Lesson	Support / Deepen
Introduction — **10 minutes** • Tell students a familiar story in synopsis, creating a cliffhanger by omitting the ending. For example: *A wicked queen becomes envious of her stepdaughter's beauty. She orders a huntsman to kill the girl. The huntsman takes pity on her, and leaves her in a forest instead.* • Ask: Did you enjoy the story? Why or why not? Draw out that the story has no resolution. • Ask: Which kinds of endings do you prefer stories to have? Why is that?	**Support** Direct students to the types of ending listed in Activity 1, question 1, to support their views on different kinds of ending. **Deepen** Ask students to suggest ways in which your story could end.
First phase — **15 minutes** • Read the three synopses. (Point out that 'synopses' is the plural of 'synopsis'.) • Take students' initial responses to the three stories. Ask: Which would you want to read in full? Why? • Ask students to complete Activity 1. • Take feedback to check understanding, asking volunteers to justify their answers. • Focus on discussion of the ending of Story C, encouraging debate about this 'twist' ending. Ask: Is this ending also a 'cliffhanger'? Is it happy? Encourage students to consider the ending from the different characters' points of view.	**Support** Work with the whole class or in supported groups using a process of elimination, asking, for example: Do any of the stories have a happy ending? **Deepen** Ask: Can you suggest any other kinds of story ending?
Second phase — **20 minutes** • Read through Activity 2 to check understanding. • Ask students to complete Activity 2, question 1. Depending on the time available, you may want students to respond either in complete sentences or with single words or phrases. • Take feedback. • Ask students to complete Activity 2, question 2.	**Support** Complete the activity in relation to Story A as a whole class or in supported groups before asking students to complete the rest of the activity independently. **Deepen** Encourage students to support their ideas with examples from the synopses.
Plenary — **10 minutes** • Take feedback on Activity 2, question 2. • Ask: Would the reader's initial impressions of any characters change due to the way the story ended? Ask students to identify and explain one example of characters for which this is true (for example, the hitch-hiker in Story C or the piper in Story B).	**Support** Recognise and validate any relevant responses. **Deepen** Challenge students to suggest different ways in which these stories could have ended.

Set workbook activities — **5 minutes**
- Point students towards the activities on pp. 28–29 of the Workbook.
- Check understanding and answer any questions.
- These activities focus on story endings.

Year 8	Unit 1: Heroes and Villains		
Section 7 Endings: Lesson 13	Skills focus: Writing: Narrative		Student Book pp. 34–35 Workbook pp. 30–31
Main Curriculum Objectives	**R8.2A** Explore a writer's or speaker's intention and viewpoint.	**W8.1A** Gather and structure a range of relevant ideas before writing.	**W8.3I** Use upper-case letters, end punctuation, commas, speech marks and apostrophes correctly, with accuracy and consistency.
Secondary Curriculum Objectives	**W8.2C** Use the organisational conventions of a range of forms, for a range of purposes and audiences, with confidence and understanding, including spoken-language forms such as presentations.		

Introduction 10 minutes • Display the following two single-clause sentences. *The hero should be rewarded. The hero saved the town.* • Ask students to create a multi-clause sentence by linking the sentences using a conjunction such as 'because', 'if', 'when' or 'after'. • Ask: What effects are created by the different conjunctions? • Note that the different conjunctions create different meanings because of the different relationships between clauses.	**Support** Provide students with a list of possible conjunctions: 'and', 'but', 'when', 'because', 'if', 'until', 'although' and 'while'. **Deepen** Challenge students to find as many different ways of linking the sentences as they can.
First phase 15 minutes • Read through the introduction to the Punctuation Boost activity to check understanding. • Ask students to complete the Punctuation Boost activity. • Take feedback. Emphasise that colons and semi-colons should not be overused, and that conjunctions often make meaning clearer. • Draw students' attention back to the story synopses, and ask them to recap the focus of the previous lesson: story endings. • Ask students to complete Activity 3. • Take feedback, encouraging debate.	**Support** In question 1 of the Punctuation Boost activity, work with students to identify the conjunctions before asking them to complete the activity independently. **Deepen** Challenge students to write further sentences related to the synopses using colons and semi-colons.
Second phase 20 minutes • Read through Activity 4 and check students' understanding. • Ask students to complete Activity 4. Challenge them to include a semi-colon and a colon in their responses.	**Support** In Activity 4, question 1, ask students to focus on parts a and d, thinking up happy and sad endings. **Deepen** Challenge students to come up with more different endings. Encourage quality and quantity.
Plenary 10 minutes • Take feedback from a range of volunteers on their preferred endings, and the responses they expect these to create. • Ask the class to explain their responses. Ask: Does your response tally with the writer's intention?	**Support** Recognise and validate any relevant choices. **Deepen** Ask students which type of ending they find most satisfying and why.

Set workbook activities 5 minutes

- Point students towards the activities on pp. 30–31 of the Workbook.
- Check understanding and answer any questions.
- These activities focus on colons and semi-colons, and writing endings.

Year 8	Unit 1: Heroes and Villains		
Section 8 Ways of telling stories: Lesson 14		**Skills focus: Writing: Narrative**	**Student Book pp. 36–37 Workbook pp. 32–33**
Main Curriculum Objectives	**R8.1B** Identify and retrieve a range of key information in a text or in spoken language.	**R8.3A** Explore the impact of some of the writer's key structural or organisational choices.	
Secondary Curriculum Objectives	**R8.2A** Explore a writer's or speaker's intention and viewpoint.	**R8.4B** Explore the impact of some of the writer's or speaker's significant vocabulary choices.	

Introduction **10 minutes** • Display the terms 'speech', 'thought', 'action' and 'description'. • Explain that most stories contain all of these elements. • Ask: Which of these elements is most important in telling a story? Encourage discussion and debate. • Draw out that events (action) form most of the plot in most stories, but not all. • Look back through the extracts used in the Student Book so far, observing that **speech** is dominant in the extracts in Section 2, **thought and action** in Section 3, and **thought and description** in Section 4.	**Support** Clarify the terms 'speech', 'thought', 'action' and 'description' to ensure understanding. **Deepen** Ask students to find passages that focus on each of the four elements using other texts.
First phase **15 minutes** • Read the extract and take students' initial responses. • Ask students to complete Activity 1 to test their understanding. • Take feedback on questions 1–4 to check accuracy. • Discuss students' answers to question 5, looking at the evidence that suggests Givens is not being honest about the way he feels: he is embarrassed and it is implied that his pride is hurt.	**Support** Complete Activity 1 orally, as a whole class or in supported groups. **Deepen** Ask students to suggest ways in which the story could end.
Second phase **20 minutes** • Return students' focus to the elements of speech, thought, action and description in storytelling. • Read through Activity 2. • Ask students to complete Activity 2, noting that thought need not be explicitly 'labelled' with an identifier such as 'he thought' or 'she wondered'.	**Support** To ensure understanding, take feedback on Activity 2, question 1 before asking students to complete question 2. **Deepen** Encourage students to comment on what each technique reveals or suggests about the two characters.
Plenary **10 minutes** • Take feedback on Activity 2, encouraging discussion and debate. • Note that one sentence features in both questions, giving different kinds of information about the two characters.	**Support** Recognise and validate all relevant responses. **Deepen** Ask: Which technique do you find most engaging: speech, thought, description or action? Why is that?

Set workbook activities **5 minutes**

- Point students towards the activities on pp. 32–33 of the Workbook.
- Check understanding and answer any questions.
- These activities focus on exploring an extract,

Year 8	Unit 1: Heroes and Villains		
Section 8 Ways of telling stories: Lesson 15	Skills focus: Writing: Narrative		Student Book pp. 38–39 Workbook pp. 34–35
Main Curriculum Objectives	**W8.2C** Use the organisational conventions of a range of forms, for a range of purposes and audiences, with confidence and understanding, including spoken-language forms such as presentations.	**W8.3G** Select vocabulary in text and spoken language with growing precision.	
Secondary Curriculum Objectives	**W8.3A** Write in Standard English and a largely appropriate register.	**W8.3J** Use grammatical terminology for parts of speech with some accuracy.	

Introduction **10 minutes** • Give students three minutes to note near-synonyms for the verb 'to say': any verbs that could appear as part of an identifier in a passage of dialogue (for example 'shout', 'whisper' or 'mutter'). • Take feedback, noting examples for reference in the Skills Boost activity.	**Support** Give students a model sentence and ask them to replace the verb 'said'. For example: *"Hello," she said.* **Deepen** Encourage students to build their vocabulary using a thesaurus and a dictionary to find and define near-synonyms.
First phase **15 minutes** • Read through Activity 3 and check students' understanding. • Ask students to complete Activity 3. • Take feedback to share and develop understanding. • Read through the Skills Boost activity. Check students' understanding of the terms 'adverb' and 'identifier'. • Ask students to complete the Skills Boost activity. • Take feedback to check accuracy.	**Support** In Activity 3, rewrite the first sentence using speech and the third sentence using description as a whole class or in supported groups, before asking students to complete the activity independently. **Deepen** In Activity 3, encourage students to try further rewrites of their responses using action.
Second phase **20 minutes** • Read through Activity 4. • Ask students to complete questions 1 and 2. • Take feedback to share and develop ideas. • Ask students to complete questions 3–8. • Ask partners to check each other's speech punctuation.	**Support** Take feedback after each step in the writing process to ensure understanding and progression. For support with speech punctuation, direct students to the Skills Boost activity in Section 2 of this unit. **Deepen** Following Activity 4, question 7, ask students to experiment with transforming some sentences from their focus on speech, action, thought or description to another technique.
Plenary **10 minutes** • Ask volunteers to share their writing with the class, clearly identifying which sentences use which technique: description, action, speech or thought. • Ask: Which technique did you find the easiest to use? Which was the most challenging? Which was most effective in telling the story and engaging readers?	**Support** Recognise and validate effective use of any one of the four techniques. **Deepen** Ask students to write a brief critical response to their own writing, noting what is suggested or revealed about their characters.

Set workbook activities **5 minutes**
- Point students towards the activities on pp. 34–35 of the Workbook.
- Check understanding and answer any questions.
- These activities focus on identifiers and telling stories.

Year 8	Unit 1: Heroes and Villains		
Section 9 Structuring sentences: Lesson 16		Skills focus: Writing: Narrative	Student Book pp. 40–41 Workbook pp. 36–37
Main Curriculum Objectives	**R8.2A** Explore a writer's or speaker's intention and viewpoint.	**R8.3A** Explore the impact of some of the writer's key structural or organisational choices.	
	R8.4A Explore the impact of some of a writer's or speaker's choices of grammatical features and sentence structure.		
Secondary Curriculum Objectives			

Lesson	Support / Deepen
Introduction — **10 minutes** • Display the term 'clause'. • Display a single-clause sentence. For example: *I went to school.* • Remind students that a clause is a single piece of information centred on one verb. • Ask students to link another clause to the first one using a conjunction. • Repeat, creating a longer and longer sentence.	**Support** Provide example conjunctions students could use to link their clauses (such as 'and', 'but', 'when', 'as', 'before', 'after', 'until', 'because', 'so', 'although' and 'if'). **Deepen** Restrict students to using each conjunction only once.
First phase — **15 minutes** • Read the extract, and take students' initial responses. Ask: Is the reader intended to sympathise with Ella or the thief? Who is the hero and who is the villain? • Ask students to complete Activity 1, first clarifying the meaning of the term 'pace' as a sense of how quickly something moves along. • Take feedback, emphasising that choices of sentence structure can add impact to a text.	**Support** Read the given sentences aloud to the whole class or supported groups, emphasising their brevity and the fast pace created. **Deepen** Ask students to identify other shorter sentences the writer has used to create impact in the extract.
Second phase — **20 minutes** • Read through Activity 2. • Note the changes needed to convert a multi-clause sentence into single-clause sentences: the removal of the conjunction, the addition of pronouns and the alteration of punctuation. • Ask students to complete Activity 2.	**Support** Display the multi-clause sentence in Activity 2, question 2 and work with students to identify the four clauses. **Deepen** Encourage students to comment in detail on their choices, focusing on their impact on the reader.
Plenary — **10 minutes** • Take feedback on Activity 2, question 1 to check accuracy. • Ask a volunteer to read aloud their single-clause sentences and then the original multi-clause version. • Take feedback on Activity 2, question 2, discussing the impact of both versions and students' preferences.	**Support** Recognise and validate any relevant responses. **Deepen** Encourage students to consider the pace of these longer sentences. Ask: Do they create a hurried or more relaxed pace?

Set workbook activities — **5 minutes**

- Point students towards the activities on pp. 36–37 of the Workbook.
- Check understanding and answer any questions.
- These activities focus on exploring short and long sentences.

Year 8	Unit 1: Heroes and Villains		
Section 9 Structuring sentences: Lesson 17	Skills focus: Writing: Narrative		Student Book pp. 42–43 Workbook pp. 38–39
Main Curriculum Objectives	**W8.3B** Divide text into paragraphs with accuracy and consistency.	**W8.3C** Use a balance of single-clause sentences, coordinate and subordinate clauses with confidence.	**W8.3D** Use a range of sentence openings in addition to subject-verb sentence openings, starting to develop variety.
	W8.3E Make deliberate choices of sentence length to achieve clarity.		
Secondary Curriculum Objectives	**W8.1A** Gather and structure a range of relevant ideas before writing.	**W8.2D** Link paragraphs in text and spoken language using adverbials to signal the development of ideas.	

Introduction **10 minutes** • Display the following example sentences. *I love cooking. I am not very good at it.* • Ask: In the second sentence, in how many places could the adverbial 'however' be positioned? • Ask students to write another pair of sentences, including the word 'eventually' in the second. • Ask: In how many places could 'eventually' be positioned? • Discuss the fact that the adverbials could be positioned in numerous places while the sentences' meanings are retained.	**Support** Use the first example as a model before asking students to write and experiment with the second. **Deepen** Ask students to look at the adverbials listed at the start of the Grammar Boost activity. Ask: Could all of these adverbials be positioned at different points in a sentence?
First phase **15 minutes** • Ask students to recall their work on sentence structure from the previous lesson. Read through the introduction to Activity 3, checking understanding. • Ask students to complete Activity 3. • Take feedback to check accuracy. • Ask students to complete the Grammar Boost activity. Point out that the activity asks students to position the adverbials at the beginning of sentences (as 'fronted' adverbials). • Take feedback to check accuracy and understanding.	**Support** Direct students to the use of adverbials of time in the extract on page 40 of the Student Book, as an exemplar of their use in context. **Deepen** Ask students to write their own sentences linked with adverbials of contrast and consequence.
Second phase **20 minutes** • Read through questions 1–5 of Activity 4 to clarify the plot that students will use. • Ask students to complete Activity 4. Encourage them to consider sentence structure as they write, but point out that they will have an opportunity to review and revise their choices.	**Support** Take feedback after each step of the writing process to ensure understanding and progression. **Deepen** Ask partners to ensure they are both paragraphing their writing correctly.
Plenary **10 minutes** • Ask volunteers to share short excerpts of their writing. • Ask students to share their responses to Activity 4, question 8, focusing on the reasons for their choices. • Ask students to summarise the sentence-structure choices that are open to them as writers.	**Support** Recognise and validate any effective choices. **Deepen** Encourage students to explain the impacts of their choices in depth and in detail.

Set workbook activities **5 minutes**
- Point students towards the activities on pp. 38–39 of the Workbook.
- Check understanding and answer any questions.
- These activities focus on adverbials and building sentences.

Year 8	Unit 1: Heroes and Villains		
Section 10 Reviewing, revising and proofreading: Lesson 18		Skills focus: Writing: Narrative	Student Book pp. 44–45 Workbook pp. 40–41
Main Curriculum Objectives	**W8.1B** Correct a range of errors in spelling, punctuation and grammar independently after writing, beginning to develop strategies for proofreading.	**W8.3H** Spell homophones, words with single/double letters and 'silent' letters with some accuracy.	
Secondary Curriculum Objectives			

Lesson	Support / Deepen
Introduction — **10 minutes** • Display the words 'there', 'too', 'no' and 'hear'. • Remind students that homophones are words that sound the same but have different meanings and spellings. • Challenge students to note as many homophones as they can for the words displayed.	**Support** Ask students to think of just one homophone for each word. **Deepen** Challenge students to think of other homophones.
First phase — **15 minutes** • Remind students of the reviewing and revising they did at the end of the previous lesson. Emphasise that proofreading is equally important after writing, and explain that these skills form the basis of this and the next lesson. • Ask students to complete the Spelling Boost activity. • Take feedback to check accuracy. • Ask students to complete Activity 1. • Take feedback, discussing and correcting any inaccuracies.	**Support** Transform Activity 1 into a matching exercise by providing students with all or some of the present-tense verb forms. **Deepen** After the Spelling Boost activity, challenge students to write other sentences featuring the homophones.
Second phase — **20 minutes** • Ask students to complete Activity 2, question 1. Suggest that students focus their full attention on one kind of mistake at a time, rather than trying to spot all three at once. • Take feedback to ensure accuracy and understanding.	**Support** Encourage students to copy the text and **then** correct it, ensuring that they copy it accurately. **Deepen** Ask students to add notes to explain precisely what each mistake was (for example, noting 'missing possessive apostrophe', 'incorrect past-tense verb form' or 'incorrect personal pronoun').
Plenary — **10 minutes** • Ask students to complete Activity 2, question 2, setting themselves proofreading targets. • Take feedback to identify future learning needs.	**Support** Ask partners to identify valid targets together. **Deepen** Ask students to identify their targets as specifically as possible.

Set workbook activities — **5 minutes**

• Point students towards the activities on pp. 40–41 of the Workbook.
• Check understanding and answer any questions.
• These activities focus on homophones and irregular past tenses.

Year 8	Unit 1: Heroes and Villains		
Section 10 Reviewing, revising and proofreading: Lesson 19		Skills focus: Writing: Narrative	Student Book pp. 46–47 Workbook pp. 42–43
Main Curriculum Objectives	**W8.1B** Correct a range of errors in spelling, punctuation and grammar independently after writing, beginning to develop strategies for proofreading.	**W8.1C** Review and revise vocabulary choice after writing.	
Secondary Curriculum Objectives			

Lesson	Support / Deepen
Introduction **10 minutes** • Using the verbs given in Activity 1 from the previous lesson, give students a spelling test by saying the verbs' infinite forms and asking them to note down the past-tense forms. • Ask partners to swap and mark each other's answers. • Discuss which spellings proved the most challenging.	**Support** Give students each verb in the context of a sentence. **Deepen** Read students ten sentences in the present tense, each featuring one of the test verbs. Ask students to write each whole sentence in the past tense.
First phase **15 minutes** • Read through Activity 3, and point out that the synonyms given are specific to their use in the passage (for example, 'run' is not always synonymous with 'pour'). • Ask students to complete Activity 3. • Take feedback, focusing on comparing the impact of the verbs chosen and those rejected. Encourage discussion and debate. • Ask students to complete the Grammar Boost activity, clarifying the meaning of the terms 'contrasting' and 'conditional'. Point out that 'as' can function as a conjunction of time or explanation. • Take feedback to check understanding.	**Support** In the Grammar Boost activity, model using a process of elimination to identify conjunctions that make sense in the context of each sentence. **Deepen** In Activity 3, encourage students to gather (and perhaps reject) other synonyms from which to make their choices.
Second phase **20 minutes** • Ask students to complete Activity 4, pointing out that they could use the conjunction banks on the opposite page of the Student Book. • Ask students to complete Activity 5.	**Support** Depending on students' confidence, you could suggest that they carry out question 1d in Activity 5 in groups. **Deepen** Encourage students to justify their choices in Activity 4. Ask: Have you created greater clarity or impact?
Plenary **10 minutes** • Take feedback on Activity 5, focusing on one question at a time. • Emphasise the process followed, and the importance of reviewing, revising and proofreading as the final stages in any writing task.	**Support** Recognise and validate any accurate corrections and/or effective revisions. **Deepen** Encourage students to consider the variety of conjunctions used, and whether they could add any adverbials.

Set workbook activities **5 minutes**
- Point students towards the activities on pp. 42–43 of the Workbook.
- Check understanding and answer any questions.
- These activities focus on reviewing vocabulary and sentence structure.

Year 8	Unit 1: Heroes and Villains		
Section 11 Assessment: Lesson 20	Skills focus: Writing: Narrative		Student Book pp. 48–49 Workbook pp. 44–45
Main Curriculum Objectives	**W8.1A** Gather and structure a range of relevant ideas before writing.	**W8.1B** Correct a range of errors in spelling, punctuation and grammar independently after writing, beginning to develop strategies for proofreading.	**W8.2C** Use the organisational conventions of a range of forms, for a range of purposes and audiences, with confidence and understanding, including spoken-language forms such as presentations.
	W8.3A Write in Standard English and a largely appropriate register.	**W8.3C** Use a balance of single-clause sentences, coordinate and subordinate clauses with confidence.	**W8.3D** Use a range of sentence openings in addition to subject-verb sentence openings, starting to develop variety.
	W8.3E Make deliberate choices of sentence length to achieve clarity.	**W8.3G** Select vocabulary in text and spoken language with growing precision.	**W8.3H** Spell homophones, words with single/double letters and 'silent' letters with some accuracy.
	W8.3I Use upper-case letters, end punctuation, commas, speech marks and apostrophes correctly, with accuracy and consistency.		
Secondary Curriculum Objectives			

Introduction **10 minutes**

- Ask students to read Activity 1.
- Point out that students should plan a complete story, and that you will assess their plans as well as their finished pieces of writing. Make it clear that they will not have time to write the whole of their story in this lesson, and should therefore focus on careful planning and the quality (not length) of their story's beginning.
- Explain to students that they will have 15 minutes to plan their story, 25 minutes to write its beginning and a further 10 minutes to review, revise and proofread their writing.

Assessment task **50 minutes**

- Ask students to complete the planning section of the assessment.
- After 15 minutes, ask students to move on to the writing section of the assessment.
- After another 25 minutes, ask students to move on to the reviewing and revising section of the assessment.
- You may wish to give students further guidance on how much they should write, and the amounts of time they should use for planning, writing and checking their responses.

Workbook assessment task

- Point students towards the task and sample student response on p. 44 of the Workbook.
- Give students the opportunity to read the task and sample response. Briefly discuss these with them and answer any questions.
- Students should identify the errors in the sample response before planning how they will improve it. They should then write an improved version, adding one or two paragraphs of text.
- Make clear your expectations of when this task will be completed. For example, it may be a homework, or students may be given time during an additional lesson.

Year 8	Unit 2: Safe and Sound		
Section 1 Spotting persuasive techniques: Lesson 1		Skills focus: Reading: Persuasive texts	Student Book pp. 52–53 Workbook pp. 46–47
Main Curriculum Objectives	**R8.1B** Identify and retrieve a range of key information in a text or in spoken language.	**R8.1D** Compare, contrast and/or combine key points of information within a text or in spoken language.	
Secondary Curriculum Objectives			

Introduction 10 minutes • Ask students to suggest situations in which they may need to be persuasive. • Ask students to describe the techniques or strategies they may use in order to be persuasive. • Look for responses that suggest giving key reasons (key points) contributes to persuasiveness. • Aim to draw attention to the importance of selecting persuasive points.	**Support** Supply examples of situations in which persuasion may be needed, for example when asking a friend for a favour. **Deepen** Take one suggestion for a situation, and ask all students to note key points they might make to achieve the desired outcome.
First phase 15 minutes • Ask students to read the poster once, quickly. • Draw attention to the Remember feature beneath it, and ask students to read the poster again. • Discuss the purpose of the poster. • Ask students to complete Activity 1. Take feedback to ensure and develop understanding. • Ask: Do you find the poster persuasive? Why is this?	**Support** To aid discussion, suggest possible purposes the poster could have (for example, to inform, explain, describe, argue or persuade). **Deepen** Ask: Which of the ideas mentioned in Activity 1, question 2 is most prominent in the poster? Which is the most persuasive?
Second phase 20 minutes • Read the first few sentences of the poster again. Ask students to interrupt when they hear a sentence that gives a reason why it is important to drink water. • Ask students to complete Activity 2. • Look again at the sentence that students identified as the first one giving a reason why it is important to drink water. • Ask: Why do you think the writer makes this point so early in the text?	**Support** Complete Activity 2, question 1 as a whole class or in supported groups, reading and pausing after each sentence. For each, ask: Does this sentence give a reason for the importance of water? **Deepen** Ask partners to discuss Activity 2, question 3, agreeing and justifying their choices.
Plenary 10 minutes • Take feedback on Activity 2, discussing which sentence most students found the most or least persuasive, and why. • Keep a record of the most persuasive sentence(s) chosen to use in the next lesson. • Discuss the fact that the writer suggests both positive and negative possible consequences: the benefits of drinking water and the drawbacks of not drinking water. • Ask: What makes a key point persuasive?	**Support** Select three sentences that highlight the benefits of drinking water. Ask students what they have in common. **Deepen** Ask students to consider which are most prevalent in the poster: benefits or drawbacks. Discuss why the writer might have made this choice.

Set workbook activities 5 minutes
- Point students towards the activities on pp. 46–47 of the Workbook.
- Check understanding and answer any questions.
- These activities focus on identifying key information and combining key points.

Year 8	Unit 2: Safe and Sound		
Section 1 Spotting persuasive techniques: Lesson 2	Skills focus: Reading: Persuasive texts		Student Book pp. 54–55 Workbook pp. 48–49
Main Curriculum Objectives	**R8.4B** Explore the impact of some of the writer's or speaker's significant vocabulary choices.	**W8.1A** Gather and structure a range of relevant ideas before writing.	**W8.3G** Select vocabulary in text and spoken language with growing precision.
	W8.3J Use grammatical terminology for parts of speech with some accuracy.		
Secondary Curriculum Objectives			

Lesson	Support / Deepen
Introduction **10 minutes** • Ask students to suggest things that a bossy person might say in order to get you to do something. • Ask students to note or suggest how a very polite person might ask the same things. • Ask: What differences can you identify? • Look for responses that recognise the different verb forms.	**Support** Draw students' attention to points of comparison, for example the first word or phrase of a suggested sentence, and then its use of verbs. **Deepen** Ask: Which method of speech is more persuasive? Why is this?
First phase **15 minutes** • Ask students to complete the first Grammar Boost activity, on imperative verbs. • Ask students to suggest one thing they enjoy and one thing they do not. As a class, compile positive and negative vocabulary to describe the two things. • Ask students to complete Activity 3, question 1. Take feedback to check and reinforce understanding. • Draw attention to the most persuasive sentence(s) from the poster that students identified in Activity 2 during the previous lesson. • Ask students to complete Activity 3, question 2. • Ask students to complete the second Grammar Boost activity, on parts of speech.	**Support** Complete Activity 3, question 1a as a whole class or in supported groups before asking students to complete question 1b and question 2 independently. **Deepen** Ask students to explore other significant vocabulary choices in the text, such as the pun in 'your body and every body'.
Second phase **20 minutes** • Take feedback on the second Grammar Boost activity, on parts of speech, to check understanding. • Ask: Would you choose to drink fizzy drinks or water? • Discuss the appeal of both. • Draw attention to the fact that the writer makes reference to fizzy drinks. • Discuss the fact that this addresses the problem that people could argue in favour of fizzy drinks instead of water, and so adds to the persuasion. • Ask students to complete Activity 4, using any relevant points from the discussion.	**Support** In Activity 4, complete questions 1 and 2 as a class or in supported groups, agreeing one key idea and gathering vocabulary together. Students should then complete question 3 independently. **Deepen** Encourage students to review and revise their writing to make it as persuasive as possible.
Plenary **10 minutes** • Take feedback and discuss responses to Activity 4. • Discuss the options students considered and the choices they made. • Ask partners to review each other's sentences orally, suggesting any ways in which points or vocabulary could be made more persuasive.	**Support** Recognise, validate and explore any choices that support persuasion. **Deepen** Ask students to share their suggested revisions, and ask the class to evaluate the suggestions.

Set workbook activities **5 minutes**

- Point students towards the activities on pp. 48–49 of the Workbook.
- Check understanding and answer any questions.
- These activities focus on imperative verbs, vocabulary choices and parts of speech.

Year 8	Unit 2: Safe and Sound		
Section 2 Persuasive vocabulary: Lesson 3		Skills focus: Reading: Persuasive texts	Student Book pp. 56–57 Workbook pp. 50–51
Main Curriculum Objectives	**R8.1B** Identify and retrieve a range of key information in a text or in spoken language.	**R8.1E** Make inferences from specific evidence found in a text or in spoken language, including specific vocabulary choices.	
Secondary Curriculum Objectives			

Lesson	Support / Deepen
Introduction **10 minutes** • Ask students to recall what they understand by the terms 'infer' and 'imply'. • Guide discussion towards the idea that people do not always state clearly what they mean, and sometimes suggest (imply) it instead, requiring others to use the skill of inference. • Ask: What might someone really mean if they said: o 'I wouldn't do that if I were you.' o 'Do you really think that's a good idea?'	**Support** Describe a scenario for students in which each example might be used. **Deepen** Ask students to suggest similar examples of sentences with implicit meanings. Encourage students to use the new key terms in their discussion.
First phase **15 minutes** • Read the webpage and take students' initial responses. Ask: Is the webpage informative? Is it persuasive? • Recall students' learning in the previous two lessons, specifically about the writer's inclusion of benefits (of drinking water) and drawbacks (of not drinking water). • Ask students to complete Activity 1. • Take feedback to check, share and develop understanding.	**Support** Model surveying each sentence of the given webpage for a positive or negative consequence. **Deepen** Ask students to supplement their responses to Activity 1, question 2 by identifying any supporting explanations given in the webpage.
Second phase **20 minutes** • Recall the key point discussed during the introduction to the lesson: that people do not always state clearly what they mean. • Ask: What effect do you think this has in persuasive texts? • Discuss or explain that writers of persuasive texts often rely on the reader's inference skills, and that this can make readers feel like they have come to their own conclusions about a topic rather than having a writer's opinion pressed on them. • Ask students to complete Activity 2.	**Support** Complete Activity 2 through discussion as a whole class or in supported groups. **Deepen** Ask: Can you identify any other sentences from the webpage in which the writer's meaning is implied rather than stated?
Plenary **10 minutes** • Take feedback on Activity 2. • Ask: How would you describe the overall tone of the webpage: positive or negative? • Ask: Which tone do you think is more likely to be persuasive in a text like this one: positive or negative?	**Support** Recognise and validate any relevant responses. **Deepen** Challenge students to rewrite the first section of the webpage, making it less positive and instead highlighting negative consequences.

Set workbook activities **5 minutes**
- Point students towards the activities on pp. 50–51 of the Workbook.
- Check understanding and answer any questions.
- These activities focus on identifying key ideas and inference.

Year 8	Unit 2: Safe and Sound		
Section 2 Persuasive vocabulary: Lesson 4	Skills focus: Reading: Persuasive texts		Student Book pp. 58–59 Workbook pp. 52–53
Main Curriculum Objectives	**R8.4B** Explore the impact of some of the writer's or speaker's significant vocabulary choices.	**W8.1A** Gather and structure a range of relevant ideas before writing.	**W8.3G** Select vocabulary in text and spoken language with growing precision.
Secondary Curriculum Objectives			

Lesson	Support / Deepen
Introduction **10 minutes** • Display the following definition. ***heart:*** *muscular organ that pumps blood through the circulatory system* • Challenge students to write a sentence using a different meaning of the word 'heart'. • Take feedback. Ask: What ideas are connected with the word 'heart'? Look for responses identifying, for example, love, affection, essence and strength. • Recap the term 'connotations' for connected ideas.	**Support** Provide prompt sentences such as 'I love you with all my heart', 'She had a hearty laugh' and 'We must get to the heart of the matter'. **Deepen** Consider the connotations of other body parts, such as the backbone or brain.
First phase **15 minutes** • Ask students to complete the Skills Boost activity. • Take feedback to share and develop understanding. • Ask students to explain further the connotations for them of each word: the personal ideas or associations each word creates. • Ask students to complete Activity 3. • Take feedback. • Discuss why the writer has chosen a phrase with such negative connotations.	**Support** In the Skills Boost activity, read out the sentence using each of the six words given. In each case, ask: Do you feel you are being positively persuaded to use a computer, or negatively persuaded not to use a computer? **Deepen** Challenge students to rewrite the phrase 'acid attack' using vocabulary with less-negative connotations.
Second phase **20 minutes** • Ask students to complete Activity 4, exploring the role of vocabulary choice in persuading the reader. • Take feedback. • Ask students to complete Activity 5, question 1. • Take feedback, discussing students' initial ideas. • Ask students to complete Activity 5, encouraging them to consider the connotations of their vocabulary choices.	**Support** In Activity 4, question 1d, encourage students to make use of the given sentence starts. **Deepen** In Activity 5, encourage students to revise their vocabulary choices with focus on using more positive or negative connotations.
Plenary **10 minutes** • Ask partners to select the most persuasive sentences in each other's response to Activity 5. • Ask students to write one or two sentences explaining why they found their chosen sentences so persuasive. • Take feedback from a variety of volunteers. • Ask the class to discuss how persuasive they find each sentence, and why.	**Support** Recognise and validate any effective points and/or vocabulary choice. **Deepen** Ask students to evaluate which makes the most persuasive contribution to a text: reference to positive consequences, reference to negative consequences or effective vocabulary choices.

Set workbook activities **5 minutes**
- Point students towards the activities on pp. 52–53 of the Workbook.
- Check understanding and answer any questions.
- These activities focus on connotations and writing persuasively.

Year 8	Unit 2: Safe and Sound		
Section 3 Responding to a text: Lesson 5	Skills focus: Reading: Persuasive texts		Student Book pp. 60–61 Workbook pp. 54–55
Main Curriculum Objectives	**R8.1B** Identify and retrieve a range of key information in a text or in spoken language.	**R8.2A** Explore a writer's or speaker's intention and viewpoint.	**R8.2C** Select relevant, focused evidence to support ideas.
Secondary Curriculum Objectives			

Lesson	Support / Deepen
Introduction **10 minutes** • Ask students to name one book aimed at very young children and another aimed at teenagers. • Ask students to suggest three or four ways in which the two styles of books differ (for example in their language levels, content and use of illustration). • Ask students why these differences are necessary. Look for responses that show awareness that texts are aimed at specific audiences.	**Support** Provide two texts that will be familiar to students: one aimed at young children and another aimed at teenagers. **Deepen** Ask students to suggest books or films aimed at other specific age groups and audiences. Ask: In what ways are they appropriate for their audiences?
First phase **15 minutes** • Read the webpage and take students' initial responses. Ask: Do you find the extract engaging and persuasive? • Read through Activity 1, noting the tactic of an elimination process suggested in the *How do I do that?* feature. • Ask students to complete Activity 1. • Take feedback to check and share understanding. Highlight the importance of identifying the key messages of a persuasive text.	**Support** Model and complete Activity 1, question 1a as a whole class or in supported groups before asking students to complete questions 1b and 1c independently. **Deepen** Ask: Which of the three key points identified in Activity 1 most succinctly and accurately sums up the whole text?
Second phase **20 minutes** • Ask students to imagine a huge room filled with an audience of men and women representing all the ages, cultures and interests of humanity. • Ask: Who in that audience might be interested in reading the webpage? Who might be the audience that the writer intended for it? • Ask students to complete Activity 2, questions 1–3.	**Support** Ask: Is this webpage relevant to you and your age group? Why is that? **Deepen** Ask students to identify evidence from the webpage to support their responses.
Plenary **10 minutes** • Take feedback on Activity 2, questions 1–3, to check understanding. Look for responses that consider both the audience's age and interests. • Allow three minutes for students to complete Activity 2, question 4. • Take feedback, asking students to justify their choices by commenting on how their ideas reflect the writer's intention and appeal to their target audience.	**Support** Recognise and validate any relevant responses. **Deepen** Ask: How would the webpage need to be adapted to make it appropriate for and accessible to younger children?

Set workbook activities **5 minutes**
- Point students towards the activities on pp. 54–55 of the Workbook.
- Check understanding and answer any questions.
- These activities focus on identifying intention and audience.

Year 8	Unit 2: Safe and Sound		
Section 3 Responding to a text: Lesson 6	Skills focus: Reading: Persuasive texts		Student Book pp. 62–63 Workbook pp. 56–57
Main Curriculum Objectives	**R8.2B** Express a critical response to a text through writing, discussion or presentation, by considering the text's features and their effects.	**R8.2C** Select relevant, focused evidence to support ideas.	**R8.4B** Explore the impact of some of the writer's or speaker's significant vocabulary choices.
Secondary Curriculum Objectives	**W8.3I** Use upper-case letters, end punctuation, commas, speech marks and apostrophes correctly, with accuracy and consistency.		

Lesson	Support / Deepen
Introduction 10 minutes • Display the following two sentences. *Lady Macbeth is full of regret What's done cannot be undone.* *Shakespeare makes it clear that this character knows What's done cannot be undone.* • Ask students to instruct you in how to punctuate the sentences. • Look for responses that recognise the difference in punctuation necessary for the two different quotations.	**Support** Work through the process in steps, first adding quotation marks and then discussing whether or not each quotation needs punctuation (a colon) to introduce it. **Deepen** Introduce the terms 'embedded quotation' and 'freestanding quotation' to differentiate between the two styles of quotation in the example sentences.
First phase 15 minutes • Ask students to complete the Skills Boost activity. • Take feedback to check accuracy. • Ask students to complete Activity 3. • Take feedback on Activity 3. • Discuss and emphasise the importance of choosing short, relevant, focused quotations.	**Support** In the Skills Boost activity, work as a class to repeat the process used in the introduction to the lesson, adding quotation marks first. **Deepen** Ask students to identify two or three short, relevant quotations that highlight the problems of using social networks.
Second phase 20 minutes • Ask students to complete Activity 4. Point out that exploring vocabulary choice is an important element in responding to a text successfully. • Take feedback on Activity 4. Discuss whether or not students have identified the same vocabulary choices. • Read through Activity 5, identifying the skills involved (and covered in this and the previous lesson). • Ask students to complete Activity 5.	**Support** Complete Activity 4 as a whole class or in supported groups. Use a process of elimination to identify significant vocabulary choices. **Deepen** Encourage students to focus on the fluency and clarity of their response to Activity 5.
Plenary 10 minutes • Ask students to work with a partner or independently to identify and label the three bulleted key elements in their response to Activity 5. • Give students a further minute or two to check the accuracy of their punctuation. • Ask volunteers to share their responses, to share and develop understanding.	**Support** Recognise and validate any effective elements in students' critical responses. **Deepen** Ask students to experiment with resequencing the three key elements, and with ways of linking them.

Set workbook activities 5 minutes
- Point students towards the activities on pp. 56–57 of the Workbook.
- Check understanding and answer any questions.
- These activities focus on quotations and vocabulary.

Year 8	Unit 2: Safe and Sound		
Section 4 Organising your response: Lesson 7	Skills focus: Reading: Persuasive texts		Student Book pp. 64–65 Workbook pp. 58–59
Main Curriculum Objectives	**R8.1B** Identify and retrieve a range of key information in a text or in spoken language.	**R8.2A** Explore a writer's or speaker's intention and viewpoint.	**R8.2C** Select relevant, focused evidence to support ideas.
Secondary Curriculum Objectives			

Introduction **10 minutes** • Display the term 'intention'. • Ask students to identify the writer's intention in each text you mention, and then name a range of found text types such as a stop sign on a road (intended to prevent accidents), instructions for a gadget (intended to help the owner work the gadget), a map (intended to help the user find their way) and a dictionary (intended to explain the meanings of words).	**Support** Prompt students with sentence starts such as 'The writer created this text in order to...' and 'A reader would want to read this text because...'. **Deepen** Ask students to name other texts and identify their intentions.
First phase **15 minutes** • Read the webpage and take students' initial responses. Ask: Do you find the webpage persuasive? • Ask students to complete Activity 1. • Take feedback, focusing on the writer's choices as identified by students. • Note that these observations will form the starting point of the final activity in this section: writing two paragraphs of a critical response.	**Support:** Remind students of the criteria for target audiences discussed in the previous section, for example age and interests. **Deepen** In response to Activity 1, question 3, encourage students to identify as many different methods as possible.
Second phase **20 minutes** • Remind students of the importance of selecting quotations as evidence that supports the point being made, and that these should be short, relevant and focused. • Ask students to complete Activity 2, noting that there is more than one arguable response to some of the questions.	**Support** Complete Activity 2, question 1a as a whole class or in supported groups to model a process of elimination. **Deepen** Challenge students to find further evidence in the text to support each point.
Plenary **10 minutes** • Take feedback on Activity 2. Encourage debate about the relative merits of different quotations. • Aim to reach a class consensus on the most effective quotation and the most significant words or phrases for each point. • Note that the skill of finding relevant evidence will also be necessary during the final activity in this section: writing two paragraphs of a critical response.	**Support** Recognise and validate any relevant responses. **Deepen** Ask students to look again at their responses to Activity 1, question 3, and to find short, focused quotations from the webpage to support each of them.

Set workbook activities **5 minutes**
- Point students towards the activities on pp. 58–59 of the Workbook.
- Check understanding and answer any questions.
- These activities focus on identifying intention and choosing evidence.

Year 8	Unit 2: Safe and Sound		
Section 4 Organising your response: Lesson 8	Skills focus: Reading: Persuasive texts		Student Book pp. 66–67 Workbook pp. 60–61
Main Curriculum Objectives	**R8.2B** Express a critical response to a text through writing, discussion or presentation, by considering the text's features and their effects.	**R8.2C** Select relevant, focused evidence to support ideas.	**R8.4B** Explore the impact of some of the writer's or speaker's significant vocabulary choices.
Secondary Curriculum Objectives	**W8.3B** Divide text into paragraphs with accuracy and consistency.		

Introduction **10 minutes** • Display the following sentences, in which commands are given but imperatives are not used. o *You must sit down.* o *It is important that you keep off the grass.* o *The eggs should be cooked in a frying pan.* • Ask students to alter the sentences orally by using imperative verbs. • Discuss how the tone of each sentence is changed.	**Support** Remind students of the characteristics of imperative verbs and model an example. **Deepen** Ask students to create their own example sentences, giving versions with and without imperatives.
First phase **15 minutes** • Ask students to complete the Skills Boost activity. • Take feedback to check and develop understanding. • Emphasise the importance of each element, and that an explanation should not be a simple repetition or rephrasing of the key point. • Ask students to complete Activity 3. • Take feedback. Ask: Which is the most emotive of all the words in both quotations? Why?	**Support** In the Skills Boost activity, encourage students to use the sequence point–evidence–explanation, and to focus on linking the elements. **Deepen** In the Skills Boost activity, encourage students to experiment with two or three different sequences and explore different ways of linking them.
Second phase **20 minutes** • Ensure students have access to their responses to Activity 1 from the previous lesson. • Read through Activity 4 to establish and check understanding. • Ask students to complete questions 1–3. • Take feedback to check understanding and reinforce the characteristics of each element. • Ask students to complete questions 4 and 5.	**Support** Suggest that students omit Activity 4, question 4, and focus on producing just one well-crafted paragraph. **Deepen** Ask students to consider how they could link their second paragraph to the first by using adverbials or similar phrases such as 'One way…' and 'Another way…'.
Plenary **10 minutes** • Take feedback, focusing on the clarity and cohesion of responses rather than their originality or perceptiveness. • Ask students to write a checklist of the different elements of an effective critical response.	**Support** Recognise and validate effective use of any of the different elements. **Deepen** Ask students to annotate their paragraphs to identify the elements of an effective response.

Set workbook activities **5 minutes** • Point students towards the activities on pp. 60–61 of the Workbook. • Check understanding and answer any questions. • These activities focus on structuring paragraphs and vocabulary choices.

Year 8	Unit 2: Safe and Sound		
Section 5 Assessment: Lesson 9	Skills focus: Reading: Persuasive texts		Student Book pp. 68–69 Workbook pp. 62–63
Main Curriculum Objectives	**R8.1B** Identify and retrieve a range of key information in a text or in spoken language.	**R8.1D** Compare, contrast and/or combine key points of information within a text or in spoken language.	**R8.2A** Explore a writer's or speaker's intention and viewpoint.
	R8.2B Express a critical response to a text through writing, discussion or presentation, by considering the text's features and their effects.	**R8.2C** Select relevant, focused evidence to support ideas.	**R8.4B** Explore the impact of some of the writer's or speaker's significant vocabulary choices.
Secondary Curriculum Objectives			

Introduction **10 minutes**

- Ask students to read the leaflet, checking their understanding of any unfamiliar vocabulary.
- Explain to students that they will have 25 minutes to complete the reading section of the assessment, and a further 25 minutes to complete the writing section.

Assessment task **50 minutes**

- Ask students to complete the reading section of the assessment. Any students finishing sooner can begin the writing task.
- After 25 minutes, ask students to move on to complete the writing section of the assessment.
- Point out that they should plan their writing, and that you will assess their plans as well as their finished pieces of writing. You may wish to suggest that students use a planning table similar to the one that they used in Section 4, Activity 4, in the previous lesson.
- You may wish to give students further guidance on how much they should write, and the amounts of time they should use for planning, writing and checking their responses.

Workbook assessment task

- Point students towards the poster and activities on pp. 62–63 of the Workbook.
- Give students the opportunity to read the poster. Briefly discuss it with them and answer any questions.
- Students should read the poster again carefully before answering the questions that follow it.
- Make clear your expectations of when this task will be completed. For example, it may be a homework, or students may be given time during an additional lesson.

Year 8	Unit 2: Safe and Sound		
Section 6 Persuasive paragraphs: Lesson 10	Skills focus: Reading: Persuasive texts		Student Book pp. 70–71 Workbook pp. 64–65
Main Curriculum Objectives	**R8.2A** Explore a writer's or speaker's intention and viewpoint.	**R8.2B** Express a critical response to a text through writing, discussion or presentation, by considering the text's features and their effects.	**R8.3A** Explore the impact of some of the writer's key structural or organisational choices.
Secondary Curriculum Objectives			

Introduction — 10 minutes	
• Display the word 'evidence'. • Ask: Why is it important for the police or the courts to have evidence? • Explain that persuasive or argument texts also need evidence, to prove or support their ideas. • Ask students to provide evidence supporting a range of statements, some more contentious than others (for example, that Earth is not flat or that a certain sports team is the best in the world). • Note that evidence can be factual or based on personal experience.	**Support** Give students an example of possible evidence for each statement before asking them what further evidence they can suggest. **Deepen** Give students two minutes to come up with their own contentious statements and three pieces of supporting evidence.
First phase — 15 minutes • Emphasise that students should not look at the webpage yet. • Ask students to complete Activity 1, question 1. Do not take feedback. • After question 1 has been completed, read the webpage. • Take students' initial responses. Ask: How aware are you of fake news? How careful are you to check it? • Ask students to complete Activity 1, questions 2 and 3. • Take feedback on Activity 1.	**Support** While taking feedback, develop awareness by asking students to be explicit, identifying the specific words or phrases in the opening that revealed most about content, audience and intention. **Deepen** Challenge students to write an alternative heading for the webpage.
Second phase — 20 minutes • Read through the introduction to Activity 2 to check students' understanding of the three elements outlined. • Ask students to complete Activity 2, question 1. • Take feedback, to be sure of understanding. • Ask students to complete Activity 2, question 2.	**Support** Complete Activity 2, question 1 as a whole class or in supported groups. Suggest that students complete question 2 in pairs, discussing their answers. **Deepen** Challenge students to create other examples of clearly fake news headlines.
Plenary — 10 minutes • Take feedback on Activity 2, question 2. • Discuss the fake news headline, asking students to identify the elements of it that revealed it as a fake, gathering as wide a range of responses as possible.	**Support** Recognise and validate any relevant responses. **Deepen** Ask students to suggest evidence that could illustrate other parts of the webpage (for example, the first paragraph of the final section).

Set workbook activities — 5 minutes

- Point students towards the activities on pp. 64–65 of the Workbook.
- Check understanding and answer any questions.
- These activities focus on structuring paragraphs and paragraphing persuasive texts.

Year 8	Unit 2: Safe and Sound		
Section 6 Persuasive paragraphs: Lesson 11	Skills focus: Reading: Persuasive texts		Student Book pp. 72–73 Workbook pp. 66–67
Main Curriculum Objectives	**R8.3A** Explore the impact of some of the writer's key structural or organisational choices.	**W8.2C** Use the organisational conventions of a range of forms, for a range of purposes and audiences, with confidence and understanding, including spoken-language forms such as presentations.	**W8.3F** Use determiners to achieve cohesion and clarity.
Secondary Curriculum Objectives	**W8.1A** Gather and structure a range of relevant ideas before writing.		

Introduction 10 minutes	**Support**
• Display a range of multi-clause cloze sentences that use the conjunction 'if'. For example: o *If __________, I will do well at school.* o *I will be fit and healthy if __________.* • Ask students to complete the sentences. • Ask: What effect does swapping the two clauses in each sentence have on its meaning?	Provide complete sentences, and focus on the order of the clauses. **Deepen** Ask students to write their own pairs of 'if' sentences, experimenting with placing the subordinate 'if' clause first and last in each.
First phase 15 minutes	**Support**
• Read through Activity 3, question 1 and check understanding of the term 'imperative'. • Ask students to complete Activity 3, question 1. • Take feedback, ensuring that the two imperative verbs in the final paragraph have been identified. • Ask students to complete questions 2 and 3. • Take feedback on Activity 3 to check understanding. • Read through the introduction to the Grammar Boost activity to check understanding of pronouns. • Ask students to complete the Grammar Boost activity. • Take feedback to check understanding.	In Activity 3, question 1, direct students to the final section of the webpage. In Activity 3, question 2, encourage them to look out for the conjunction 'if' in the webpage. **Deepen** Following the Grammar Boost activity, ask students to create their own sentences using the pronouns 'this', 'that', 'these' and 'those'.
Second phase 20 minutes	**Support**
• Read through Activity 4. • Ask students to complete Activity 4, questions 1–3. • Take feedback to check ideas. • Ask students to complete Activity 4, questions 4–6.	Take feedback after each step in the writing process to check progression and understanding. **Deepen** Encourage students to pause and review the clarity and fluency of each paragraph as they write.
Plenary 10 minutes	**Support**
• Ask partners to identify an effective paragraph in each other's responses to Activity 4. • Ask volunteers to share their chosen paragraphs. • Ask students to identify one or two opportunities to improve the cohesion and clarity of their writing using the pronouns 'this', 'that', 'these' and 'those'. • Ask volunteers to share examples of sentences featuring these pronouns, imperative verbs and subordinating conjunctions.	Recognise and validate any effective choices in text or sentence structure. **Deepen** Encourage students to review and consider revising their sentence structure and/or vocabulary choices.

Set workbook activities 5 minutes
• Point students towards the activities on pp. 66–67 of the Workbook. • Check understanding and answer any questions. • These activities focus on demonstrative pronouns and writing persuasive paragraphs.

Year 8	Unit 2: Safe and Sound	
Section 7 Persuasive structures: Lesson 12	Skills focus: Reading: Persuasive texts	Student Book pp. 74–75 Workbook pp. 68–69
Main Curriculum Objectives	**R8.1B** Identify and retrieve a range of key information in a text or in spoken language.	**R8.3A** Explore the impact of some of the writer's key structural or organisational choices.
Secondary Curriculum Objectives		

Lesson	Differentiation
Introduction **10 minutes** • Display the key vocabulary 'mental health', 'wellbeing', 'bereavement', 'loneliness', 'connect', 'confidence' and 'resilient'. • Ask students to explain what they understand by each word. • Clarify the meaning of any gaps in students' vocabulary, and discuss different impressions of the concepts.	**Support** Display a sentence containing each word, and encourage students to use context to work out their meanings. **Deepen** Challenge students to use each word in a sentence.
First phase **15 minutes** • Read the webpage. • Take students' initial responses. Ask: Do you think this webpage gives good advice? • Check students' understanding of the terms 'heading', 'subheading' and 'bullet point'. • Ask students to complete Activity 1. • Take feedback to check students' understanding and awareness of organisational features of the webpage.	**Support** Monitor understanding by completing Activity 1, question 1 as a whole class or in supported groups. **Deepen** In Activity 1, question 1, challenge students to summarise the text in only four words, three words or even two words.
Second phase **20 minutes** • Check students' understanding of the term 'introduction'. • Ask students to identify the introduction in the webpage. • Ask students to complete Activity 2.	**Support** Complete Activity 2, question 1 as a whole class or in supported groups. **Deepen** Encourage students to use their own words to describe the purposes of the features, rather than the given suggestions.
Plenary **10 minutes** • Take feedback on Activity 2, noting the range of purposes that each feature can achieve. • Emphasise that these key features, although frequently used in persuasive or advisory texts, are not compulsory. They are used because they are effective.	**Support** Recognise and validate all relevant responses. **Deepen** Ask: Do you find the organisational features of the webpage effective? Can you suggest any improvements?

Set workbook activities **5 minutes**

- Point students towards the activities on pp. 68–69 of the Workbook.
- Check understanding and answer any questions.
- These activities focus on key information, and text structure and features.

Year 8	Unit 2: Safe and Sound		
Section 7 Persuasive structures: Lesson 13	Skills focus: Reading: Persuasive texts		Student Book pp. 76–77 Workbook pp. 70–71
Main Curriculum Objectives	**R8.2A** Explore a writer's or speaker's intention and viewpoint.	**W8.1A** Gather and structure a range of relevant ideas before writing.	**W8.2C** Use the organisational conventions of a range of forms, for a range of purposes and audiences, with confidence and understanding, including spoken-language forms such as presentations.
	W8.3F Use determiners to achieve cohesion and clarity.		
Secondary Curriculum Objectives	**R8.2B** Express a critical response to a text through writing, discussion or presentation, by considering the text's features and their effects.		

Introduction — **10 minutes**	
• Display the following list of determiners: 'this', 'that', 'these', 'those', 'the', 'a', 'some', 'his', 'her', 'their'. • Ask students to write five sentences, each one featuring at least one of the determiners. • Take feedback.	**Support** Model an example sentence featuring each of the determiners in turn, asking students then to compose verbally a new sentence including each. **Deepen** Challenge students to get as many determiners as possible into just one sentence.
First phase — **15 minutes** • Read through the Grammar Boost activity before asking students to complete it. • Take feedback to check accuracy and understanding. • Read through Activity 3, checking understanding and clarifying the nature of the three suggested responses. • Ask students to complete Activity 3. • Take feedback, explaining that students should aim to emulate the writer's key intentions when they complete Activity 4.	**Support** Complete question 1 of the Grammar Boost activity as a whole class or in supported groups. **Deepen** Ask students to identify vocabulary choices that help the writer to achieve their intention, for example imperative verbs such as 'build' and 'make', positive language such as 'positive' and 'strengthen', and negative language such as 'loneliness'.
Second phase — **20 minutes** • Read through Activity 4 to clarify the task: planning a short text. • Ask students to complete Activity 4.	**Support** Take feedback after each step in the planning process to monitor understanding and progress. **Deepen** Encourage students to note positive and/or negative vocabulary choices for use in their writing.
Plenary — **10 minutes** • Ask partners to evaluate the effectiveness of each other's plans, considering whether each feature achieves the desired purpose explored in Activity 2, and intention explored in Activity 3. • Take feedback on Activity 4, focusing on the effectiveness of students' choices.	**Support** Recognise and validate any effective choices. **Deepen** Ask students to evaluate the effectiveness of planned vocabulary choices.

Set workbook activities — **5 minutes**
- Point students towards the activities on pp. 70–71 of the Workbook.
- Check understanding and answer any questions.
- These activities focus on determiners and responding to a text.

Year 8	Unit 2: Safe and Sound		
Section 8 Exploring the writer's choices: Lesson 14	Skills focus: Reading: Persuasive texts		Student Book pp. 78–79 Workbook pp. 72–73
Main Curriculum Objectives	**R8.1B** Identify and retrieve a range of key information in a text or in spoken language.	**R8.2B** Express a critical response to a text through writing, discussion or presentation, by considering the text's features and their effects.	**R8.4B** Explore the impact of some of the writer's or speaker's significant vocabulary choices.
Secondary Curriculum Objectives	**R8.2A** Explore a writer's or speaker's intention and viewpoint.		

Introduction 10 minutes	
• Remind students of the term 'emotive language': language intended to prompt an emotional response in the reader. • Display the following trios of words. o *killed – murdered – slaughtered* o *broken – shattered – smashed* o *annoyed – angry – furious* • Ask students to identify the most and least emotive word in each trio, and to explain their reasons.	**Support** Place each word in the context of a sentence, such as 'The man was killed.' **Deepen** Ask students to suggest their own trios containing words that are increasingly emotive, such as 'happy – joyful – ecstatic'.
First phase 15 minutes	
• Read the webpage and take students' initial responses. Ask: Do you find the advice convincing and persuasive? • Ask students to complete Activity 1. • Take feedback to check and share understanding. • Focus discussion on question 3b. Ask: How has the writer tried to make the webpage persuasive?	**Support** Direct students to the section 'Why is sleep so difficult?' for Activity 1, question 2 and the section 'Sleep matters!' for question 3. **Deepen** Encourage students to give focused evidence to support their responses to Activity 1, question 3b.
Second phase 20 minutes	
• Remind students of the activity completed at the start of the lesson, focusing on emotive language. • Ask students to complete Activity 2. • For question 2, you may wish to provide students with access to a thesaurus, or work with the whole class to collate a range of synonyms.	**Support** Complete Activity 2, question 1 as a whole class or in supported groups until students are ready to continue independently. **Deepen** Ask students to repeat Activity 2, question 2 in relation to a sentence of their own choosing from the webpage.
Plenary 10 minutes	
• Take feedback on Activity 2. • Discuss why emotive vocabulary makes a text more persuasive. • Note that most of the emotive vocabulary choices in the webpage are negative but that positive emotive language could be used to greater effect, to create a positive emotional response in the reader.	**Support** Recognise and validate any effective responses. **Deepen** Ask: Why might the writer have avoided emotive language for the more sensitive aspects of this topic?

Set workbook activities **5 minutes**

- Point students towards the activities on pp. 72–73 of the Workbook.
- Check understanding and answer any questions.
- These activities focus on identifying persuasive ideas and emotive language.

Year 8	Unit 2: Safe and Sound		
Section 8 Exploring the writer's choices: Lesson 15	Skills focus: Reading: Persuasive texts		Student Book pp. 80–81 Workbook pp. 74–75
Main Curriculum Objectives	**R8.4A** Explore the impact of some of a writer's or speaker's choices of grammatical features and sentence structure.	**R8.4B** Explore the impact of some of the writer's or speaker's significant vocabulary choices.	**W8.3C** Use a balance of single-clause sentences, coordinate and subordinate clauses with confidence.
Secondary Curriculum Objectives	**W8.3E** Make deliberate choices of sentence length to achieve clarity.	**W8.3G** Select vocabulary in text and spoken language with growing precision.	

Introduction **10 minutes** • Display the following two sentences. o *I go to bed at 9 p.m. every night.* o *I go to bed at 9 p.m. every night and get up at 7 a.m. every morning.* • Ask: In each sentence, how many actions are described? How many verbs are there? How many clauses are there? • Guide responses to recognise the relationship between the numbers of actions, verbs and clauses.	**Support** Begin by asking students to eliminate any words in the sentences that are definitely not verbs. **Deepen** Challenge students to create their own pairs of single-clause and multi-clause sentences.
First phase **15 minutes** • Read through the Grammar Boost activity to check understanding. • Ask students to complete the Grammar Boost activity. • Take feedback to check and share understanding. • Read through Activity 3 to check understanding. • Ask students to complete Activity 3. • Take feedback.	**Support** In Activity 3, complete the first sentence in question 1 as a whole class or in supported groups, before students complete the last two sentences independently. **Deepen** In the Grammar Boost activity, challenge students to link the single-clause sentences in Activity 1 with conjunctions to create multi-clause sentences.
Second phase **20 minutes** • Read through Activity 4. • Note that, while the activities in previous lessons have focused on forming a key point first, this activity uses quotations as its starting point. Assure students that this does not, however, mean that their response paragraphs must begin with a quotation: as always, they may decide for themselves how to sequence their ideas. • Ask students to complete Activity 4.	**Support** Take feedback after each step of the writing process. Encourage students to follow a point–evidence–explanation paragraph structure in response to Activity 4, question 4. **Deepen** Encourage students to experiment with the structure of their response paragraphs.
Plenary **10 minutes** • Ask partners to identify the three elements of each paragraph of each other's work, and check that each has been used correctly. • Take feedback, asking volunteers to share examples of how they have expressed each element. Discuss which of the elements students find most and least easy to formulate.	**Support** Recognise and validate all effective aspects of any one element in students' responses, identifying explicitly the reasons for its success. **Deepen** Encourage students to review and revise their writing for clarity and accuracy.

Set workbook activities **5 minutes**
- Point students towards the activities on pp. 74–75 of the Workbook.
- Check understanding and answer any questions.
- These activities focus on sentence types and developing a response using evidence.

Year 8	Unit 2: Safe and Sound		
Section 9 Rhetorical devices: Lesson 16		Skills focus: Reading: Persuasive texts	Student Book pp. 82–83 Workbook pp. 76–77
Main Curriculum Objectives	**R8.4A** Explore the impact of some of a writer's or speaker's choices of grammatical features and sentence structure.	**R8.4B** Explore the impact of some of the writer's or speaker's significant vocabulary choices.	
Secondary Curriculum Objectives	**R8.1B** Identify and retrieve a range of key information in a text or in spoken language.	**R8.2A** Explore a writer's or speaker's intention and viewpoint.	

Lesson	Support / Deepen
Introduction **10 minutes** • Ask students to suggest persuasive reasons for not taking up smoking. • Discuss how compelling the class thinks each suggestion is. • Explain that, in this lesson, students will look at more ways of making persuasive ideas still more persuasive.	**Support** Provide prompts for students' suggestions, such as the topics of health, hygiene and personal appearance. **Deepen** Challenge students to make each other's points more persuasive by altering their vocabulary and/or sentence structures.
First phase **15 minutes** • Read the extract and take students' initial responses. Ask: Is the extract persuasive? • Discuss whether or not the writer has covered the same points that students gathered. • Take feedback to check and share understanding. • Ask students to complete Activity 1.	**Support** For Activity 1, questions 2 and 3, direct students to the bullet points in the extract. **Deepen** Encourage students to give focused evidence to support one or two of their three responses to Activity 1, questions 2 and 3.
Second phase **20 minutes** • Read through Activity 2. Discuss students' recollection of each rhetorical device (from their learning in Year 7). • Ask students to complete Activity 2, question 1. • Take feedback on question 1 to check understanding. • Read through the extract again. Ask students to stop you when they notice a rhetorical device. • Ask students to complete Activity 2, question 2.	**Support** Focus on each example in turn as a whole class or in supported groups. Suggest methods of identification, for example scanning for a question mark to identify rhetorical questions. **Deepen** Ask students to identify all examples of each kind of rhetorical device in the extract.
Plenary **10 minutes** • Take feedback on Activity 2, question 2, to check understanding and awareness. • Ask: Why does each device make its point more persuasive? • Challenge students to use one or more rhetorical devices in persuading you of something, for example to extend the time allowed for break.	**Support** Prompt students with suggestions such as that some devices add emphasis and some help to engage the reader. **Deepen** Challenge students to identify other language features in the text, for example alliteration.

Set workbook activities **5 minutes**

- Point students towards the activities on pp. 76–77 of the Workbook.
- Check understanding and answer any questions.
- These activities focus on identifying rhetorical devices.

Year 8	Unit 2: Safe and Sound		
Section 9 Rhetorical devices: Lesson 17	Skills focus: Reading: Persuasive texts		Student Book pp. 84–85 Workbook pp. 78–79
Main Curriculum Objectives	**R8.2B** Express a critical response to a text through writing, discussion or presentation, by considering the text's features and their effects.	**W8.3C** Use a balance of single-clause sentences, coordinate and subordinate clauses with confidence.	**W8.3G** Select vocabulary in text and spoken language with growing precision.
	W8.3I Use upper-case letters, end punctuation, commas, speech marks and apostrophes correctly, with accuracy and consistency.		
Secondary Curriculum Objectives	**W8.3E** Make deliberate choices of sentence length to achieve clarity.		

Lesson	Support / Deepen
Introduction — **10 minutes** • Briefly recap students' learning about clauses, referring to the Grammar Boost activity in Section 8, Lesson 14 for support, if needed. • Display the following sentence. *Dolphins swim in the sea, eat fish, live in groups of up to a thousand and are highly intelligent.* • Ask students to identify the number of clauses in the sentence, and then to rewrite the sentence as four single-clause sentences. • Take feedback. Ask: What words or punctuation marks have you needed to omit or add?	**Support** Work as a class or in supported groups to identify each clause in the example sentence. **Deepen** Ask students to experiment with how many other ways they can structure information in the example sentence.
First phase — **15 minutes** • Ask students to complete the Punctuation Boost activity. • Take feedback, asking students to read their sentences (including the punctuation) aloud. • Ensure students have access to their responses to Activity 2 from the previous lesson. • Read through Activity 3. Emphasise that responses should not simply state that a device is persuasive but rather consider *why* this is. • Ask students to complete Activity 3. • Take feedback to share and develop ideas.	**Support** In Activity 3, direct students to the bullet-pointed prompts and then ask, for example: Which idea is being emphasised by the repetition? **Deepen** Encourage partners to discuss their responses to Activity 3 in depth, aiming to come to agreement.
Second phase — **20 minutes** • Read through Activity 4. Point out that students are being asked to write isolated sentences, not a complete text, to develop their skills in crafting rhetorical devices. • Ask students to complete Activity 4.	**Support** Take feedback after each task, to build confidence. Complete Activity 4, question 4 as a whole class. **Deepen** Challenge students to rewrite a point using two or more different rhetorical devices before deciding which is most effective.
Plenary — **10 minutes** • Take feedback on Activity 4. • Focus on one rhetorical device at a time, asking a range of volunteers to share examples. • Ask: Which devices are particularly effective? Which are particularly challenging to use?	**Support** Recognise and validate any effective use of rhetorical devices. **Deepen** Ask students to comment on *why* each device makes each point more persuasive.

Set workbook activities — **5 minutes**

- Point students towards the activities on pp. 78–79 of the Workbook.
- Check understanding and answer any questions.
- These activities focus on exploring and creating rhetorical devices.

Year 8	Unit 2: Safe and Sound		
Section 10 Getting ready to respond: Lesson 18	Skills focus: Reading: Persuasive texts		Student Book pp. 86–87 Workbook pp. 80–81
Main Curriculum Objectives	**R8.2A** Explore a writer's or speaker's intention and viewpoint.	**R8.3A** Explore the impact of some of the writer's key structural or organisational choices.	**R8.4B** Explore the impact of some of the writer's or speaker's significant vocabulary choices.
Secondary Curriculum Objectives			

Lesson	Support / Deepen
Introduction 10 minutes • Explain to students that the next two lessons focus on gathering material for a response to a text. • Ask: Based on your experience in this unit so far, what structural features and kinds of vocabulary might you expect to find in a persuasive text? • Take feedback, noting responses for reference at the end of the lesson.	**Support** Refer students to specific previous texts studied, for example in Sections 4 and 9. Ask: What kinds of vocabulary and structural features are included in these texts? **Deepen** Ask students to identify how these features differ from those in, for example, narrative texts.
First phase 15 minutes • Read the webpage and take students' initial responses. • Ask students to complete Activity 1. • Take feedback to check and share understanding.	**Support** Encourage students to use the subheadings to guide them in locating the correct answers to Activity 1, question 1. **Deepen** Ask students to complete Activity 1, question 1 by noting down all the relevant details in the webpage rather than only the number of details requested.
Second phase 20 minutes • Read through Activity 2. Remind students of their work on structure throughout the unit, and in Section 7 particularly. • Ask students to complete Activity 2. • Take feedback, noting that clearly organised information and engaging subheadings all contribute to the clarity and persuasive power of a text. • Ask students to complete Activity 3.	**Support** Take feedback after each question to check understanding and monitor progress. **Deepen** Encourage students to consider and express the impact of the emotive vocabulary choices on the reader.
Plenary 10 minutes • Take feedback on Activity 3. • Ask students to compile a list of key ideas explored in this lesson that might be included in a written response. • Ask students to compare the structural features and kinds of vocabulary they expect to find in a persuasive text, established in the introduction to this lesson, with their findings in this webpage. • Note that different text types can, to an extent, be defined by their key features.	**Support** Recognise and validate any relevant responses. **Deepen** Ask students to gather and compare key features in a range of different text types, such as description, argument and information texts.

Set workbook activities 5 minutes
- Point students towards the activities on pp. 80–81 of the Workbook.
- Check understanding and answer any questions.
- These activities focus on structure, and vocabulary and intention.

Year 8	Unit 2: Safe and Sound		
Section 10 Getting ready to respond: Lesson 19	Skills focus: Reading: Persuasive texts		Student Book pp. 88–89 Workbook pp. 82–83
Main Curriculum Objectives	**R8.2B** Express a critical response to a text through writing, discussion or presentation, by considering the text's features and their effects.	**R8.2C** Select relevant, focused evidence to support ideas.	**R8.4A** Explore the impact of some of a writer's or speaker's choices of grammatical features and sentence structure.
	W8.3G Select vocabulary in text and spoken language with growing precision.		
Secondary Curriculum Objectives			

Lesson	Support / Deepen
Introduction — **10 minutes** • Ask a volunteer to recap the content of the webpage. • Ask: How would you respond to the webpage if you were experiencing dangerously hot weather? Encourage students to answer you with adjectives that would describe the webpage in this context (such as 'helpful'). • Note students' responses for display, grouping them according to meaning. • Ask students to add synonyms to each group. • Ask: Which word most accurately describes your response?	**Support** Provide suggestions of descriptors from which students can select, such as 'helpful', 'worthless', 'reassuring' and 'worrying'. **Deepen** Provide thesauruses to prompt and develop students' vocabulary skills. Warn them to beware of inappropriate or inaccurate synonyms.
First phase — **15 minutes** • Remind students that this lesson continues the process of gathering ideas for a written response. • Ask students to complete the Skills Boost activity. • Take feedback, discussing the merits of the different options, and noting that the longest word is not necessarily the best.	**Support** Suggest students look for just one significant feature in the given sentences. **Deepen** Can students identify further possible vocabulary choices to use in the Skills Boost activity?
Second phase — **20 minutes** • Ask students to complete Activity 4. • Take feedback, sharing ideas in preparation for Activity 5. • Read the exemplar paragraph in Activity 5. Ask: Is this paragraph effective? Why is that? Ask students to comment on specific features, such as its structure, relevant evidence or carefully chosen vocabulary. • Ask students to complete Activity 5.	**Support** In Activity 5, take feedback after each step in the writing process to ensure understanding and progression. **Deepen** Ask students to use the exemplar paragraph to develop success criteria for evaluating their own response.
Plenary — **10 minutes** • Take feedback, asking volunteers to share their paragraphs. • Ask the class to verify that each element of each paragraph is used effectively. • Recap the process of preparing a critical response that has been covered in this and the previous lesson.	**Support** Ask students to note down the process of preparing a response, to be used as a reference to support them in the coming assessment. **Deepen** Challenge students to experiment with the structure, sentence lengths and vocabulary choices in their response to Activity 5.

Set workbook activities — **5 minutes**

- Point students towards the activities on pp. 82–83 of the Workbook.
- Check understanding and answer any questions.
- These activities focus on rhetorical devices.

Year 8	Unit 2: Safe and Sound		
Section 11 Assessment: Lesson 20		Skills focus: Reading: Persuasive texts	Student Book pp. 90–91 Workbook pp. 84–85
Main Curriculum Objectives	**R8.1B** Identify and retrieve a range of key information in a text or in spoken language.	**R8.2A** Explore a writer's or speaker's intention and viewpoint.	**R8.2B** Express a critical response to a text through writing, discussion or presentation, by considering the text's features and their effects.
	R8.2C Select relevant, focused evidence to support ideas.	**R8.3A** Explore the impact of some of the writer's key structural or organisational choices.	**R8.4A** Explore the impact of some of a writer's or speaker's choices of grammatical features and sentence structure.
	R8.4B Explore the impact of some of the writer's or speaker's significant vocabulary choices.		
Secondary Curriculum Objectives			

Introduction **10 minutes**

- Ask students to read the newspaper article, and check their understanding of any unfamiliar vocabulary.
- Explain to students that they will have 25 minutes to complete the reading section of the assessment, and a further 25 minutes to complete the writing section.

Assessment task **50 minutes**

- Ask students to complete the reading section of the assessment. Any students finishing sooner can begin the writing task.
- After 25 minutes, ask students to move on to complete the writing section of the assessment.
- Point out that they should plan their writing, and that you will assess their plans as well as their finished pieces of writing.
- You may wish to give students further guidance on how much they should write, and the amounts of time they should use for planning, writing and checking their responses.

Workbook assessment task

- Point students towards the extract, task and sample student response on pp. 84–85 of the Workbook.
- Give students the opportunity to read the extract, task and sample response. Briefly discuss these with them and answer any questions.
- Students should identify the errors in the sample response before planning how they will improve it. They should then write an improved version, adding two or three paragraphs of text.
- Make clear your expectations of when this task will be completed. For example, it may be a homework, or students may be given time during an additional lesson.

Year 8	Unit 3: A Perfect World		
Section 1 Exploring a fictional future: Lesson 1	Skills focus: Writing: Argument		Student Book pp. 94–95 Workbook pp. 86–87
Main Curriculum Objectives	**R8.1B** Identify and retrieve a range of key information in a text or in spoken language.	**R8.1C** Summarise a short text or speech effectively, selecting appropriate and relevant detail.	**R8.1E** Make inferences from specific evidence found in a text or in spoken language, including specific vocabulary choices.
Secondary Curriculum Objectives			

Introduction **10 minutes** • Display and read just the first seven lines of the extract – but not the introduction or the rest of the extract. • What can students deduce about this story? • What might be meant by the 'Great Pollution'? • Can students guess anything further about the world in which the story is set? • Give students two or three minutes to discuss their ideas with a partner. Take feedback.	**Support** Prompt students with additional questioning, for example was the Great Pollution a positive or negative event? What might have been polluted? **Deepen** Encourage students to identify the specific clues that prompted their responses.
First phase **15 minutes** • Read the complete extract. Take students' initial responses but point out that Activities 1 and 2 will further challenge their skills of inference and deduction. • Ask students to complete Activity 1. • Take feedback. Ask volunteers to share their summaries and invite the class to evaluate the relevance of each detail and the brevity of the summary as a whole.	**Support** Take feedback after each question in Activity 1 to check understanding and ensure progression. **Deepen** Challenge students to include all key details in their summaries but in as few words as possible.
Second phase **20 minutes** • Read through Activity 2. Point out that students must note their inferences (or guesses!) but also explicitly note the specific clues that led to them, where possible. • Ask students to complete Activity 2.	**Support** Complete Activity 2, question 1a as a whole class or in a supported group. **Deepen** Can students infer any other ideas or details from the extract?
Plenary **10 minutes** • Take feedback on Activity 2, focusing in particular on the clues from which students deduced or inferred their responses. • Discuss as a whole class: has the writer engaged students' interest in this world, and in the story? How?	**Support** Recognise and validate any relevant suggestions. **Deepen** Challenge students to predict how the story might develop (although there are no significant clues in the extract).

Set workbook activities **5 minutes**
- Point students towards the activities on pp. 86–87 of the Workbook.
- Check understanding and answer any questions.
- These activities focus on summarising key ideas and inference.

Year 8	Unit 3: A Perfect World		
Section 1 Exploring a fictional future: Lesson 2	Skills focus: Writing: Argument		Student Book pp. 96–97 Workbook pp. 88–89
Main Curriculum Objectives	**R8.2B** Express a critical response to a text through writing, discussion or presentation, by considering the text's features and their effects.	**W8.3A** Write in Standard English and a largely appropriate register.	**W8.1A** Gather and structure a range of relevant ideas before writing.
Secondary Curriculum Objectives			

Introduction 10 minutes	**Support**
• Display the definition and example of subject and verb in the Grammar Boost activity. • Ask students to identify a subject and verb in a range of sentences, for example five sentences from the extract adapted as single-clause sentences. • Take feedback to check accuracy.	**Support** Point out that many sentences begin subject–verb. Make clear that the subject and verb are not always the first two words in a sentence. **Deepen** Challenge students to find all the subjects and verbs in the first paragraph of the extract.
First phase 15 minutes • Recap briefly the extract, read in the previous lesson. • Ask students to complete Activity 3. • Take feedback on Activity 3. • Point out that responses to question 2 are entirely subjective but may have been manipulated by the writer's choices. Discuss how. • Ask students to complete the Grammar Boost activity. • Take feedback to check accuracy.	**Support** Suggest students first complete three details from the extract before comparing them with their own world. **Deepen** Ask students to repeat the Grammar Boost activity, rewriting sentences in the simple past tense, with special attention to inflections of 'to be'.
Second phase 20 minutes • Read through Activity 4. • Discuss initial ideas as a whole class to share and develop thinking. • Ask students to complete Activity 4.	**Support** Take feedback at each stage of the writing process to check progression. **Deepen** Challenge students to produce two openings: a dystopian vision in addition to their utopia.
Plenary 10 minutes • Ask students to work with a partner to identify particularly effective ideas/sentences. • Ask volunteers to share their choices with the class. • Are these story openings effective and engaging, or not? Look for responses that recognise the lack of conflict in a perfect world – an essential element in an engaging story. How could conflict be introduced?	**Support** Recognise and validate any appropriate choices. **Deepen** Encourage students to revise their writing to include a hint of potential conflict, for example a positive aspect of life that, it is suggested, has a sinister side.

Set workbook activities 5 minutes

- Point students towards the activities on pp. 88–89 of the Workbook.
- Check understanding and answer any questions.
- These activities focus on responding to ideas, and subjects and verbs.

Year 8	Unit 3: A Perfect World	
Section 2 Building an argument: Lesson 3	Skills focus: Writing: Argument	Student Book pp. 98–99 Workbook pp. 90–91
Main Curriculum Objectives	**R8.1B** Identify and retrieve a range of key information in a text or in spoken language.	**R8.1C** Summarise a short text or speech effectively, selecting appropriate and relevant detail.
Secondary Curriculum Objectives	**R8.1E** Make inferences from specific evidence found in a text or in spoken language, including specific vocabulary choices.	

Lesson	Support / Deepen
Introduction **10 minutes** • Display the sentence '*School is important.*' • Ask: Do you agree with this statement? • Ask students to suggest ways in which the argument could be strengthened. • Explicitly identify the ways in which students' suggestions strengthen the argument (for example, that they act as evidence or provide explanation).	**Support** Prompt students to suggest explanations and then examples of why or how school can be important. **Deepen** Ask students themselves to identify the ways in which their suggestions strengthen the argument.
First phase **15 minutes** • Read the article and take students' immediate responses. Ask: Do you find this argument powerful and convincing? • Ask students to complete the Skills Boost activity. • Take feedback to check and share understanding. • Note that the two paragraphs are structured differently: in Paragraph 1, the topic sentence comes first, followed by the evidence and then the explanation; in Paragraph 2, the evidence comes first, followed by the explanation and then the topic sentence.	**Support** Work with students using a process of elimination, examining one sentence at a time. **Deepen** Challenge students to write a further paragraph arguing for or against homework. Ask them to annotate this to identify each feature.
Second phase **20 minutes** • Read through Activity 1, ensuring understanding of the function of topic sentences. Emphasise that they are not always the first sentence in a paragraph. • Ask students to complete Activity 1. • Take feedback on Activity 1, aiming to find agreement. • Discuss the positions of the topic sentences. For each paragraph, ask: What was the writer's intention in structuring the paragraph like this?	**Support** Begin Activity 1 as a whole class or in supported groups, working together until students are confident enough to complete it independently. **Deepen** Ask students to summarise each topic sentence in their own words.
Plenary **10 minutes** • Read aloud the topic sentences identified (paraphrasing them when necessary). Note that this creates an effective summary of the text. • Ask students to use the topic sentences they have identified to write a summary of the text in their own words.	**Support** Work with students to identify key information in the topic sentences to include in a summary. **Deepen** Challenge students to write their summary in 20 words or fewer.

Set workbook activities **5 minutes**
- Point students towards the activities on pp. 90–91 of the Workbook.
- Check understanding and answer any questions.
- These activities focus on identifying key ideas and exploring structure.

Year 8	Unit 3: A Perfect World		
Section 2 Building an argument: Lesson 4	Skills focus: Writing: Argument		Student Book pp. 100–101 Workbook pp. 92–93
Main Curriculum Objectives	**R8.2A** Explore a writer's or speaker's intention and viewpoint.	**R8.3A** Explore the impact of some of the writer's key structural or organisational choices.	**W8.1A** Gather and structure a range of relevant ideas before writing.
Secondary Curriculum Objectives			

Lesson	Differentiation
Introduction **15 minutes** • Ask: What do you understand by the term 'argument'? • Consolidate students' understanding that an argument in the context of an 'argument text' is not an aggressive exchange between two people: it is an expression of a point of view. • Present students with an argument scenario (for example, a child trying to convince a parent that they should have a later bedtime). • Ask students to identify the problem the argument is addressing (for example, that the child believes their bedtime is too early).	**Support** Establish a more concrete argument scenario, making both participants' points of view clear before asking students to identify the problem. **Deepen** Ask students to suggest similar scenarios and to identify possible problems at the heart of them.
First phase **15 minutes** • Read through Activity 2, checking that students understand each of the three stages in the given structure. • Ask students to complete Activity 2. • Take feedback, noting the paragraph-by-paragraph structure of the article: an introduction outlining the problem; paragraphs explaining the problem; a conclusion calling for action. • Ask students to complete Activity 3. • Take feedback on Activity 3, discussing which side of the argument most students find more compelling.	**Support** In Activity 2, ask students to summarise the problem, the reason given and the action suggested in the article verbally, before asking them to complete the activity. **Deepen** Ask students to identify evidence or examples from their own experience to support the points they note in Activity 3.
Second phase **15 minutes** • Read through Activity 4. • Ask students to complete Activity 4 • Take feedback to ensure that students have identified specific problems, not simply decided whether they believe homework is a good or bad idea.	**Support** Take feedback after each step of the planning process. **Deepen** Place students in pairs, asking one student in each pair to plan an argument for and the other against homework, regardless of their own personal views.
Plenary **10 minutes** • Ask partners to check that each of the three planning stages achieves its aim in each other's work. • Ask volunteers to share ideas from their planning with the class. Discuss whether or not the class finds the argument convincing and compelling, and why this is.	**Support** Recognise and validate any relevant responses. **Deepen** Ask partners with opposing arguments to debate which of them has created the most compelling argument and why.

Set workbook activities **5 minutes**

- Point students towards the activities on pp. 92–93 of the Workbook.
- Check understanding and answer any questions.
- These activities focus on planning an argument.

Year 8	Unit 3: A Perfect World		
Section 3 Choosing vocabulary 1: Lesson 5		Skills focus: Writing: Argument	Student Book pp. 102–103 Workbook pp. 94–95
Main Curriculum Objectives	**R8.1B** Identify and retrieve a range of key information in a text or in spoken language.	**R8.1E** Make inferences from specific evidence found in a text or in spoken language, including specific vocabulary choices.	
Secondary Curriculum Objectives			

Lesson	Differentiation
Introduction **10 minutes** • Display an image from a newspaper website: a portrait of a person, a group of people or a place. • Ask: What can you infer about this person (or people or place) from the clues in the picture? What can you infer about the situation? • Take feedback, gathering as wide a variety of inferences as possible.	**Support** Prompt students with relevant details. For example: 'She is smiling, so that implies that …' **Deepen** Challenge students to make five or more inferences.
First phase **15 minutes** • Read the webpage and take students' initial responses. Ask: Do you find the argument convincing? Would you sign the petition? Why is this? • Ask students to complete Activity 1. • Take feedback to check understanding. • Note that question 4 focuses on the writer's intention. Ask: Who do you think must have been the writer of this webpage? Whose views and ideas does the page include? • Guide students' discussion to recognise that the writer must have created the page on behalf of the company Theirworld, and that it represents the views of the company.	**Support** Check students' understanding of the term 'statistics', giving examples if necessary. **Deepen** Ask students to write a summary of the ideas in the webpage in 15 words or fewer.
Second phase **20 minutes** • Remind students of the key terms 'inference' and 'imply', and their meanings. • Ask students to complete Activity 2. • Make it clear that, in their responses, students should avoid simply repeating words or phrases from the webpage; instead, they should focus on identifying what the writer is implying.	**Support** Take feedback after each question to ensure understanding and progression. **Deepen** Challenge students to identify other sentences in which the writer implies the difference that access to quality care can make.
Plenary **10 minutes** • Take feedback on Activity 2, and reinforce the key terms again. • Remind students that the charity Theirworld campaigns to improve the lives of young children. Ask: What is implied by the name of the charity?	**Support** Recognise and validate all relevant responses. **Deepen** Encourage students to evaluate the webpage. Ask: Are you convinced by the argument presented? Why is this?

Set workbook activities **5 minutes**

- Point students towards the activities on pp. 94–95 of the Workbook.
- Check understanding and answer any questions.
- These activities focus on key points and intentions.

Year 8	Unit 3: A Perfect World		
Section 3 Choosing vocabulary 1: Lesson 6	Skills focus: Writing: Argument		Student Book pp. 104–105 Workbook pp. 96–97
Main Curriculum Objectives	**R8.4B** Explore the impact of some of the writer's or speaker's significant vocabulary choices.	**W8.3G** Select vocabulary in text and spoken language with growing precision.	**W8.3H** Spell homophones, words with single/double letters and 'silent' letters with some accuracy.
Secondary Curriculum Objectives			

Lesson	Support / Deepen
Introduction **10 minutes** • Display the nouns 'ant', 'Alice', 'air', 'Antarctica', 'ambulance', 'anger', 'Abdul' and 'adventure'. • Ask students to sort these nouns into three groups. • Look for and guide responses that recognise the distinctions between common nouns, abstract nouns and proper nouns (noting that the latter can be identified by their initial capital letters).	**Support** Supply the three categories (common, proper and abstract) into which the nouns should be sorted. **Deepen** Ask: How many more nouns can you add to each of the three groups?
First phase **15 minutes** • Read through Activity 3. Note that the activity asks students to identify only nouns, not noun phrases or any other word classes. • Ask students to complete Activity 3. • Take feedback, exploring the connotations of each noun choice (for example, that the noun 'journey' suggests progress and a destination). • Read through the Spelling Boost activity. Discuss the fact that the word 'silent' appears in speech marks. Explain that this is because, even though the letters aren't sounded independently, they can have an effect on the other sounds in a word. • Ask students to complete the Spelling Boost activity. • Take feedback, noting common patterns such as the fact that 'k' always appears before 'n'.	**Support** After the Spelling Boost activity, read each row of words aloud to ensure that students recognise each one. **Deepen** In Activity 3, encourage students to comment on each of their chosen nouns in as much depth and detail as possible. In the Spelling Boost activity, challenge students to add other examples to the lists of words featuring each 'silent' consonant.
Second phase **20 minutes** • Read through Activity 4. Point out that the focuses of this activity are effective structure and vocabulary choice, not the length of the letter. (Students should write no more than 150 words.) • Look at the Vocabulary Bank and note that the majority of the words also appear in the webpage. • Ask students to complete Activity 4.	**Support** Suggest that students complete only Activity 4, question 1, using one of the given nouns and one of the given verbs in each of their three sentences. **Deepen** Challenge students to imply rather than clearly state their opinions where possible.
Plenary **10 minutes** • Ask partners to identify effective sentences in each other's writing. • Ask volunteers to share their effective sentences. • Ask the class to identify whether the ideas in each volunteered sentence are implied or clearly stated, and to consider the impact of specific vocabulary choices.	**Support** Recognise and validate any effective vocabulary in students' writing. **Deepen** Ask students to suggest positive and constructive targets for improvement in their partner's writing.

Set workbook activities	5 minutes
• Point students towards the activities on pp. 96–97 of the Workbook. • Check understanding and answer any questions. • These activities focus on positive nouns and verbs.	

Year 8	Unit 3: A Perfect World		
Section 4 Choosing vocabulary 2: Lesson 7	Skills focus: Writing: Argument		Student Book pp. 106–107 Workbook pp. 98–99
Main Curriculum Objectives	**R8.1B** Identify and retrieve a range of key information in a text or in spoken language.	**R8.1E** Make inferences from specific evidence found in a text or in spoken language, including specific vocabulary choices.	**R8.4B** Explore the impact of some of the writer's or speaker's significant vocabulary choices.
Secondary Curriculum Objectives	**R8.2A** Explore a writer's or speaker's intention and viewpoint.		

Lesson	Support / Deepen
Introduction — **10 minutes** • Display two or three sentences containing adjectives and adverbs. For example: o *The sleeping baby breathed quietly.* o *Some tall buildings sway slightly in strong winds.* • Ask students to identify the nouns, verbs, adjectives and adverbs in the sentences. • Work with students to identify methods of determining word classes (noting, for example, that many adverbs end in –ly and that nouns can be preceded by a determiner). • Note that verbs ending –ing can act as adjectives (for example, 'swaying').	**Support** Prompt students to identify, for example, words that name objects and words that name actions. Take and display notes on the discussion to support students throughout the lesson. **Deepen** Challenge students to write their own sentences that each contain a noun, a verb, an adjective and an adverb.
First phase — **15 minutes** • Read the webpage. • Take students' immediate responses. Ask: How do you feel about the plight of the orangutan, after reading the webpage? • Ask students to complete Activity 1. • Take feedback, explicitly highlighting that students have had to use their skills of inference to identify the writer's intention.	**Support** Take feedback after Activity 1, question 1 to ensure understanding. Complete question 2 as a whole class or in supported groups. **Deepen** Ask students to identify which questions required inference.
Second phase — **20 minutes** • Read the introduction to Activity 2 to check understanding. • Ask students to complete Activity 2.	**Support** Refer students to their earlier discussion on word classes, and the notes taken. **Deepen** Challenge students to identify other significant adverb or adjective choices in the webpage.
Plenary — **10 minutes** • Take feedback on Activity 2 to share and develop understanding. • Ask: Is the impact of the webpage created mainly by the ideas it contains, or by the writer's vocabulary choices? Discuss the merits of both.	**Support** Recognise and validate all relevant responses. **Deepen** Ask students to select effective sentences from the webpage and to rewrite them omitting adjectives and adverbs. Ask: What is lost?

Set workbook activities — **5 minutes**

- Point students towards the activities on pp. 98–99 of the Workbook.
- Check understanding and answer any questions.
- These activities focus on understanding the text, and commenting on adjectives and adverbs.

Year 8	Unit 3: A Perfect World		
Section 4 Choosing vocabulary 2: Lesson 8	Skills focus: Writing: Argument		Student Book pp. 108–109 Workbook pp. 100–101
Main Curriculum Objectives	**R8.4B** Explore the impact of some of the writer's or speaker's significant vocabulary choices.	**W8.3G** Select vocabulary in text and spoken language with growing precision.	**W8.3H** Spell homophones, words with single/double letters and 'silent' letters with some accuracy.
Secondary Curriculum Objectives			

Introduction — **10 minutes** • Display a selection of words from the Spelling Boost activity, with the unspoken or unstressed vowel missing. For example: 'seprate', 'vegtable', 'famly'. • Ask students to identify the spelling errors and to correct them. • Ask: What do these spellings have in common?	**Support** Reveal that none of the words is spelled correctly, and that each is missing a vowel. Ask students to select and position the correct vowel. **Deepen** Display all 16 words with the relevant vowels omitted.
First phase — **15 minutes** • Ask students to complete question 1 of the Spelling Boost activity. • You may wish to complete question 2 as a spelling test rather than including the elements of a memory game. If not, note that the activity is similar to a party game in which an array of objects are displayed on a tray then covered. • Ask students to complete question 2. • Take feedback, discussing how many spellings students have learned. • Ask students to complete Activity 3. • Take feedback. Referring to the example sentence in question 2, ask: What impact do the vocabulary choices have on the presentation of the orangutan?	**Support** In the Spelling Boost activity, ask students to work on just the first two rows of words. **Deepen** In the Spelling Boost activity, ask students to identify the word class of each given word. In Activity 3, challenge students to create a wholly positive and then a wholly negative noun phrase describing the orangutan.
Second phase — **20 minutes** • Ask students to complete Activity 4, question 1a. • Take feedback to share and develop ideas. • Ask students to complete questions 1 and 2. • Read through question 3. • Emphasise that vocabulary choice is the key focus of the activity, and that students' intention should be to influence the reader's opinion and encourage agreement with their point of view. • Ask students to complete question 3.	**Support** Take feedback after each step of the writing process in Activity 4, question 2. Encourage students to make full use of the Vocabulary Bank provided. **Deepen** Encourage students to use their own vocabulary choices in preference to those provided.
Plenary — **10 minutes** • Ask students to share before and after examples of their writing: sentences featuring unmodified nouns and/or verbs from their first draft, and the improved versions after review. • Ask the class to comment on the impact added in each case.	**Support** Recognise and validate any effective vocabulary choices. **Deepen** Encourage partners to review each other's work, suggesting further revisions to their choices of verbs, adverbs and adjectives.

Set workbook activities — **5 minutes**
- Point students towards the activities on pp. 100–101 of the Workbook.
- Check understanding and answer any questions.
- These activities focus on silent vowels, and adding impact with noun phrases and adverbs.

Year 8	Unit 3: A Perfect World		
Section 5 Assessment: Lesson 9	Skills focus: Writing: Argument		Student Book pp. 110–111 Workbook pp. 102–103
Main Curriculum Objectives	**R8.1B** Identify and retrieve a range of key information in a text or in spoken language.	**R8.1E** Make inferences from specific evidence found in a text or in spoken language, including specific vocabulary choices.	**R8.2A** Explore a writer's or speaker's intention and viewpoint.
	R8.4B Explore the impact of some of the writer's or speaker's significant vocabulary choices.	**W8.1A** Gather and structure a range of relevant ideas before writing.	**W8.2C** Use the organisational conventions of a range of forms, for a range of purposes and audiences, with confidence and understanding, including spoken-language forms such as presentations.
	W8.3G Select vocabulary in text and spoken language with growing precision.		
Secondary Curriculum Objectives			

Introduction **10 minutes**

- Ask students to read the webpage. Check their understanding of any unfamiliar vocabulary, and of the context of the webpage: from a website aimed at helping young people take action to protect the environment against global warming.
- Explain to students that they will have 25 minutes to complete the reading section of the assessment, and a further 25 minutes to complete the writing section.

Assessment task **50 minutes**

- Ask students to complete the reading section of the assessment. Any students finishing sooner can begin the writing task.
- After 25 minutes, ask students to move on to complete the writing section of the assessment.
- Point out that they should plan their writing, and that you will assess their plans as well as their finished pieces of writing.
- You may wish to give students further guidance on how much they should write, and the amounts of time they should use for planning, writing and checking their responses.

Workbook assessment task

- Point students towards the article and activities on pp. 102–103 of the Workbook.
- Give students the opportunity to read the article. Briefly discuss it with them and answer any questions.
- Students should read the article again carefully before answering the questions that follow it.
- Make clear your expectations of when this task will be completed. For example, it may be a homework, or students may be given time during an additional lesson.

Year 8	Unit 3: A Perfect World		
Section 6 Supporting key points: Lesson 10		Skills focus: Writing: Argument	Student Book pp. 112–113 Workbook pp. 104–105
Main Curriculum Objectives	**R8.3A** Explore the impact of some of the writer's key structural or organisational choices.		
Secondary Curriculum Objectives			

Lesson	Support / Deepen
Introduction **15 minutes** • Display the following viewpoint. *Human beings use too much plastic.* • Take students' responses. Ask: Do you agree? • Add the following statistic. *Over 90% of the plastic ever used has never been recycled – that's an estimated 6300 million tons used just once, then burned or buried.* • Ask: What does the statistic tell us? What does it imply? Emphasise the difference between the two questions. (It tells us that most plastic is burned or buried rather than recycled; it implies that we should recycle more plastic.) • Discuss to what extent the viewpoint is supported and strengthened by the statistic.	**Support** Recap the difference between ideas or information that are clearly stated, and implied ideas that require readers to use their inference skills. **Deepen** Encourage students to identify the reasons that supporting evidence makes a point both more plausible and more significant.
First phase **15 minutes** • Read the newspaper article. Check students' understanding of its vocabulary and its key ideas. • Ask: What is the writer's opinion? • Ask students to complete Activity 1. • Take feedback to check understanding.	**Support** In Activity 1, remind students of the difference between what is shown (question 1a) and what is suggested (question 1c) as explored at the start of the lesson. **Deepen** How convincing is this evidence? Why? Why not?
Second phase **15 minutes** • Read through Activity 2, noting that the information from each section of text is paraphrased. • Clarify and check students' understanding of the roles of points, examples and explanations. • Ask students to complete Activity 2.	**Support** In Activity 2, work with the whole class or supported groups to identify the three elements in A–C. Students can work on D–F independently. **Deepen** Ask students to summarise the two sections in their own words.
Plenary **10 minutes** • Take feedback on Activity 2 to check understanding. • Challenge pairs to discuss and note down alternative examples that could support the key points made in these two sections. • Take feedback.	**Support** Recognise and validate any relevant new examples suggested. **Deepen** Ask: Where and how might you look for an expert opinion or statistic to support these points?

Set workbook activities **5 minutes**

- Point students towards the activities on pp. 104–105 of the Workbook.
- Check understanding and answer any questions.
- These activities focus on evidence, and points, examples and comments.

Year 8	Unit 3: A Perfect World		
Section 6 Supporting key points: Lesson 11	Skills focus: Writing: Argument		Student Book pp. 114–115 Workbook pp. 106–107
Main Curriculum Objectives	**R8.3A** Explore the impact of some of the writer's key structural or organisational choices.	**W8.2D** Link paragraphs in text and spoken language using adverbials to signal the development of ideas.	**W8.3B** Divide text into paragraphs with accuracy and consistency.
Secondary Curriculum Objectives			

Introduction 10 minutes	**Support**
• Display the following sentence from the newspaper article. *In the years ahead, AI will have an extraordinary impact on our lives, from self-driving cars to robot surgeons, but we would be foolish to allow ourselves to become too reliant on them.* • Ask students to recall the three elements often found in paragraphs or sections of argument text, as discussed in the previous lesson: a key point, an example and a link to the main argument. • Ask students to identify these three elements in the displayed sentence.	Work as a whole class or in supported groups to identify the example in the sentence first, and then to distinguish the point from the link. **Deepen** Encourage students to note and share their thinking as they deduce which element is which.
First phase 15 minutes	**Support**
• Read through Activity 3, pointing out that its focus is on sequencing the three elements. Note that the example given in question 2 relies on small revisions to the sentence, and that students will need to make similar small revisions to create sentences that make sense. • Ask students to complete Activity 3. • Take feedback to check understanding and clarity of expression. • Ask students to complete the Grammar Boost activity. • Take feedback to check fluency.	In Activity 3, question 2, work with the whole class to rewrite the sentence, focusing first on sequencing the elements and then on making small revisions so the sentence makes sense. **Deepen** In Activity 3, question 2, challenge students to rewrite and link the three elements of the sentence in as many different ways as they can. (They could refer to question 1 for a list of the possible sequences.)
Second phase 20 minutes	**Support**
• Read through Activity 4, checking students' understanding. • If time allows, encourage students to conduct some research to identify evidence or examples to support their ideas. If not, explain that they may make up expert views and statistics to support their arguments. • Ask students to complete Activity 4.	Recall students' work in Activities 2 and 3 and the Grammar Boost activity to support their writing. **Deepen** Encourage students to gather or formulate two or three possible examples and/or pieces of evidence to support their points before deciding which is the most effective.
Plenary 10 minutes	**Support**
• Ask partners to identify and label the point, example and link in each of the paragraphs in each other's work. • Ask volunteers to share a paragraph with the class. • Ask students to discuss whether they find the view expressed compelling.	Recognise and validate any effective point, example or link. **Deepen** Note the ways in which volunteers' paragraphs are sequenced. Ask: Which sequences are more effective?

Set workbook activities **5 minutes**

- Point students towards the activities on pp. 106–107 of the Workbook.
- Check understanding and answer any questions.
- These activities focus on ordering points, examples and comments, and using fronted adverbials to link sentences.

Year 8	Unit 3: A Perfect World		
Section 7 Structuring sentences: Lesson 12		Skills focus: Writing: Argument	Student Book pp. 116–117 Workbook pp. 108–109
Main Curriculum Objectives	**R8.2A** Explore a writer's or speaker's intention and viewpoint.	**R8.4A** Explore the impact of some of a writer's or speaker's choices of grammatical features and sentence structure.	
Secondary Curriculum Objectives			

Introduction 10 minutes • Display the following two sentences. o *I would be very grateful if you could please sit down and, if possible, stop talking.* o *Sit down and stop talking.* • Discuss: Which sentence has greater impact? Why? Ensure that both sentence lengths and the tone of the vocabulary are discussed. • Reinforce the point by asking volunteers to perform each sentence. • Ask: How do the sentences suggest or create the tone each performer has chosen to use?	**Support** Prompt students with elements of the sentences they could compare, such as sentence length and vocabulary choice. **Deepen** Ask students to create their own pairs of sentences with similar meanings but different lengths and tones.
First phase 15 minutes • Read the article and take students' initial responses. • Discuss: How important are manners? Why is this? • Read through Activity 1, checking students' understanding of the term 'statistics' and the concept of a scientific study. • Take feedback to check understanding. • Explain that evidence that contradicts a writer's main point may also be included in an argument text. Ask: Why might this be? • Guide discussion to appreciate that this may make the 'problem' of the argument clearer.	**Support** Complete Activity 1, question 1 as a whole class or in supported groups before asking students to complete question 2 independently. **Deepen** Ask: What do you think you can work out about the writer, based on his opinions? You could prompt students to consider the elements of age, values and gender.
Second phase 20 minutes • Remind students of the activity at the beginning of the lesson, and the effect of the shorter sentence. • Read through Activity 2, questions 1a and 1b. • Ask students to complete Activity 2, questions 1a and 1b. • Take feedback to check understanding, and read through question 1c. Read the rewritten sentences aloud, highlighting the staccato tone created by the short sentences. • Ask students to complete the rest of Activity 2.	**Support** For Activity 2, question 1b, work with the whole class or a supported group to read the second paragraph aloud and hear the emphases created. **Deepen** Ask students to select other sentences from the article and experiment with swapping clauses to explore the impact.
Plenary 10 minutes • Take feedback on the rest of Activity 2. • Ask students to suggest other ways in which sentence structure can be varied, for example with fronted adverbials and additional clauses. • Note the lesson's key learning points: writers can emphasise an idea by using short sentences and by positioning it at the end of a sentence.	**Support** Take two minutes to model examples of the different ways sentence structure can be manipulated. **Deepen** Ask students to formulate their own examples of different ways sentences can be structured and lengthened.

Set workbook activities 5 minutes
- Point students towards the activities on pp. 108–109 of the Workbook.
- Check understanding and answer any questions.
- These activities focus on evidence and sentence length.

Year 8	**Unit 3: A Perfect World**		
Section 7 Structuring sentences: Lesson 13	**Skills focus: Writing: Argument**	**Student Book pp. 118–119** **Workbook pp. 110–111**	
Main Curriculum Objectives	**W8.3C** Use a balance of single-clause sentences, coordinate and subordinate clauses with confidence.	**W8.3E** Make deliberate choices of sentence length to achieve clarity.	**W8.3I** Use upper-case letters, end punctuation, commas, speech marks and apostrophes correctly, with accuracy and consistency.
Secondary Curriculum Objectives	**W8.1A** Gather and structure a range of relevant ideas before writing.	**W8.3D** Use a range of sentence openings in addition to subject–verb sentence openings, starting to develop variety.	

Introduction **10 minutes** • Display the following three sentences. o *The old wooden door creaked loudly.* o *The door creaked and opened wide.* o *The door creaked because it was old.* • Ask students to identify the 'odd one out'. • Look for responses that recognise the single-clause sentence. • Note the similar length of all three sentences, pointing out that short sentences can be multi-clause sentences, and that long sentences can be single-clause sentences.	**Support** Ask students to identify the single clause sentence and then explain how they selected it. **Deepen** Ask students to rewrite the multi-clause sentences using different conjunctions and then as two single-clause sentences.
First phase **15 minutes** • Read through the Punctuation Boost activity, ensuring students understand how the writer has used this punctuation in the given examples. • Ask students to complete the Punctuation Boost activity. • Take feedback to check accuracy and understanding. • Ask students to complete Activity 3. • Take feedback, focusing on accuracy and clarity as well as impact.	**Support** Complete question 1 of the Punctuation Boost activity as a whole class or in supported groups, adding semi-colons together before students add dashes independently in question 2. **Deepen** In Activity 3, challenge students to restructure the sentences in as many more different ways as they can.
Second phase **20 minutes** • Read through Activity 4. • Point out that the activity highlights the importance of sentence variety. Note that this is valuable in creating clarity, impact and variety. • Ask students to complete question 1. • Take feedback to share and develop ideas. • Ask students to complete the rest of Activity 4.	**Support** Take feedback after Activity 4, question 2 to ensure and discuss the clarity and accuracy of students' responses. **Deepen** Encourage students to consider their vocabulary choice as well as their sentence structure.
Plenary **10 minutes** • Ask partners to identify any sentences, or groups of sentences, in each other's work that are structured particularly effectively. • Ask volunteers to share examples. Ask the class to comment on what and how impact has been created.	**Support** Recognise and validate any sentences that achieve clarity and/or impact. **Deepen** Focus students' attention and comments on only sentences they have restructured for impact.

Set workbook activities **5 minutes**
- Point students towards the activities on pp. 110–111 of the Workbook.
- Check understanding and answer any questions.
- These activities focus on using dashes and semi-colons, and experimenting with and writing sentences.

Year 8	**Unit 3: A Perfect World**		
Section 8 Using rhetorical devices: Lesson 14	**Skills focus: Writing: Argument**		**Student Book pp. 120–121** **Workbook pp. 112–113**
Main Curriculum Objectives	**R8.1B** Identify and retrieve a range of key information in a text or in spoken language.	**R8.2A** Explore a writer's or speaker's intention and viewpoint.	**R8.4B** Explore the impact of some of the writer's or speaker's significant vocabulary choices.
Secondary Curriculum Objectives			

Introduction **10 minutes** • Ask students to write one sentence arguing that students should always do their homework (highlighting its benefits and/or the problems caused by not doing it). • Take feedback, gathering a range of examples from volunteers. Ask the class to identify how the volunteers have tried to give their ideas impact. • Focus on two or three examples. Ask: How could more impact be added? Look for responses that recognise the value of vocabulary choice, sentence structure and/or rhetorical devices.	**Support** Prompt students with a sentence starter such as 'Homework is …' or 'Students who don't do their homework …'. **Deepen** Give students an opportunity to review and revise independently the vocabulary and sentence structures they have used to create impact.
First phase **15 minutes** • Read the extract. • Ask students to complete Activity 1. • Take feedback to check understanding. Ask: Do you agree with the writer? Why is this? • Focus on how the extract is written. Ask: How has the writer tried to persuade you? • Ask students to identify one or two effective choices of vocabulary or sentence structure.	**Support** In Activity 1, focus students on one paragraph of the extract at a time, exploring how each one could contribute to their responses. **Deepen** Challenge students to write a summary of the extract in 20 words or fewer.
Second phase **20 minutes** • Read through Activity 2 to refresh students' awareness of rhetorical devices. • Ask students to complete Activity 2, question 1. • Take feedback to check understanding. • Ask students to complete Activity 2. Encourage them to use complete sentences as their examples.	**Support** Complete Activity 2, question 1 as a whole class. In question 2, focus students' attention on scanning for one device at a time. **Deepen** Challenge students to identify multiple examples of each device.
Plenary **10 minutes** • Take feedback to check understanding. Use directed questioning to focus students' attention on considering the impact each device adds to the writer's key ideas, viewpoint and intention. • Ask: How effective are rhetorical devices? Why? • Ask students to write a short encyclopaedia entry on the topic of rhetorical devices: what they are, how they are used and why they are used.	**Support** Model removing one or two rhetorical devices in the extract, for example replacing the rhetorical question with a statement. Ask: What effect is lost? **Deepen** Ask students to rewrite their examples with the rhetorical device removed, for example replacing the rhetorical question with a statement. Ask: What effect is lost?

Set workbook activities **5 minutes**
- Point students towards the activities on pp. 112–113 of the Workbook.
- Check understanding and answer any questions.
- These activities focus on identifying rhetorical devices.

<table>
<tr><td>Year 8</td><td colspan="3">Unit 3: A Perfect World</td></tr>
<tr><td colspan="2">Section 8 Using rhetorical devices: Lesson 15</td><td>Skills focus: Writing: Argument</td><td>Student Book pp. 122–123
Workbook pp. 114–115</td></tr>
<tr><td>Main Curriculum Objectives</td><td>W8.3I Use upper-case letters, end punctuation, commas, speech marks and apostrophes correctly, with accuracy and consistency.</td><td>W8.1A Gather and structure a range of relevant ideas before writing.</td><td>W8.3G Select vocabulary in text and spoken language with growing precision.</td></tr>
<tr><td>Secondary Curriculum Objectives</td><td colspan="3"></td></tr>
</table>

<table>
<tr><td>Introduction — 10 minutes
• Display the terms 'possession' and 'contraction'.
• Ask students to write one sentence including an apostrophe showing possession, and one including an apostrophe showing contraction.
• Ask volunteers to share examples to check understanding. Display a correct example of each to model correct usage.
• Ask partners to check correct usage in each other's sentences.
• To explore common misunderstandings, ask students to share any errors found.</td><td>Support
Use the examples from the Punctuation Boost activity as models.

Deepen
Ask students to write a paragraph including three or four apostrophes and one intentional error. Challenge partners to spot the errors in each other's work.</td></tr>
<tr><td>First phase — 15 minutes
• Ask students to complete the Punctuation Boost activity.
• Take feedback to check accuracy.
• Ask volunteers to recap the definitions of rhetorical devices.
• Ask students to complete Activity 3.
• Take feedback on Activity 3, discussing the usage, structure and impact of each device.</td><td>Support
In Activity 3, suggest that students refer to Activity 2 in the previous lesson to recap understanding of rhetorical devices.

Deepen
In the Punctuation Boost activity, challenge students to write five sentences demonstrating correct usage of 'it's' and 'its'.</td></tr>
<tr><td>Second phase — 20 minutes
• Read through Activity 4.
• Ask students to complete question 1.
• Take feedback to share ideas.
• Ask students to complete question 2.
• Again, take feedback to share ideas.
• Ask students to complete questions 3 and 4.</td><td>Support
Ask the class or supported groups to select one idea from Activity 4, question 1 on which all students can focus, encouraging them to develop ideas together.

Deepen
Encourage students to consider vocabulary and sentence structure carefully in their writing.</td></tr>
<tr><td>Plenary — 10 minutes
• Ask students to check their response to Activity 4 for accurate use of apostrophes. Take examples of correct usage and any corrections found.
• Ask students to share examples of rhetorical devices they used in response to Activity 4. Focus students on the usage, structure and impact of each device.</td><td>Support
Recognise and validate accurate usage of any rhetorical device.

Deepen
Encourage students to consider how many rhetorical devices is too many. Warn students to beware of overuse.</td></tr>
</table>

Set workbook activities — **5 minutes**

- Point students towards the activities on pp. 114–115 of the Workbook.
- Check understanding and answer any questions.
- These activities focus on apostrophes and using rhetorical devices.

Year 8	Unit 3: A Perfect World		
Section 9 Introductions and conclusions: Lesson 16		Skills focus: Writing: Argument	Student Book pp. 124–125 Workbook pp. 116–117
Main Curriculum Objectives	**R8.2A** Explore a writer's or speaker's intention and viewpoint.	**R8.2B** Express a critical response to a text through writing, discussion or presentation, by considering the text's features and their effects.	**R8.3A** Explore the impact of some of the writer's key structural or organisational choices.
Secondary Curriculum Objectives			

Introduction 10 minutes	Support
• Ask students to imagine they are planning a speech to persuade other students to take better care of the school grounds. • Ask: How would you introduce your point of view? How would you conclude your argument? • Allow three minutes for students to discuss and note down their ideas. • Take feedback. Discuss what the functions of an introduction and of a conclusion are, and how these are best achieved.	Ask partners to support each other as they compose their speeches orally. **Deepen** Suggest that students next use a different medium to express their argument, by writing the first and last paragraphs of a persuasive letter on the subject.
First phase 15 minutes • Read the explanation before the extracts and ensure students' understanding of what content they will contain. • Read the 'Introduction' sections of both Extract A and Extract B. You may also wish to reread the complete extracts at the start of Sections 7 and 8. • Ask students to complete Activity 1. • Take feedback to check and develop understanding, encouraging discussion. • Note that the writers' topics and points of view are not explicitly introduced (for example, neither extract states 'In this article, I will …' or 'In my opinion …').	**Support** Focus first on answering all questions in relation to Extract A before moving on to Extract B. **Deepen** When taking feedback, ask students to identify the most significant word(s) in the sentences and phrases they have identified.
Second phase 20 minutes • Read through Activity 2 and check students' understanding. • Discuss why each technique is engaging, for example what the appeal of stories is or why surprising the reader is effective. • Ask students to complete Activity 2.	**Support** Complete Activity 2, question 1 as a whole class or in supported groups before asking students to complete question 2 independently. **Deepen** Encourage students to develop their responses to Activity 2, questions 1b and 2b, identifying the impacts of specific ideas and vocabulary choices.
Plenary 10 minutes • Take feedback on Activity 2, to share and develop understanding. • Ask: Which introduction is most effective, and why? • Ensure that students recognise the importance of making both the topic and the point of view engaging.	**Support** Recognise and validate any relevant responses to Activity 2. **Deepen** Ask: How could each writer have used another one of the techniques to engage the reader?

Set workbook activities **5 minutes**
- Point students towards the activities on pp. 116–117 of the Workbook.
- Check understanding and answer any questions.
- These activities focus on introductions.

Year 8	Unit 3: A Perfect World		
Section 9 Introductions and conclusions: Lesson 17	Skills focus: Writing: Argument		Student Book pp. 126–127 Workbook pp. 118–119
Main Curriculum Objectives	**W8.1A** Gather and structure a range of relevant ideas before writing.	**W8.2C** Use the organisational conventions of a range of forms, for a range of purposes and audiences, with confidence and understanding, including spoken-language forms such as presentations.	**W8.3A** Write in Standard English and a largely appropriate register.
Secondary Curriculum Objectives	**W8.2B** Use appropriate linguistic conventions to achieve a wider range of purposes and address a wider range of audiences, e.g. to explain, to describe or to persuade, with confidence and understanding.	**W8.3C** Use a balance of single-clause sentences, coordinate and subordinate clauses with confidence.	**W8.3E** Make deliberate choices of sentence length to achieve clarity.
	W8.3G Select vocabulary in text and spoken language with growing precision.		

Introduction **10 minutes** • Display the following statement. *Money cannot buy happiness.* • Ask: Do you agree? • Encourage students to discuss both money's benefits and the causes of happiness that cannot be bought. • Note points both for and against the statement for reference in the final writing task of the lesson.	**Support** Discuss and note points for and against the statement before asking students if they agree with it. **Deepen** Ask partners to discuss the statement and note points both for and against it, before taking feedback.
First phase **15 minutes** • Read the 'Conclusion' sections of both Extract A and Extract B. You may also wish to reread the complete extracts at the start of Sections 7 and 8. • Ask students to complete Activity 3. • Take feedback to check and develop understanding. • Note that the conclusion to Extract B begins 'In short, ...' • Discuss the fact that phrases such as this one are helpful but not necessary. • Ask students to complete the Skills Boost activity. • Take feedback to check accuracy and understanding.	**Support** In Activity 3, complete question 1 as a whole class or in supported groups before asking students to complete question 2 independently. **Deepen** In Activity 3, encourage students to develop their responses to questions 1c and 2c, identifying the impacts of specific ideas and vocabulary choices.
Second phase **20 minutes** • Recap the ideas gathered at the start of the lesson. • Read through Activity 4. • Ask students to complete questions 1 and 2. • Take feedback, discussing the reasons for students' choices of key points. • Recall students' learning on sentence lengths in the 'Introduction' of Extract A from Section 7. • Ask students to complete Activity 4.	**Support** Focus students on completing and discussing their introductions, moving on to conclusions only if time allows. **Deepen** Challenge students to write two or three introductions, experimenting with different techniques to engage the reader.
Plenary **10 minutes** • Ask volunteers to share introductions, and then conclusions, with the class. • Ask the class to identify and evaluate successful features in each, and possible improvements that could add more impact.	**Support** Recognise and validate any effective choices. **Deepen** Ask students to annotate the key features of their writing.

Set workbook activities **5 minutes**
- Point students towards the activities on pp. 118–119 of the Workbook.
- Check understanding and answer any questions.
- These activities focus on conclusions.

Year 8	Unit 3: A Perfect World		
Section 10 Reviewing and revising: Lesson 18		Skills focus: Writing: Argument	Student Book pp. 128–129 Workbook pp. 120–121
Main Curriculum Objectives	**R8.3A** Explore the impact of some of the writer's key structural or organisational choices.	**W8.2C** Use the organisational conventions of a range of forms, for a range of purposes and audiences, with confidence and understanding, including spoken-language forms such as presentations.	
Secondary Curriculum Objectives			

Introduction **10 minutes** • Read the extract, ensuring students' understanding of its context: this is a model of an article written by a (fictional) student. • Ask the class to suggest elements for a checklist of the key features of an argument text and the job that each one does, based on their learning so far in this unit. • Note their responses.	**Support** Prompt students with leading questions, such as 'What is the job of the first and last paragraphs?' and 'Can you name the three key elements that should be found in each paragraph?' **Deepen** Encourage students to include linguistic as well as structural features in their checklists.
First phase **25 minutes** • Read through the Argument Text Checklist at the beginning of Activity 1. Ensure students' understanding of the term 'main body' (the majority of the writing in the text, as opposed to, for example, an introduction and/or conclusion). • Compare the checklist in the Student Book to the checklist created during the introduction to the lesson, discussing any points that students did not suggest. • Ask students to complete Activity 1, questions 1–3. • Take feedback, aiming to agree as a class which features are present in the text and which features are missing.	**Support** Take feedback after each of questions 1–3 in Activity 1 to monitor understanding and reinforce key learning. **Deepen** Ask students to identify which sentence performs which function in the introduction and in the conclusion.
Second phase **15 minutes** • Read through Activity 1, question 4. • Explain that students can create fictional scientific research, expert opinions or statistics in order to add evidence to the extract. • Ask students to complete Activity 1, question 4. • If time allows, suggest that students suggest two or three ideas for each missing feature.	**Support** Work as a whole class or in supported groups to craft sentences for one or two missing points. **Deepen** Challenge students to identify any explanations or evidence that are present but could be more effective, and suggest improvements.
Plenary **10 minutes** • Ask volunteers to share examples of the sentences written in response to Activity 1, question 4. • Ask the class, in each case, to choose one sentence that they would award a place in the text, and to explain why they think it is effective.	**Support** Recognise and validate any responses that include the desired feature. **Deepen** Ask students to share examples of explanations or evidence that they have improved.

Set workbook activities **5 minutes**
- Point students towards the activities on pp. 120–121 of the Workbook.
- Check understanding and answer any questions.
- These activities focus on identifying points, examples and comments

Year 8	Unit 3: A Perfect World		
Section 10 Reviewing and revising: Lesson 19		Skills focus: Writing: Argument	Student Book pp. 130–131 Workbook pp. 122–123
Main Curriculum Objectives	**W8.1B** Correct a range of errors in spelling, punctuation and grammar independently after writing, beginning to develop strategies for proofreading.	**W8.1C** Review and revise vocabulary choice after writing.	
Secondary Curriculum Objectives	**W8.3H** Spell homophones, words with single/double letters and 'silent' letters with some accuracy.	**W8.3I** Use upper-case letters, end punctuation, commas, speech marks and apostrophes correctly, with accuracy and consistency.	

Introduction 10 minutes • Display the following multi-clause sentence. *We are damaging our planet and we should change our ways.* • Ask students to suggest ways in which sentence structure and vocabulary choices could be adjusted to give this sentence more impact.	**Support** Suggest breaking the sentence into two shorter sentences and replacing the words 'should' and 'damaging'. **Deepen** Suggest that students consider using an adverb, adjective or rhetorical device to add impact.
First phase 20 minutes • Read through Activity 2, ensuring understanding. Note that this activity focuses on reviewing and revising a range of textual elements: vocabulary, sentence structure and rhetorical devices. • Ask students to complete Activity 2. • Take feedback, discussing as wide a range of suggestions as possible, and their impacts.	**Support** Take feedback after each question to monitor progress and understanding. **Deepen** Encourage students to suggest as many impact-adding improvements as they can.
Second phase 15 minutes • Discuss the concept of 'careless' errors: errors that you may make while rushing, rather than those made due to a lack of understanding. • Read through the list of common careless errors at the beginning of the Skills Boost activity, checking understanding. • Ask students to complete question 1 of the Skills Boost activity. Emphasise the importance of noting the errors in the order in which they are found.	**Support** Briefly recap the rules/guidance for each error, for example when an apostrophe is needed, the various meanings of different homophones. **Deepen** Ask students to compile a checklist of common but easily misspelt words. Suggest looking through their own writing and the Student Book to prompt them.
Plenary 10 minutes • Take feedback on question 1 of the Skills Boost activity to check and validate accuracy. • Discuss any categories of error overlooked by a significant number of students. Note these, to guide future learning and target setting. • Explain that question 2 of the Skills Boost activity is intended to prompt students to identify which errors they tend to overlook. • Ask students to complete question 2 of the Skills Boost activity. • Take feedback.	**Support** Recap the rules for any errors that students did not find. **Deepen** Ask students to write two or three sentences containing each of the five kinds of error. Ask partners to identify and correct each other's errors.

Set workbook activities 5 minutes • Point students towards the activities on pp. 122–123 of the Workbook. • Check understanding and answer any questions. • These activities focus on reviewing vocabulary choices and sentence structure, and checking for careless errors.

Year 8	Unit 3: A Perfect World		
Section 11 Assessment: Lesson 20		Skills focus: Writing: Argument	Student Book pp. 132–133 Workbook pp. 124–125
Main Curriculum Objectives	**W8.1A** Gather and structure a range of relevant ideas before writing.	**W8.1C** Review and revise vocabulary choice after writing.	**W8.2C** Use the organisational conventions of a range of forms, for a range of purposes and audiences, with confidence and understanding, including spoken-language forms such as presentations.
	W8.3A Write in Standard English and a largely appropriate register.	**W8.3B** Divide text into paragraphs with accuracy and consistency.	**W8.3C** Use a balance of single-clause sentences, coordinate and subordinate clauses with confidence.
	W8.3E Make deliberate choices of sentence length to achieve clarity.	**W8.3G** Select vocabulary in text and spoken language with growing precision.	**W8.3H** Spell homophones, words with single/double letters and 'silent' letters with some accuracy.
	W8.3I Use upper-case letters, end punctuation, commas, speech marks and apostrophes correctly, with accuracy and consistency.		
Secondary Curriculum Objectives			

Introduction **10 minutes**

- Ask students to read Activity 1. Point out that they should plan their writing, and that you will assess their plans as well as their finished pieces of writing.
- Time may have been allocated before the lesson for students to research topics for the writing task. If not, explain that students should make up evidence in answer to question 2.
- Explain to students that they will have 15 minutes to complete the planning section of the assessment, a further 25 minutes to complete the writing section and a further 10 minutes to review, revise and proofread their writing.

Assessment task **50 minutes**

- Ask students to complete the planning section of the assessment.
- After 15 minutes, ask students to move on to complete the writing section of the assessment.
- After a further 25 minutes, ask students to move on to complete the reviewing and revising section of the assessment.
- You may wish to give students further guidance on how much they should write, and the amounts of time they should use for planning, writing and checking their responses.

Workbook assessment task

- Point students towards the task and sample student response on p. 124 of the Workbook.
- Give students the opportunity to read the task and sample response. Briefly discuss these with them and answer any questions.
- Students should identify the errors in the sample response before planning how they will improve it. They should then write an improved version, adding one or two paragraphs of text.
- Make clear your expectations of when this task will be completed. For example, it may be a homework, or students may be given time during an additional lesson.

Year 8	Unit 4: World of Sport		
Section 1 Summarising: Lesson 1		Skills focus: Reading: Information texts	Student Book pp. 136–137 Workbook pp. 126–127
Main Curriculum Objectives	**R8.1A** Use a range of strategies to decode unfamiliar words.	**R8.1B** Identify and retrieve a range of key information in a text or in spoken language.	**R8.1D** Compare, contrast and/or combine key points of information within a text or in spoken language with a given focus.
Secondary Curriculum Objectives			

Introduction **10 minutes** • Model the formation of the following word, building the form prefix + root + suffix. *help > help + ful > un + help + ful* • Ask: What other words of the 'help' family do you know? (If necessary, guide students towards the words 'helped', 'helping', 'helper' and 'helpless'.) • Display the root word 'excite'. • Ask: How many words of the 'excite' family do you know? Allow students three minutes' independent thinking time. • Take feedback.	**Support** Provide the following prefixes and suffixes from which students can choose (including those not appropriate for 'excite'). • un–; dis–; re– • –ed; –ing; –ble; –ly; –ful **Deepen** Challenge students to suggest other root words with large word families.
First phase **15 minutes** • Ask students to complete the Skills Boost activity. • Take feedback to check accuracy of usage and spelling, and to share vocabulary and definitions. • Read the information text. Ask students to identify any unfamiliar vocabulary. • Ask students to complete Activity 1. • Repeat the activity using any other unfamiliar vocabulary that students identified. • Take feedback focusing on the usefulness and accuracy of the clues identified.	**Support** In the Skills Boost activity, take feedback to check understanding. **Deepen** If students are familiar with all the vocabulary in the information text, ask them to complete Activity 1 by identifying what methods it would be best for someone unfamiliar with the terms to use.
Second phase **20 minutes** • Read through Activity 2 and refresh students' understanding of scanning. Draw students' attention to the model partial responses to question 2. • Point out that this activity develops the skill of gathering related information from different parts of a text. • Ask students to complete Activity 2.	**Support** Work with the class or supported groups to scan for the first reference in the information text to 'rules'. Take feedback after Activity 2, question 1 to check accuracy. **Deepen** Encourage students to use both methods of linking information and their own words to express it.
Plenary **10 minutes** • Take feedback on Activity 2, comparing responses and different ways of expressing them. • Emphasise the usefulness of the skill of linking related information, for example when responding to and writing information texts.	**Support** Recognise and validate any relevant elements of responses. **Deepen** Challenge students to repeat Activity 2, linking information about people who have played cricket.

Set workbook activities **5 minutes**
- Point students towards the activities on pp. 126–127 of the Workbook.
- Check understanding and answer any questions.
- These activities focus on prefixes and suffixes, understanding unfamiliar words and combining points.

Year 8	Unit 4: World of Sport		
Section 1 Summarising: Lesson 2		Skills focus: Reading: Information texts	Student Book pp. 138–139 Workbook pp. 128–129
Main Curriculum Objectives	**R8.1B** Identify and retrieve a range of key information in a text or in spoken language	**R8.1C** Summarise a short text or speech effectively, selecting appropriate and relevant detail.	
Secondary Curriculum Objectives			

Introduction 10 minutes • Explain to students that this lesson will focus on writing a summary, and that one of the key skills needed is identifying key information. • Display the following three linked sentences. *I got my first pair of football boots when I was four. They were red. I loved them.* • Ask: Which of the three sentences contains the most important information? Why is that? • Repeat the discussion using the following three linked sentences. *I played football every day. We went to the park after school. It didn't matter if it was raining.*	**Support** Use a process of elimination, reading the sentences aloud three times and omitting a different sentence each time. Discuss which sentence is least important. **Deepen** Challenge students to combine the three pieces of information into one sentence, using as few words as possible while retaining all the meaning.
First phase 15 minutes • Read through Activity 3, Method 1, to check understanding. • Ask: Do you agree with the choice of most-important sentence? Why is that? • Read the second paragraph of the information text again. Ask students to select its most important sentence, and compare choices. • Ask students to complete Activity 3, question 1. • Take feedback.	**Support** Complete Activity 3, question 1a as a whole class or in supported groups. Ask students to complete questions 1b–1e independently, but take feedback after each step. **Deepen** Encourage students to consider different ways of rephrasing and restructuring sentences in their own words.
Second phase 20 minutes • Read through Activity 3, Method 2, to check understanding. • Ask students to complete questions 2a and 2b. Take feedback to compare and discuss responses. • Ask students to complete question 2c. Again, take feedback to compare and discuss responses. • Ask students to complete question 3.	**Support** You may wish not to use Method 2, allowing students to focus on Method 1 when completing their summaries. **Deepen** Encourage students to consider different ways of rephrasing and restructuring their responses.
Plenary 10 minutes • Ask students to combine their responses to Activity 3, questions 1–3 to form their full summaries. • Ask students to check that their total word count does not exceed 75, and to adjust their summaries if necessary. • Ask partners to evaluate the thoroughness of each other's summaries. • Take feedback. Discuss which elements of the process students found most accessible and most challenging.	**Support** Focus students on each paragraph summary individually. **Deepen** Challenge students to reduce their summaries to 50 words or fewer, without losing key information.

Set workbook activities 5 minutes
- Point students towards the activities on pp. 128–129 of the Workbook.
- Check understanding and answer any questions.
- These activities focus on writing a summary.

Year 8	Unit 4: World of Sport		
Section 2 Informing and describing: Lesson 3	Skills focus: Reading: Information texts		Student Book pp. 140–141 Workbook pp. 130–131
Main Curriculum Objectives	**R8.1B** Identify and retrieve a range of key information in a text or in spoken language.	**R8.2B** Express a critical response to a text through writing, discussion or presentation, by considering the text's features and their effects.	
Secondary Curriculum Objectives			

Lesson	Support / Deepen
Introduction **10 minutes** • Ask students to recall how to scan a text for information. • Return to the information text studied in the previous two lessons (Section 1): 'The History of Cricket'. • Display the following question. *When was the first match between Australia and England?* • Discuss which would be an effective key word or phrase for which to scan. Point out that a word that is unlikely to appear often is the best choice. • Ask students to scan the information text for the chosen key word and give the answer.	**Support** Use a process of elimination to identify an appropriate key word or phrase, evaluating a final shortlist of two or three options as a whole class. **Deepen** Challenge students to scan texts in the classroom (for example posters or a display) to find the answer to a specific question.
First phase **15 minutes** • Read the article extract. • Read through Activity 1, emphasising the need to note the key word or phrase scanned for as part of the response. • Ask students to complete Activity 1. • Take feedback to check scanning skills and accuracy. • Discuss whether all students agreed on the key word/phrase for which to scan.	**Support** Work with the whole class or in supported groups to identify key words/phrases for the first two or three questions. **Deepen** Ask students to write their own questions on the extract to challenge a partner.
Second phase **20 minutes** • Read through Activity 2, checking students' understanding. • Ask students to complete Activity 2. • Point out that some information is implied rather than directly stated, and must be inferred (for example, the fact that the object of gurning is to pull the 'nastiest expressions').	**Support** Work with the whole class or in supported groups to complete the table in relation to the first one or two events. **Deepen** Students need not copy the table; they may simply note which events are missing which information type.
Plenary **10 minutes** • Take feedback to check accuracy. • Ask: Are any other types of information given about any of these events? • Ask: Why do you think this has been included?	**Support** Prompt students to identify examples of statistics before discussing their role. **Deepen** Ask students to note five pieces of information about a sporting event in which they participate.

Set workbook activities **5 minutes**
- Point students towards the activities on pp. 130–131 of the Workbook.
- Check understanding and answer any questions.
- These activities focus on understanding and responding.

Year 8	Unit 4: World of Sport		
Section 2 Informing and describing: Lesson 4		Skills focus: Reading: Information texts	Student Book pp. 142–143 Workbook pp. 132–133
Main Curriculum Objectives	**R8.2A** Explore a writer's or speaker's intention and viewpoint.	**R8.4B** Explore the impact of some of the writer's or speaker's significant vocabulary choices.	**W8.3G** Select vocabulary in text and spoken language with growing precision.
Secondary Curriculum Objectives	**R8.1E** Make inferences from specific evidence found in a text or in spoken language, including specific vocabulary choices.		

Introduction **10 minutes** • Display a jumbled list of six facts and locally relevant opinions. For example: *Paris is the capital of France. Football is the best sport in the world. Science is brilliant. George Washington was the first US president. Our school is in [town]. Fruits are delicious.* • Ask students to note which are facts and which are opinions, and to explain how they identified this. • Note that opinion may be implied in an information text, but is rarely explicitly stated.	**Support** Remind students that opinions can be disputed but facts cannot. **Deepen** Ask students to suggest three facts and three opinions of their own.
First phase **15 minutes** • Read through Activity 3 to check understanding. • Ask students to complete Activity 3, encouraging them to respond to question 1c by identifying the impression created rather than vocabulary choice. • Take feedback to share and develop understanding. • Ask students to complete the Skills Boost activity. • Take feedback, noting that a text may have more than one intention, and that different readers often respond in different ways.	**Support** In the Skills Boost activity, discuss, as a whole class or in supported groups, the types of text from which the extracts might have been taken. Discuss what may have happened immediately before the given point in each extract. **Deepen** In Activity 3, challenge students to identify any other significant or effective descriptive vocabulary choices in the extract. Ask: What does this contribute?
Second phase **20 minutes** • Read through the 'Imagine' section of Activity 4. • Ask students to complete question 1. • Take feedback to share and develop ideas. • Ask students to complete questions 2–6. • Ensure students have completed all the planning tasks before they start to write.	**Support** Take feedback after each step in the process to monitor progression and develop understanding. **Deepen** Challenge students to condense their ideas in fewer than 50 words, while still fulfilling the other given criteria. Note that they could imply rather than state ideas to achieve this.
Plenary **10 minutes** • Ask partners to read each other's texts and try to guess the writer's intention. • Take feedback. Ask: What clues helped you to guess your partner's intention?	**Support** Recognise any effective elements in students' writing. **Deepen** Focus on students' effective use of implication to help condense texts.

Set workbook activities **5 minutes**

- Point students towards the activities on pp. 132–133 of the Workbook.
- Check understanding and answer any questions.
- These activities focus on informing and describing, and identifying intentions.

Year 8	Unit 4: World of Sport		
Section 3 Selecting evidence: Lesson 5	Skills focus: Reading: Information texts		Student Book pp. 144–145 Workbook pp. 134–135
Main Curriculum Objectives	**R8.1B** Identify and retrieve a range of key information in a text or in spoken language.	**R8.1E** Make inferences from specific evidence found in a text or in spoken language, including specific vocabulary choices.	**R8.4B** Explore the impact of some of the writer's or speaker's significant vocabulary choices.
Secondary Curriculum Objectives			

Introduction **10 minutes** • Display the following sentence. *Deepak eventually finished his homework and crawled into bed.* • Ask: What can be inferred about Deepak from this sentence? • Look for detailed responses. For example: 'He has spent a long time on his homework and is exhausted, which suggests he is hard-working.' • Ask students to identify the specific words that prompted their inferences.	**Support** Prompt students to consider what can be inferred about Deepak's physical state and his attitudes to education. **Deepen** Challenge students to make a strongly opinionated inference, perhaps an extremely negative or positive one.
First phase **15 minutes** • Read the extract. • Read through Activity 1. Ask students to identify the questions that require the skill of scanning, and which require the skill of inference. • Ask students to complete Activity 1. • Take feedback, asking students to identify the key words or phrases for which they scanned the text.	**Support** Work with students to identify key words or phrases to use for scanning. **Deepen** Challenge students to identify further evidence to support the inferences made in their responses to Activity 1.
Second phase **20 minutes** • Explain that, in the next lesson, students will be writing a response to the extract, and that identifying and commenting on significant vocabulary choices will be a key part of that. • Ask students to complete Activity 2. You may wish to reveal that one of the given quotations is a distractor, and that therefore one quotation supports two of the statements.	**Support** Model a process of elimination using Activity 2, question 1a. Ask: Which quotation suggests the sport's popularity? Which word suggests it? **Deepen** Challenge students to identify further quotations and vocabulary choices that support each answer.
Plenary **10 minutes** • Take feedback on Activity 2 to check accuracy and understanding. • Discuss the fact that some of the answers directly state the various aspects of the sport, while others imply it. • Emphasise the need for inference skills when exploring a writer's vocabulary choices.	**Support** Recognise and validate any relevant responses. **Deepen** Challenge students to develop the given statements, commenting more fully on what each vocabulary choice implies.

Set workbook activities **5 minutes**
- Point students towards the activities on pp. 134–135 of the Workbook.
- Check understanding and answer any questions.
- These activities focus on finding and inferring information, and vocabulary choices.

Year 8	Unit 4: World of Sport		
Section 3 Selecting evidence: Lesson 6	Skills focus: Reading: Information texts		Student Book pp. 146–147 Workbook pp. 136–137
Main Curriculum Objectives	**R8.2A** Explore a writer's or speaker's intention and viewpoint.	**R8.2B** Express a critical response to a text through writing, discussion or presentation, by considering the text's features and their effects.	**R8.2C** Select relevant, focused evidence to support ideas.
Secondary Curriculum Objectives	**W8.3C** Use a balance of single-clause sentences, coordinate and subordinate clauses with confidence.		

Introduction **10 minutes** • Display the following sentence. *Dina quickly hid the old map and ran.* • Ask students to identify the word classes in the sentence: the nouns, adverbial, verbs, adjective, determiner and conjunction. • Ask: How many single-clause sentences could be created from this multi-clause sentence? • Ask students to rewrite the sentence as two single-clause sentences. • Take feedback to check understanding.	**Support** Reveal that there are two nouns, one adverbial, two verbs, one determiner and one conjunction. Use a process of elimination to identify less-familiar word classes (such as the determiner). **Deepen** Challenge students to add a third clause to the original sentence.
First phase **15 minutes** • Read through the introduction to the Grammar Boost activity, to check and consolidate students' understanding. • Ask students to complete the Grammar Boost activity. • Take feedback. • Ask students to recap the rules of punctuating quotations. • Ask students to complete Activity 3. • Take feedback to check understanding.	**Support** In the Grammar Boost activity, work as a class or in supported groups to identify the verb(s) in each sentence. In Activity 3, question 2, suggest that students use question 1's exemplar sentence as a model for their response. **Deepen** In Activity 3, question 2c, challenge students to express their ideas in their own words, not using question 1's exemplar sentence as a model.
Second phase **20 minutes** • Read through Activity 4, emphasising that the task is to write two paragraphs, each consisting of a point, evidence and explanation. • Ask students to complete questions 1 and 2. Take feedback to share and develop thinking. • Ask students to complete questions 3–6.	**Support** Take feedback after each step in the process to monitor progression and understanding. **Deepen** Ask students to focus on the clarity and fluency of their written expression as well as the fullness of their responses.
Plenary **10 minutes** • Ask partners to ensure that each sentence in each other's responses focuses on the writer's intention: the impression created of Sepak Takraw. • Ask volunteers to share one of their paragraphs.	**Support** Recognise and validate any effective elements of students' paragraphs. **Deepen** Ask students to start building a bank of useful phrases for writing a response, such as 'This suggests' and 'This creates the impression that'.

Set workbook activities **5 minutes**
- Point students towards the activities on pp. 136–137 of the Workbook.
- Check understanding and answer any questions.
- These activities focus on clauses and using evidence.

Year 8	Unit 4: World of Sport		
Section 4 Exploring vocabulary choice: Lesson 7	Skills focus: Reading: Information texts		Student Book pp. 148–149 Workbook pp. 138–139
Main Curriculum Objectives	**R8.1B** Identify and retrieve a range of key information in a text or in spoken language.	**R8.2A** Explore a writer's or speaker's intention and viewpoint.	
Secondary Curriculum Objectives			

Lesson	Support / Deepen
Introduction — **10 minutes** • Recap the term 'intention': the effect the writer wants their text to have. • Ask students to describe a favourite moment from a story, television programme or film. • Ask the class to identify the writer's or director's intention in that moment.	**Support** Display a range of possible intentions from which students can choose (for example surprise, excitement, tension, humour, fear, mystery). **Deepen** Ask students to identify some of the ways in which the writer or director tried to achieve their intention.
First phase — **15 minutes** • Read the article and take students' initial responses. Ask: Does the article make you want to see or take part in Fierljeppen? Why is that? Look for responses that identify specific details from the article. • Ask students to complete Activity 1. • Take feedback after each question to monitor and share understanding.	**Support** Complete Activity 1, question 1 as a whole class or in supported groups, looking at each of the three paragraphs in turn to identify what information is given. Ask: Which details add to your understanding of the sport? **Deepen** Challenge students to identify any interesting or important information in the article that is not needed to complete Activity 1.
Second phase — **20 minutes** • Look at the vocabulary list included within Activity 2, question 1a: terms that could describe impressions of sports. • Ask: Which are relevant to the game of Fierljeppen? • Ask students to complete Activity 2. Emphasise the importance of considering every sentence, phrase and word to identify the vocabulary choices that have created the identified impressions.	**Support** Discuss Activity 2, questions 1a and 2a as a whole class or in supported groups. **Deepen** Encourage students to use their own ideas and/or a thesaurus to express their impressions as fully and precisely as possible.
Plenary — **10 minutes** • Take feedback on Activity 2 to share and develop ideas. • Model writing a sentence to express one of the students' responses in the following form. *The word _____ creates the impression that Fierljeppen is _____.* • Ask students to write two or three sentences following your example. • Take feedback to check understanding and accuracy of expression.	**Support** Recognise and validate any relevant elements of responses to Activity 2, looking for only one or two words or phrases from the article. **Deepen** Encourage students to express their ideas in different ways, using a variety of sentence starts. For example: *The writer creates …* *The text suggests …*

Set workbook activities — **5 minutes**

- Point students towards the activities on pp. 138–139 of the Workbook.
- Check understanding and answer any questions.
- These activities focus on identifying key information, and intention and vocabulary.

Year 8	Unit 4: World of Sport		
Section 4 Exploring vocabulary choice: Lesson 8	Skills focus: Reading: Information texts		Student Book pp. 150–151 Workbook pp. 140–141
Main Curriculum Objectives	**R8.2B** Express a critical response to a text through writing, discussion or presentation, by considering the text's features and their effects.	**R8.2C** Select relevant, focused evidence to support ideas.	**R8.4B** Explore the impact of some of the writer's or speaker's significant vocabulary choices.
Secondary Curriculum Objectives			

Introduction — **10 minutes**	**Support**
• Display the vocabulary 'leaps', 'grabs' and 'lurches' from the article. • Focus on each word in turn. Ask: What ideas or associations does this term create in your minds? • Give students one minute to discuss and note their ideas. • Take feedback.	Prompt students with questions such as 'What are the qualities of animals that leap?' **Deepen** Ask students to identify other evocative vocabulary choices in the article.
First phase — **15 minutes**	**Support**
• Read through the introduction to the Skills Boost activity to ensure understanding of the terms 'formal register' and 'informal register'. • Ask students to complete the Skills Boost activity. • Take feedback, noting that vocabulary choice affects the register and therefore the tone of a text. • Recap the content of the article. • Ask students to complete Activity 3. • Take feedback, emphasising the difference between words that convey information and those that elicit an emotional or imaginative response.	In Activity 3, display the given sentence and use a process of elimination to identify words that create a powerful response. **Deepen** Ask students to repeat Activity 3, identifying a quotation that creates a powerful impression of the sport of Fierljeppen.
Second phase — **20 minutes**	**Support**
• Ask students to recap the definitions of the terms 'connotation', 'implication' and 'infer'. • Ask students to complete Activity 4. • Take feedback from as wide a variety of students as time allows, sharing and developing understanding. • Ask students to complete question 1 of Activity 5. • If time allows, ask students to complete question 2 of Activity 5.	Complete Activity 4 as a whole class or in supported groups, displaying responses for reference in Activity 5. **Deepen** In Activity 4, encourage students to express their own ideas in their own words.
Plenary — **10 minutes**	**Support**
• Ask students to review their responses to Activity 5, ensuring that they consider the writer's intention, feature appropriate short quotations and offer relevant comments on effective vocabulary choices. • Ask volunteers to share responses, or parts of responses, that exemplify these criteria.	Recognise and validate any relevant elements of responses, clearly identifying effective features. **Deepen** Challenge students to support their points with two quotations and comments on two different vocabulary choices.

Set workbook activities — **5 minutes**
• Point students towards the activities on pp. 140–141 of the Workbook. • Check understanding and answer any questions. • These activities focus on register, choosing evidence and connotations.

Year 8	Unit 4: World of Sport		
Section 5 Writing a response: Lesson 9	Skills focus: Reading: Information texts		Student Book pp. 152–153 Workbook pp. 142–143
Main Curriculum Objectives	**R8.2A** Explore a writer's or speaker's intention and viewpoint.	**R8.2B** Express a critical response to a text through writing, discussion or presentation, by considering the text's features and their effects.	**R8.2C** Select relevant, focused evidence to support ideas.
Secondary Curriculum Objectives	**R8.4B** Explore the impact of some of the writer's or speaker's significant vocabulary choices.		

Introduction — 10 minutes	Support / Deepen
• Read the first section of the newspaper article: the paragraphs under the subheading 'Bobsleigh'. • Give partners two or three minutes to gather ideas to include in a description of the experience of taking part in bobsleigh. • Take feedback to share and develop understanding.	**Support** If possible, search for and show a short online video of a bobsleigh event to support understanding. **Deepen** Encourage students to include comments on what would be experienced by all five senses.
First phase — 15 minutes • Read the whole of the newspaper article and take students' immediate responses. Ask: Does the article effectively convey the experience of taking part in these sports? Why is that? • Ask students to complete Activity 1. • Take feedback to check understanding, and prompt discussion of students' initial responses. • Explain that students will be developing their responses to the article during this lesson and the next.	**Support** Take feedback on Activity 1, question 1 to ensure understanding before students complete question 2. **Deepen** Encourage students to justify each of their responses to Activity 1, question 2 with a quotation and an explanation.
Second phase — 20 minutes • Remind students of the importance of supporting critical responses with evidence from the article, and of selecting short, focused, relevant quotations. • Ask students to complete Activity 2.	**Support** Work with the whole class or in supported groups to complete Activity 2, question 2, working through the article sentence by sentence to hunt for relevant quotations. **Deepen** Ask students to identify significant vocabulary choices in their quotations.
Plenary — 10 minutes • Ask students to review their choices of quotations in Activity 2, question 2. Ask them to check that all the quotations are short, focused and relevant. • Ask volunteers to share their quotations. Ask the remainder of the class to evaluate their length and relevance.	**Support** Recognise and validate any relevant choices. **Deepen** Ask students to explain their choices of quotations, encouraging them to comment on, for example, what makes the description so vivid.

Set workbook activities — **5 minutes**

- Point students towards the activities on pp. 142–143 of the Workbook.
- Check understanding and answer any questions.
- These activities focus on gathering information and responding to the text, and evidence of intention.

Year 8	Unit 4: World of Sport		
Section 5 Writing a response: Lesson 10	**Skills focus: Reading: Information texts**		**Student Book pp. 154–155** **Workbook pp. 144–145**
Main Curriculum Objectives	**R8.2B** Express a critical response to a text through writing, discussion or presentation, by considering the text's features and their effects.	**W8.3B** Divide text into paragraphs with accuracy and consistency.	**W8.3D** Use a range of sentence openings in addition to subject–verb sentence openings, starting to develop variety.
Secondary Curriculum Objectives	**R8.4B** Explore the impact of some of the writer's or speaker's significant vocabulary choices.	**W8.1A** Gather and structure a range of relevant ideas before writing.	

Introduction **10 minutes** • Take suggestions of two-clause sentences in which the clauses are linked with different conjunctions. • Ensure that some sentences contain subordinating conjunctions such as 'because', 'when' and 'if', suggesting these yourself if necessary. • Ask: In which, if any, of these sentences could the two clauses be swapped while the meaning of the sentences remains unchanged? • Look for responses that recognise that subordinate clauses can precede the main clause.	**Support** Model identifying and swapping clauses. For example: *The bobsleigh slowed when I braked.* *When I braked, the bobsleigh slowed.* **Deepen** Ask: How is meaning changed or lost when clauses linked with coordinating conjunctions are swapped? For example: *I put on my helmet and I lay down.* *And I lay down, I put on my helmet.*
First phase **15 minutes** • Ask students to complete the Grammar Boost activity. • Ask a volunteer to recap the content of the newspaper article. • Remind students that a critical paragraph often makes a point, supports this with a quotation and then explains the quotation's effect. Point out that these elements can be sequenced in different ways. • Ask students to complete Activity 3. • Take feedback to share and develop understanding.	**Support** In Activity 3, work with the class or in supported groups to complete questions 1a–c, identifying the quotation and the explanations first. **Deepen** In Activity 3, encourage students to create two fluent, accurate versions of the paragraph written in response to question 1d.
Second phase **20 minutes** • Ask students to complete Activity 4. • Take feedback to check understanding and clarity of expression. • Ask students to annotate their responses, identifying the point, quote and explanation in each paragraph.	**Support** Work with the whole class or in supported groups to develop the vocabulary prompts and sentence starts into fluent sentences. **Deepen** Encourage students to respond in two different ways to some or all of the questions, using their own words rather than the suggested vocabulary.
Plenary **10 minutes** • Ask partners to verify the accuracy of annotation and evaluate the fluency of written expression in each other's work. • Ask volunteers to share examples with the class.	**Support** Recognise and validate any effective choices or fluent expression in students' responses. **Deepen** Ask students to investigate different ways their paragraphs can be successfully structured.

Set workbook activities **5 minutes**
- Point students towards the activities on pp. 144–145 of the Workbook.
- Check understanding and answer any questions.
- These activities focus on sentence starts and writing paragraphs.

Year 8	Unit 4: World of Sport		
Section 6 Assessment: Lesson 11	Skills focus: Reading: Information texts		Student Book pp. 156–157 Workbook pp. 146–147
Main Curriculum Objectives	**R8.1B** Identify and retrieve a range of key information in a text or in spoken language.	**R8.1C** Summarise a short text or speech effectively, selecting appropriate and relevant detail.	**R8.1D** Compare, contrast and/or combine key points of information within a text or in spoken language.
	R8.1E Make inferences from specific evidence found in a text or in spoken language, including specific vocabulary choices.	**R8.2A** Explore a writer's or speaker's intention and viewpoint.	**R8.2B** Express a critical response to a text through writing, discussion or presentation, by considering the text's features and their effects.
	R8.2C Select relevant, focused evidence to support ideas.	**R8.4B** Explore the impact of some of the writer's or speaker's significant vocabulary choices.	
Secondary Curriculum Objectives			

Introduction **10 minutes**

- Ask students to read the extract, and check their understanding of any unfamiliar vocabulary.
- Explain to students that they will have 25 minutes to complete the reading section of the assessment, and a further 25 minutes to complete the writing section.

Assessment task **50 minutes**

- Ask students to complete the reading section of the assessment. Any students finishing sooner can begin the writing task.
- After 25 minutes, ask students to move on to complete the writing section of the assessment.
- Point out that they should plan their writing, and that you will assess their plans as well as their finished pieces of writing.
- You may wish to give students further guidance on how much they should write, and the amounts of time they should use for planning, writing and checking their responses.

Workbook assessment task

- Point students towards the extract and activities on pp. 146–147 of the Workbook.
- Give students the opportunity to read the extract. Briefly discuss it with them and answer any questions.
- Students should read the extract again carefully before answering the questions that follow it.
- Make clear your expectations of when this task will be completed. For example, it may be a homework, or students may be given time during an additional lesson.

Year 8	Unit 4: World of Sport		
Section 7 Structuring an information text: Lesson 12	Skills focus: Reading: Information texts		Student Book pp. 158–159 Workbook pp. 148–149
Main Curriculum Objectives	**R8.1A** Read largely accurately and with understanding.	**R8.2A** Explore a writer's or speaker's intention and viewpoint.	**R8.2B** Express a critical response to a text through writing, discussion or presentation, by considering the text's features and their effects.
Secondary Curriculum Objectives			

Lesson	Support / Deepen
Introduction **10 minutes** • Ask students to define the terms 'formal' and 'informal' in terms of clothing (for example, a suit versus jeans and a t-shirt). • Ask students to name three situations in which they might be expected to wear each outfit. • Ask students to name three situations in which they might be expected to speak formally, and three in which they might be expected to speak informally. • Take feedback, ranking suggestions in order of formality, from the most formal to the most informal.	**Support** Provide students with examples of situations to rank in order of formality, for example a school assembly, a job application, a conversation with friends and a meeting with the headteacher. **Deepen** Ask students to write the opening one or two lines of speech for each occasion, using appropriately formal or informal language.
First phase **15 minutes** • Read the extract. • Ask students to complete Activity 1, question 1. • Take feedback to check understanding. • Ask students to complete Activity 1, question 2. • Take feedback, asking students to justify their choices. • Look for responses that identify what makes points of information important and/or engaging.	**Support** Complete Activity 1, question 2 through discussion, as a whole class or in supported groups. **Deepen** Ask students to suggest other ideas they think the writer could have included in the extract.
Second phase **20 minutes** • Ask students to recap the definition of the terms 'intention', 'formal language' and 'informal language'. • Ask students to complete Activity 2. • Take feedback. • Experiment with and discuss the impact of omitting some of the key features identified in question 2 (for example dates, examples and informal language).	**Support** Take feedback after Activity 2, question 1, to check and ensure understanding. **Deepen** Ask students to identify other intentions the writer may have had.
Plenary **10 minutes** • Discuss the tone of the language in the extract, looking at the balance of informal phrases (such as '… but not their hands – which sounds very similar to football, until you learn that …') and more formal ones (such as '… in which two sides tried to keep possession of a small ball …'). • Ask students to note other key features of the extract (for example, the image and the fact box) for reference in the next lesson.	**Support** Work with students to find examples of each identifiable feature. **Deepen** Ask students to suggest ways in which some of the unused key features named in Activity 2 could have been used in the extract.

Set workbook activities **5 minutes**
- Point students towards the activities on pp. 148–149 of the Workbook.
- Check understanding and answer any questions.
- These activities focus on reading and understanding, and intention.

Year 8	Unit 4: World of Sport		
Section 7 Structuring an information text: Lesson 13	Skills focus: Reading: Information texts		Student Book pp. 160–161 Workbook pp. 150–151
Main Curriculum Objectives	**R8.3A** Explore the impact of some of the writer's key structural or organisational choices.	**W8.1A** Gather and structure a range of relevant ideas before writing.	**W8.2C** Use the organisational conventions of a range of forms, for a range of purposes and audiences, with confidence and understanding, including spoken-language forms such as presentations.
Secondary Curriculum Objectives	**W8.2A** Use the presentational conventions of a range of forms, for a range of purposes and audiences (for example, academic essays, stories, scripts and notes for talks and presentations), with confidence and understanding.		

Lesson	Support / Deepen
Introduction **10 minutes** • Ask volunteers to summarise verbally the purpose, form and positioning of subheadings in information texts. • Display the guidance gathered for reference later in the lesson.	**Support** Provide an example of the use of subheadings by looking at the Section 5 newspaper article, 'Exhilarating Winter Olympic sports'. **Deepen** Ask students to summarise their ideas as a list of dos and don'ts.
First phase **15 minutes** • Ask a volunteer to recap the extract. • Read through the short introduction to Activity 3, checking understanding of the ideas. • Ask students to complete Activity 3. • Take feedback to check understanding. • Discuss and display the types of supporting information and examples given. • Recap the opening activity on subheadings, and then ask students to complete the Skills Boost activity. • Point out to students that they should focus on the key points/topic sentences in each paragraph of the extract to help them.	**Support** In Activity 3, complete question 1 as a whole class or in supported groups to model the thought process required. **Deepen** In the Skills Boost activity, challenge students to use engaging language techniques such as alliteration to create effective subheadings.
Second phase **20 minutes** • Read through Activity 4 and check understanding. • Ask students to complete questions 1a and 1b. • Take feedback to share and develop initial ideas. • Ask students to complete the remainder of Activity 4. • Encourage students to plan their texts thoroughly before starting to write, even if this means they do not have time to finish their texts during the lesson.	**Support** Take feedback after each step in the process to monitor progress. **Deepen** Challenge students to plan at least two or three items of supporting information or examples for each paragraph.
Plenary **10 minutes** • Ask volunteers to share examples of their writing. • Ask the class to evaluate effective use of subheadings, clarity and accurate use of key points, and variety and relevance of supporting information.	**Support** Recognise and validate any relevant or effective choices. **Deepen** Challenge partners to review and suggest revisions to each other's texts.

Set workbook activities **5 minutes**
- Point students towards the activities on pp. 150–151 of the Workbook.
- Check understanding and answer any questions.
- These activities focus on paragraph structure and presenting an information text.

Year 8	Unit 4: World of Sport		
Section 8 Exploring vocabulary and sentence choices: Lesson 14	Skills focus: Reading: Information texts		Student Book pp. 162–163 Workbook pp. 152–153
Main Curriculum Objectives	**R8.2A** Explore a writer's or speaker's intention and viewpoint.	**R8.2B** Express a critical response to a text through writing, discussion or presentation, by considering the text's features and their effects.	**R8.4B** Explore the impact of some of the writer's or speaker's significant vocabulary choices.
Secondary Curriculum Objectives			

Introduction 10 minutes	Support
• Ask students to suggest verbs that might appear in a description of a popular sport (such as 'kick' or 'throw'). • Display these for later reference. • Ask students to remind you what a noun phrase is. • Ask students to suggest a noun phrase that might appear in a description of the same sport (such as 'a quick, easy goal' or 'the home team's players'). • Display these, too, for later reference.	Work with the class to build noun phrases, asking students to suggest a noun and then adjectives that could describe it. **Deepen** Encourage students to add a prepositional phrase to a noun phrase (such as 'the player with the injury').
First phase 15 minutes • Read the article and take students' initial responses. • Ask: Does any sport in your area attract this kind of devotion? • Ask students to complete Activity 1. • Take feedback on Activity 1 to check and develop understanding.	**Support** Ask students to find just one piece of information in the article to support their answers to Activity 1, question 2. **Deepen** Ask students to find all the pieces of information in the article that support their answers to Activity 1, question 2.
Second phase 20 minutes • Return students' focus to the verbs and noun phrases noted during the introductory activity. • Ask students to complete Activity 2, referring to their responses to Activity 1, question 2, for support.	**Support** In Activity 2, question 1, read the sentences aloud, omitting the focus phrases. Ask: What is lost? **Deepen** Encourage students to give detailed and precisely expressed responses.
Plenary 10 minutes • Take feedback on Activity 2. • Aim to discuss the impact of each of the focus phrases. • Emphasise that both vocabulary choice and selection of information can have an impact on the reader – and that students should aim to comment on both when responding to a text.	**Support** Recognise and validate any relevant responses. **Deepen** Encourage students to identify and comment on the impression built up by the writer's choices throughout the article.

Set workbook activities 5 minutes
• Point students towards the activities on pp. 152–153 of the Workbook. • Check understanding and answer any questions. • These activities focus on responding to vocabulary choices.

Year 8	Unit 4: World of Sport		
Section 8 Exploring vocabulary and sentence choices: Lesson 15	Skills focus: Reading: Information texts		Student Book pp. 164–165 Workbook pp. 154–155
Main Curriculum Objectives	**R8.2B** Express a critical response to a text through writing, discussion or presentation, by considering the text's features and their effects.	**R8.4A** Explore the impact of some of a writer's or speaker's choices of grammatical features and sentence structure.	
Secondary Curriculum Objectives	**W8.1A** Gather and structure a range of relevant ideas before writing.	**W8.2C** Use the organisational conventions of a range of forms, for a range of purposes and audiences, with confidence and understanding, including spoken-language forms such as presentations.	**W8.3C** Use a balance of single-clause sentences, coordinate and subordinate clauses with confidence.

Introduction **10 minutes**	
• Display a range of familiar coordinating and subordinating conjunctions. • Display the stem sentence 'I enjoy playing sport ...'. • Ask students to complete the sentence using a conjunction and an additional clause. • Use students' responses to demonstrate that each clause can operate as a single-clause sentence. • Ask students to suggest similar multi-clause sentences to rephrase as single-clause sentences.	**Support** Prompt students to use the correct terminology ('clause', 'single-clause', 'multi-clause' and 'conjunction') to embed their understanding. **Deepen** Encourage students to experiment with swapping the two clauses in each sentence. Ask: Which sentences lose sense?
First phase **15 minutes** • Read through the introduction to the Grammar Boost activity before asking students to complete it. • Take feedback to check understanding and reinforce use of terminology. • Ask students to complete Activity 3. • Take feedback on Activity 3, focusing on students' explanations of the impact created. • Note that positioning key information in a short sentence or at the end of a longer sentence gives it emphasis.	**Support** In Activity 3, question 1, orally link the short sentence to the longer sentence with 'and'; in Activity 3, question 2, orally swap the clauses in the sentence. In each case, ask: How is the emphasis altered? **Deepen** You may wish to develop students' awareness of sentence structure using the terms 'coordinate' and 'subordinate'.
Second phase **20 minutes** • Remind students of the three key elements of a paragraph of critical response: a key point, evidence and an explanation. • Ask students to complete Activity 4, questions 1–3. Suggest that they refer to Activities 1–3 for support. • Take feedback to share and develop ideas. • Ask students to complete questions 4 and 5.	**Support** Complete Activity 4, questions 1–3 as a whole class or in supported groups, referring to Activities 1–3 closely. **Deepen** Encourage students to develop their responses beyond the ideas gathered in Activities 1–3.
Plenary **10 minutes** • Ask partners to evaluate each other's paragraphs, to check that each is clear, includes a point, evidence and explanation, and comments on both sentence structure and vocabulary. • Ask volunteers to share any particularly effective extracts from their partner's responses.	**Support** Recognise and validate any effective elements of students' responses. **Deepen** Encourage students to add additional supporting evidence and comments for each of their paragraphs.

Set workbook activities **5 minutes**
- Point students towards the activities on pp. 154–155 of the Workbook.
- Check understanding and answer any questions.
- These activities focus on single- and multi-clause sentences, and sentence structure.

Year 8	Unit 4: World of Sport		
Section 9 Planning a critical response: Lesson 16	Skills focus: Reading: Information texts		Student Book pp. 166–167 Workbook pp. 156–157
Main Curriculum Objectives	**R8.1B** Identify and retrieve a range of key information in a text or in spoken language.	**R8.2A** Explore a writer's or speaker's intention and viewpoint.	**R8.3A** Explore the impact of some of the writer's key structural or organisational choices.
Secondary Curriculum Objectives	**R8.2B** Express a critical response to a text through writing, discussion or presentation, by considering the text's features and their effects.		

Introduction **10 minutes** • Ask partners to recap the key elements of an effective critical response to a text, allowing five minutes for discussion. • Take feedback, using students' level of awareness and understanding to guide the focus and emphasis of this lesson and the next.	**Support** Suggest that students aim to note five key elements. **Deepen** Ask students to discuss the relative importance of the elements needed, and how they can be combined.
First phase **15 minutes** • Read the article extract and take students' initial responses. • Explain that this lesson and the next will consolidate students' skills in responding critically to texts, each step helping to build an effective response. • Ask students to complete Activity 1. • Take feedback to check and develop understanding.	**Support** Complete Activity 1, questions 3–5 as a whole class or in supported groups, modelling and discussing choices. **Deepen** Challenge students to identify the key ideas in the article extract on which this activity has not focused (for example, the length of the fight itself).
Second phase **20 minutes** • Clarify what is meant by a text's 'structure': the selection and sequence of ideas or information it contains. • Read through Activity 2, clarifying the process: identifying the content of each paragraph then considering the writer's intention in choosing that sequence of ideas. • Ask students to complete Activity 2.	**Support** Encourage students to 'test' each of the possible responses suggested in Activity 2, question 2. Ask: Do any of these suggestions match your own ideas about the text? **Deepen** Encourage students to add an explanation of their own to any of the suggested responses they choose in answer to Activity 2, question 2.
Plenary **10 minutes** • Take feedback on Activity 2, gathering as wide a range of responses as possible. • Review and reinforce the process of planning a critical response explored so far. Look ahead to the content of the next lesson (exploring vocabulary choice and sentence structure) to give students a 'whole picture' of the process.	**Support** Recognise and validate any relevant contributions. **Deepen** Ask students to evaluate the effectiveness of the article extract. Ask: Do you find it engaging and informative? Why is that?

Set workbook activities **5 minutes**
- Point students towards the activities on pp. 156–157 of the Workbook.
- Check understanding and answer any questions.
- These activities focus on structure.

Year 8	Unit 4: World of Sport		
Section 9 Planning a critical response: Lesson 17	Skills focus: Reading: Information texts		Student Book pp. 168–169 Workbook pp. 158–159
Main Curriculum Objectives	**R8.4A** Explore the impact of some of a writer's or speaker's choices of grammatical features and sentence structure.	**R8.4B** Explore the impact of some of the writer's or speaker's significant vocabulary choices.	**W8.1A** Gather and structure a range of relevant ideas before writing.
Secondary Curriculum Objectives	**R8.2B** Express a critical response to a text through writing, discussion or presentation, by considering the text's features and their effects.	**R8.2C** Select relevant, focused evidence to support ideas.	**W8.2C** Use the organisational conventions of a range of forms, for a range of purposes and audiences, with confidence and understanding, including spoken-language forms such as presentations.

Introduction **10 minutes** • Ask students to note the facts they have learned about sumo, and compile a bulleted class list using their suggestions. • Ask students to note adjectives they could use to describe sumo, and compile a class spidergram. • Ask: Which method do you favour for noting ideas? • Ask students to justify their opinions. • Point out that choosing methods of planning is a matter of personal preference. • Retain the list and spidergram for later reference.	**Support** Prompt students with leading questions to support their suggestions, including key vocabulary. For example: What do rikishi wear? Is the dohyo large or small? **Deepen** Ask: Have you ever used other planning formats? Ask students to comment on the advantages and disadvantages of the different methods.
First phase **15 minutes** • Recap the activities completed in the previous lesson. • Read through the introduction to Activity 3. • Ask students to complete Activity 3. • Take feedback to share and develop ideas. • Read through the introduction to Activity 4. • Ask students to complete Activity 4. • Take feedback to share and develop ideas.	**Support** Spend time discussing the example sentences in the introduction to Activity 4. **Deepen** Encourage students to identify significant sentence structures in the whole of the article extract.
Second phase **20 minutes** • Draw students' attention back to the list and spidergram compiled during the introduction activity. • Ask students to complete the Skills Boost activity. • Take feedback, noting both the selection of ideas and the variety of preferences. • Ensure students have access to their responses to Activity 2 from the previous lesson. • Ask students to complete Activity 5, referring to their responses to Activities 2–4. Emphasise that the activity asks them to plan, not write, a response.	**Support** Take feedback after each step in the planning process to support and develop understanding. **Deepen** Encourage students to comment on text structure, sentence structure and vocabulary in each of their three paragraphs.
Plenary **10 minutes** • Take feedback on students' planning, drawing attention to the fact that they have included a key point, example and explanation in each paragraph.	**Support** Recognise and validate any relevant contributions. **Deepen** Encourage students to develop their notes, adding as much detail as possible to their explanations.

Set workbook activities	**5 minutes**

- Point students towards the activities on pp. 158–159 of the Workbook.
- Check understanding and answer any questions.
- These activities focus on vocabulary, sentence structure and planning.

Year 8	Unit 4: World of Sport		
Section 10 Comparing information texts: Lesson 18	Skills focus: Reading: Information texts		Student Book pp. 170–171 Workbook pp. 160–161
Main Curriculum Objectives	**R8.1B** Identify and retrieve a range of key information in a text or in spoken language.	**R8.2C** Select relevant, focused evidence to support ideas.	**R8.2D** Make developed comparisons of writers' ideas and perspectives between two texts.
Secondary Curriculum Objectives			

Lesson	Support / Deepen
Introduction **10 minutes** • Ask students to suggest any information they already know about the sport of volleyball. • If possible, show a short video of a volleyball match. Ask students to describe the game, and infer some of its rules. Take feedback.	**Support** Prompt students with suggestions of information about the rules, play and object of the game. **Deepen** Introduce the idea of comparison. Ask, for example: How does volleyball differ from basketball?
First phase **15 minutes** • Read Extract A and take students' initial responses. • Ask: Why might a reader want to read this extract? • Look for responses that recognise the extract as a purely informative text. • Ask students to complete Activity 1, noting that they are asked to compile a list of single words or phrases. • Take feedback to check accuracy and understanding.	**Support** Model examples of words that could be used to complete the activity, using both possible sentence endings. **Deepen** Ask students to provide evidence to support their responses.
Second phase **20 minutes** • Read Extract B and take students' initial responses. • Ask: How does this extract differ from Extract A? In what ways is it similar? • Ask students to complete Activity 2, again noting that they are asked to compile a list of single words or phrases.	**Support** Model examples of words that could be used to complete the activity, using both possible sentence endings for each sentence. **Deepen** Ask students to provide evidence to support their responses.
Plenary **10 minutes** • Take feedback on Activity 2, focusing on the methods that students used to complete it (for example, scanning Extract B for key words). • Ask students to sum up verbally some key differences between the two extracts, including their responses to each one.	**Support** Ask students to express and justify a simple preference for one extract. **Deepen** Encourage students to consider differences beyond the factual information in each extract, such as the writers' intentions.

Set workbook activities **5 minutes**
- Point students towards the activities on pp. 160–161 of the Workbook.
- Check understanding and answer any questions.
- These activities focus on comparing key information.

Year 8	Unit 4: World of Sport		
Section 10 Comparing information texts: Lesson 19		Skills focus: Reading: Information texts	Student Book pp. 172–173 Workbook pp. 162–163
Main Curriculum Objectives	**R8.2D** Make developed comparisons of writers' ideas and perspectives between two texts.	**R8.4B** Explore the impact of some of the writer's or speaker's significant vocabulary choices.	**W8.2D** Link paragraphs in text and spoken language using adverbials to signal the development of ideas.
Secondary Curriculum Objectives	**R8.2A** Explore a writer's or speaker's intention and viewpoint.	**R8.2B** Express a critical response to a text through writing, discussion or presentation, by considering the text's features and their effects.	**R8.4A** Explore the impact of some of a writer's or speaker's choices of grammatical features and sentence structure.
	W8.1A Gather and structure a range of relevant ideas before writing.	**W8.2C** Use the organisational conventions of a range of forms, for a range of purposes and audiences, with confidence and understanding, including spoken-language forms such as presentations.	

Lesson	Support / Deepen
Introduction **10 minutes** • Ask students to name two familiar celebrities. • Challenge the class to note five similarities and five differences between the two celebrities, in less than five minutes. • Take feedback, noting the various areas of comparison.	**Support** Prompt students to consider points of comparison such as professions, appearance and achievements. **Deepen** Encourage students to use adverbials of comparison in their responses.
First phase **15 minutes** • Ask students to remind you of their learning about adverbials of comparison. • Ask students to complete the Grammar Boost activity. • Take feedback, checking accuracy and clarity. • Ask volunteers to recap the content of each extract. • Introduce Activity 3, highlighting the difference between its focus and the focus of Activities 1 and 2: intention rather than information. • Ask students to complete Activity 3.	**Support** In Activity 3, discuss the writer's intention in Extract A as a class, before students focus on Extract B to complete Activity 3. **Deepen** In the Grammar Boost activity, encourage students not to use the same adverbial twice.
Second phase **20 minutes** • Ensure students have access to their responses to Activity 2 from the previous lesson. • Read through Activity 4, clarifying the difference between comparing information and comparing the writers' intentions. • Ask students to complete Activity 4. You may wish to take feedback on question 1 before asking students to complete question 2, in order to monitor progress and understanding more closely.	**Support** Encourage students to make use of the sample sentence structures provided. **Deepen** Encourage students to use their own sentence structures and vocabulary choices to complete the activity.
Plenary **10 minutes** • Ask volunteers to share excerpts from their paragraphs. Note effective use of key points, evidence, explanation and adverbials of comparison. • Ask students to recap the process of comparing information and intention. Point out that the assessment in the next lesson will also ask students to compare two information texts.	**Support** Recognise and validate any relevant contributions. **Deepen** Give partners three minutes to review and revise excerpts before sharing, checking for precision of expression.

Set workbook activities **5 minutes**

- Point students towards the activities on pp. 162–163 of the Workbook.
- Check understanding and answer any questions.
- These activities focus on comparing intention.

Year 8	**Unit 4: World of Sport**		
Section 11 Assessment: Lesson 20	**Skills focus: Reading: Information texts**		**Student Book pp. 174–175** **Workbook pp. 164–165**
Main Curriculum Objectives	**R8.1B** Identify and retrieve a range of key information in a text or in spoken language.	**R8.2A** Explore a writer's or speaker's intention and viewpoint.	**R8.2B** Express a critical response to a text through writing, discussion or presentation, by considering the text's features and their effects.
	R8.2C Select relevant, focused evidence to support ideas.	**R8.2D** Make developed comparisons of writers' ideas and perspectives between two texts.	**R8.4A** Explore the impact of some of a writer's or speaker's choices of grammatical features and sentence structure.
	R8.4B Explore the impact of some of the writer's or speaker's significant vocabulary choices.	**W8.3B** Divide text into paragraphs with accuracy and consistency.	
Secondary Curriculum Objectives			

Introduction **10 minutes**

- Ask students to read the two extracts.
- Explain to students that they will have 15 minutes to complete the reading section for Extract A, 15 minutes to complete the reading section for Extract B and a further 20 minutes to complete the writing section.

Assessment task **50 minutes**

- Ask students to complete Activity 1: Responding to Extract A. Any students finishing sooner can begin Activity 2: Reading Extract B.
- After 15 minutes, ask students to complete Activity 2: Reading Extract B. Any students finishing sooner can begin the writing task.
- After another 15 minutes, ask students to move on to complete Activity 3: the writing section of the assessment.
- You may wish to give students further guidance on how much they should write, and the amounts of time they should use for writing and checking their responses.

Workbook assessment task

- Point students towards the extract, question and sample student response on pp. 164–165 of the Workbook.
- Give students the opportunity to read the extract, question and sample response. Briefly discuss these with them and answer any questions.
- Students should identify the errors in the sample response before planning how they will improve it. They should then write an improved version, adding at least three paragraphs of text.
- Make clear your expectations of when this task will be completed. For example, it may be a homework, or students may be given time during an additional lesson.

Year 8	Unit 5: A Moment in Time		
Section 1 Writing autobiographically: Lesson 1	Skills focus: Writing to explain and describe		Student Book pp. 178–179 Workbook pp. 166–167
Main Curriculum Objectives	**R8.1B** Identify and retrieve a range of key information in a text or in spoken language.	**R8.1D** Compare, contrast and/or combine key points of information within a text or in spoken language with a given focus.	**R8.1E** Make inferences from specific evidence found in a text or in spoken language, including specific vocabulary choices.
Secondary Curriculum Objectives			

Lesson	
Introduction **10 minutes** • Ask volunteers from the class to recount their very earliest memories. • Ask students to consider why those memories have lasted. Look for responses that recognise these were memorable occasions, events or emotions experienced. • Note a summary of these observations for reference in the next lesson.	**Support** Prompt students with suggestions, for example a birthday, a family celebration. **Deepen** Ask students to identify the types of detail that appear in a significant proportion of their memories: for example sensory detail, dialogue, emotion.
First phase **15 minutes** • Read the extract. Take students' initial responses, noting the intentionally episodic nature of the extract. The subject matter of the extract is a sensitive topic so take the opportunity to discuss it sensitively as a class. • Ask students to complete Activity 1. Point out that some questions identify relevant paragraphs but all will call upon students' scanning skills. • Take feedback to check and develop understanding.	**Support** Complete Activity 1, questions 1 and 2 as a whole class or in supported groups, modelling the skills needed for the remainder of the activity. **Deepen** What other information can students infer from the extract about the writer and his childhood?
Second phase **20 minutes** • Compare the extract (and, to an extent, any text) to a jigsaw: disjointed parts of a bigger picture that begin to make sense when pieced together. • Reread the first paragraph of the extract and ask students to complete Activity 2.	**Support** Discuss and ask students to recap the first paragraph verbally, using their own words, before tackling Activity 2. **Deepen** What further information can students infer about the writer and/or his family?
Plenary **10 minutes** • Take feedback, noting the key ideas that students have included in their summaries. • Which piece of information and/or inferences are essential, and which could be omitted without reducing the efficacy of a summary?	**Support** Recognise and validate any relevant responses. **Deepen** Ask students to describe the writer waking up in hospital. On which clues in the extract did they base their ideas?

Set workbook activities **5 minutes**
- Point students towards the activities on pp. 166–167 of the Workbook.
- Check understanding and answer any questions.
- These activities focus on identifying key ideas and pulling ideas together.

Year 8	Unit 5: A Moment in Time		
Section 1 Writing autobiographically: Lesson 2	Skills focus: Writing to explain and describe		Student Book pp. 180–181 Workbook pp. 168–169
Main Curriculum Objectives	**R8.1C** Summarise a short text or speech effectively, selecting appropriate and relevant detail.	**R8.2B** Express a critical response to a text through writing, discussion or presentation, by considering the text's features and their effects.	**W8.1A** Gather and structure a range of relevant ideas before writing.
Secondary Curriculum Objectives			

Introduction — 10 minutes	
• Display two headings: *emotions, senses*. • Ask students to note ideas under both headings: so far today, what have they seen, heard, smelt, touched, or tasted? What emotions have they felt? • Take feedback, collating and displaying ideas for reference later in the lesson.	**Support** Suggest that students remember their day event by event, for example waking up, getting ready, coming into school. **Deepen** Encourage students to note something for all five senses and a variety of emotions.
First phase — 15 minutes • Recap the extract and reread the final two paragraphs. • Ask students to complete the Skills Boost activity. • Take feedback to check accuracy and completeness. • Ask students to complete Activity 3. Point out that questions 1 and 2b require an entirely personal, subjective response. • Take feedback, highlighting the variety of the class's responses.	**Support** In Activity 3, discuss questions 1 and 2 as a whole class or in supported groups. **Deepen** In the Skills Boost activity, ask students to summarise the 2nd and 4th paragraphs in one sentence each, as well as the final two paragraphs.
Second phase — 20 minutes • Recap students' responses to the opening activity, suggesting they refer to them for inspiration in their response to Activity 4. • Ask students to complete Activity 4.	**Support** Ask students to plan and write just one paragraph, including a range of facts, senses, emotions and dialogue. **Deepen** Challenge students to link their three memories to suggest a coherent narrative.
Plenary — 10 minutes • Ask students to work with a partner, reviewing and commenting on their responses to Activity 4. Have they included a range of sensory details, emotion and dialogue? Is it effective? • Ask volunteers to share one effective paragraph from their partner's response to Activity 4. What does the class find effective about it?	**Support** Recognise and validate any effective choices. **Deepen** Encourage students to identify any unnecessary details that do not make a significant contribution to the picture they are trying to create.

Set workbook activities — 5 minutes
• Point students towards the activities on pp. 168–169 of the Workbook. • Check understanding and answer any questions. • These activities focus on summarising and responding to ideas.

Year 8	Unit 5: A Moment in Time		
Section 2 Exploring structure and intention: Lesson 3	Skills focus: Writing to explain and describe		Student Book pp. 182–183 Workbook pp. 170–171
Main Curriculum Objectives	**R8.1E** Make inferences from specific evidence found in a text or in spoken language, including specific vocabulary choices.	**R8.2B** Express a critical response to a text through writing, discussion or presentation, by considering text's features and their effects.	**R8.3A** Explore the impact of some of the writer's key structural or organisational choices.
Secondary Curriculum Objectives			

Introduction 10 minutes • Ask students to imagine sailing out to sea in a boat, and to describe how this would make them feel. • Then ask them to imagine jumping into the water, and again to describe how they would feel. • Finally, ask them to imagine that they are swimming with sharks, and how this would make them feel. • Ask: How might an observer be able to infer your feelings from your actions or expressions?	**Support** Prompt students with feelings they could experience, such as joy, sea sickness, fear and excitement. **Deepen** Ask students to write three or four sentences describing their actions and expressions in each scenario.
First phase 15 minutes • Read the newspaper article and take students' initial responses. • Ask: Would you like to dive with sharks? Why is that? • Ask students to complete Activity 1. • Take feedback to check, share and develop understanding.	**Support** Work through the first two or three quotations with the class or in supported groups. **Deepen** Ask students to identify one or two further quotations that support their responses.
Second phase 20 minutes • Discuss the way that responses can change and develop as stories develop – sometimes very quickly. • Read through Activity 2, and ask students to draw the flowchart they will be completing, including one section for each of the five paragraphs. • Ask students to complete Activity 2.	**Support** Discuss students' responses to the first paragraph as a whole class or in supported groups, before asking students to complete the activity in pairs. **Deepen** Encourage students to use their own ideas and vocabulary choices rather than the ones suggested.
Plenary 10 minutes • Take feedback. Note the variety of students' responses and range of vocabulary used to express them. • Ask students to identify a story or a film that they have enjoyed, and to discuss with a partner their changing responses as they watched or read it. • Take feedback.	**Support** Recognise and validate any relevant responses. **Deepen** Discuss: Why and how has the writer created this developing response in the reader?

Set workbook activities 5 minutes
- Point students towards the activities on pp. 170–171 of the Workbook.
- Check understanding and answer any questions.
- These activities focus on inferring ideas.

Year 8	Unit 5: A Moment in Time		
Section 2 Exploring structure and intention: Lesson 4	Skills focus: Writing to explain and describe		Student Book pp. 184–185 Workbook pp. 172–173
Main Curriculum Objectives	**R8.2A** Explore a writer's or speaker's intention and viewpoint.	**W8.2B** Use appropriate linguistic conventions to achieve a wider range of purposes and address a wider range of audiences, e.g. to explain, to describe or to persuade, with confidence and understanding.	**W8.2C** Use the organisational conventions of a range of forms, for a range of purposes and audiences, with confidence and understanding, including spoken-language forms such as presentations.
Secondary Curriculum Objectives	**W8.1A** Gather and structure a range of relevant ideas before writing.		

Activity	Differentiation
Introduction **10 minutes** • Display all subject and object pronouns: 'I', 'you', 'he', 'she', 'it', 'we', 'they', 'me', 'him', 'her', 'us' and 'them'. • Ask a volunteer from the class to choose two pronouns at random. • Challenge the class to write one sentence using both of them. • Take feedback, assessing the sentences for clarity. • Ask: Can you identify to whom or to what each pronoun refers?	**Support** Provide students with a range of nouns to include in their sentences, such as 'students', 'teacher', 'lesson' and 'homework'. **Deepen** Challenge students to work with four, five or even six randomly selected pronouns in one sentence.
First phase **15 minutes** • Ask students to complete the Grammar Boost activity. • Take feedback to check accuracy and understanding. • Remind students of their responses to the newspaper article, as discussed in the previous lesson. • Ask students to complete Activity 3, pointing out that it focuses on identifying significant vocabulary choices. • Take feedback, comparing students' responses.	**Support** In the Grammar Boost activity, work with students to identify the pronouns in the given sentences. **Deepen** Challenge students to identify any more-positive feelings evoked by the writer's vocabulary choices in her description of the sharks.
Second phase **20 minutes** • Read through Activity 4, clarifying the process and expected outcome. • Ensure that students have access to their responses to Activity 2 from the previous lesson. • Ask students to complete Activity 4, question 1. • Take feedback to share and develop ideas. • Ask students to complete questions 2–4.	**Support** Suggest that students base their planned responses on the article, intending disgust, fear and then relief. **Deepen** Encourage students to gather a wider range of ideas and vocabulary than they will need.
Plenary **10 minutes** • Ask partners to exchange their work. Ask students to consider whether their partner's writing achieves the intended responses, and to identify particularly effective vocabulary choices. • Ask volunteers to share effective sentences from their partner's writing.	**Support** Recognise and validate any effective choices. **Deepen** Encourage partners to discuss, review and revise their vocabulary choices.

Set workbook activities **5 minutes**

- Point students towards the activities on pp. 172–173 of the Workbook.
- Check understanding and answer any questions.
- These activities focus on first, second and third person, and creating a response.

Year 8	Unit 5: A Moment in Time		
Section 3 Using narrative structures: Lesson 5		Skills focus: Writing to explain and describe	Student Book pp. 186–187 Workbook pp. 174–175
Main Curriculum Objectives	**R8.1B** Identify and retrieve a range of key information in a text or in spoken language.	**R8.3A** Explore the impact of some of the writer's key structural or organisational choices.	
Secondary Curriculum Objectives			

Introduction **10 minutes** • Ask students to note five important events, in either world history or their own history. • Discuss the term and concept of 'chronological order'. • Ask: Did any of you note your events in chronological order automatically? Why is that? • Work as a class to sort any students' events that were not already in chronological order.	**Support** Prompt students by suggesting categories of important events, such as school milestones or changes at home. **Deepen** Ask: Why is chronological order easier for us to follow and understand?
First phase **15 minutes** • Read the article and take students' initial responses. • Ask: Is the article structured chronologically? How can you tell? • Ask students to complete Activity 1. Point out that they can use their scanning skills to identify dates in the article, but that some events are not specifically dated. • Take feedback, checking accuracy and noting any differences in responses (for example, whether all students noted the drought of 1974 as the earliest event described).	**Support** Work as a class or in supported groups to find dates, scanning the article for numbers amongst the words. **Deepen** Ask students to respond to Activity 1, question 3 by writing a concise diary from the perspective of Zhifa, briefly describing the events of 1974.
Second phase **20 minutes** • Read through Activity 2. • Clarify the definitions of the four elements of narrative structure. • Ask students to complete Activity 2. • Before taking feedback, ask partners to evaluate each other's responses. Prompt them to check that their partner's four responses effectively summarise the story of Zhifa's discovery.	**Support** Complete Activity 2, questions 1 and 2 as a class or in supported groups, before asking students to complete the activity independently. **Deepen** Challenge students to shorten their responses, giving the key information in as few words as possible.
Plenary **10 minutes** • Take feedback on Activity 2. Ask volunteers to share their responses to each of the four questions, building up a group summary of the story. • Explicitly identify each element of the story, consolidating understanding of the terminology 'exposition', 'conflict', 'climax' and 'resolution'.	**Support** Recognise and validate any relevant responses. **Deepen** Ask: Is the story fully and satisfyingly resolved in the article? How might it be more satisfyingly resolved?

Set workbook activities **5 minutes** • Point students towards the activities on pp. 174–175 of the Workbook. • Check understanding and answer any questions. • These activities focus on key information and narrative structure.

<table>
<tr><td>Year 8</td><td colspan="3">Unit 5: A Moment in Time</td></tr>
<tr><td colspan="2">Section 3 Using narrative structures: Lesson 6</td><td>Skills focus: Writing to explain and describe</td><td>Student Book pp. 188–189
Workbook pp. 176–177</td></tr>
<tr><td rowspan="2">Main Curriculum Objectives</td><td>R8.2A Explore a writer's or speaker's intention and viewpoint.</td><td>R8.3A Explore the impact of some of the writer's key structural or organisational choices.</td><td>W8.1A Gather and structure a range of relevant ideas before writing.</td></tr>
<tr><td colspan="3">W8.2C Use the organisational conventions of a range of forms, for a range of purposes and audiences, with confidence and understanding, including spoken-language forms such as presentations.</td></tr>
<tr><td>Secondary Curriculum Objectives</td><td colspan="3"></td></tr>
</table>

<table>
<tr><td rowspan="2">Introduction 10 minutes
• Allow two or three minutes for students to remind themselves of the article.
• Test students on key points of information in the article using 'who', 'what', 'where', 'when' and 'why' questions. For example: 'Who was digging a hole?' 'Why were they digging the hole?' 'What did they find in the hole?' 'How did the different characters respond to the find?' 'When did they decide to change what they were doing?'
• Discuss the answers, or supply them for peer reviews.</td><td>Support
Allow students to refer to the article during the test.</td></tr>
<tr><td>Deepen
Allow just one minute for students to remind themselves of the article before they begin the test.</td></tr>
<tr><td rowspan="2">First phase 15 minutes
• Read through Activity 3, checking students' understanding of the suggested vocabulary (in particular 'engage' and 'withhold').
• Briefly recap the concept of chronological structure.
• Ask students to complete Activity 3.
• Take feedback to share and develop understanding.
• Ask students to complete the Skills Boost activity.
• Take feedback to check the accuracy of responses to question 1, and to compare students' ideas about effective openings.</td><td>Support
In Activity 3, discuss questions 1c and 2c as a whole class or in supported groups, with close reference to the suggested vocabulary.</td></tr>
<tr><td>Deepen
In question 2 of the Skills Boost activity, challenge students to compose a gripping opening sentence for the story.</td></tr>
<tr><td rowspan="2">Second phase 20 minutes
• Read through Activity 4, ensuring understanding of the task: planning (rather than completing) an article.
• Ask volunteers to refresh the class's understanding of the key terms 'exposition', 'conflict', 'climax' and 'resolution'.
• Ask students to complete questions 1 and 2. Take feedback to share and develop ideas.
• Ask students to complete question 3.</td><td>Support
Take feedback after each step in the writing process. In Activity 4, question 3c, refer students to the vocabulary suggested in Activity 3.</td></tr>
<tr><td>Deepen
Challenge students to include an element of rising tension in their planning, and to consider how they will suggest it.</td></tr>
<tr><td rowspan="2">Plenary 10 minutes
• Take feedback on Activity 4, question 3, asking volunteers to share their opening sentences.
• Ask the class to discuss how effective each opening sentence would be.</td><td>Support
Recognise and validate any effective elements in students' planning.</td></tr>
<tr><td>Deepen
Ask partners to discuss the elements of tension in their planning, and to review their effectiveness.</td></tr>
</table>

Set workbook activities **5 minutes**

- Point students towards the activities on pp. 176–177 of the Workbook.
- Check understanding and answer any questions.
- These activities focus on writer's intention and chronological or non-chronological structure.

Year 8	Unit 5: A Moment in Time		
Section 4 Choosing precise vocabulary: Lesson 7	Skills focus: Writing to explain and describe		Student Book pp. 190–191 Workbook pp. 178–179
Main Curriculum Objectives	**R8.2A** Explore a writer's or speaker's intention and viewpoint.	**R8.2B** Express a critical response to a text through writing, discussion or presentation, by considering the text's features and their effects.	**R8.4B** Explore the impact of some of the writer's or speaker's significant vocabulary choices.
Secondary Curriculum Objectives			

Lesson	Support / Deepen
Introduction **10 minutes** • Ask volunteers from the class to suggest experiences they have truly enjoyed, or activities they frequently enjoy. • Ask students to justify their choices and persuade their classmates to try their named experiences. • Note the techniques that students use: the selection of ideas and information to explain their enjoyment and the vocabulary used to describe it.	**Support** Look for a class consensus on an enjoyable experience or activity. Work as a class to explain and describe it, collating ideas for display. **Deepen** Give students an opportunity to develop their ideas and vocabulary choices to make their descriptions still more vivid and persuasive.
First phase **15 minutes** • Read the newspaper article and take students' initial responses. Ask: Do you think you would enjoy scuba diving? Why is that? • Check students' awareness of the meaning of, and difference between, explanation and description. • Ask students to complete Activity 1. • Take feedback to check and develop understanding.	**Support** Work with students to identify the relevant parts of the article before they answer each question. **Deepen** Encourage students to incorporate as much relevant detail as possible in their responses to Activity 1, question 1.
Second phase **20 minutes** • Read through Activity 2, emphasising that students should aim to make careful comments on the impact of the writer's vocabulary choices. • Ask students to complete Activity 2. • Point out that question 4 requires a personal response based on the effectiveness of the writer's choices.	**Support** Complete Activity 2, question 1 as a whole class or in supported groups, discussing the impact of relevant vocabulary. **Deepen** Encourage students to consider all significant vocabulary choices in each part of the article.
Plenary **10 minutes** • Take feedback on Activity 2, focusing on students' comments on significant vocabulary choices. • Note the range and variety of responses, exploring whether students agree on the most significant vocabulary choices, and on the impressions those choices create. • Ask: Do you think this is an effective article? Why is that?	**Support** Recognise and validate any identifications of relevant vocabulary choices and/or effective comments on them. **Deepen** Encourage students to make use of their critical vocabulary, such as the terms 'imply', 'intention' and emphasises'.

Set workbook activities **5 minutes**
- Point students towards the activities on pp. 178–179 of the Workbook.
- Check understanding and answer any questions.
- These activities focus on responding to vocabulary choice.

Year 8	Unit 5: A Moment in Time		
Section 4 Choosing precise vocabulary: Lesson 8	Skills focus: Writing to explain and describe		Student Book pp. 192–193 Workbook pp. 180–181
Main Curriculum Objectives	**W8.1A** Gather and structure a range of relevant ideas before writing.	**W8.2C** Use the organisational conventions of a range of forms, for a range of purposes and audiences, with confidence and understanding, including spoken-language forms such as presentations.	**W8.3G** Select vocabulary in text and spoken language with growing precision.
Secondary Curriculum Objectives			

Introduction 10 minutes	**Support**
• Provide students with thesauruses or display an online thesaurus. • Model how to use a thesaurus by looking up a familiar word such as 'small', and discuss its synonyms, including the word 'short'. Ensure students' understanding of the term 'synonym'. • Display the sentence *'I live in a small house.'* • Ask: Would 'short' be an appropriate synonym for 'small' in this sentence? Why is that? • Emphasise the importance of using a thesaurus only to suggest, not determine, vocabulary choices.	Demonstrate replacing 'small' in the example sentence with each synonym and discuss the effect of each one. **Deepen** Repeat the activity using the sentence 'I live in a big house', considering synonyms for 'big'. Ask students to write sentences to explore how appropriate the different synonyms are.
First phase 15 minutes	**Support**
• Read through the Skills Boost activity. • Ask students to complete the Skills Boost activity, warning against the use of unfamiliar vocabulary. • Take feedback to check understanding and accuracy. • Read through Activity 3. Ask students to follow the steps given in the Skills Boost activity to complete it. • Take feedback, discussing the reasons for students' choices.	Complete the Skills Boost activity as a whole class or in supported groups, ensuring understanding before students tackle Activity 3. **Deepen** Challenge students to consider revising other vocabulary in the given paragraphs.
Second phase 20 minutes	**Support**
• Read through Activity 4. • Ask students to complete question 1. • Take feedback to share and develop ideas. • Ask students to complete questions 2–4, and to begin question 5. Point out that they should focus on planning their text, and on writing its first paragraph.	Take feedback after each step in the writing process to ensure progress and understanding. **Deepen** Encourage students to consider organising their ideas in the most effective way in Activity 4, question 3, as well as in question 4.
Plenary 10 minutes	**Support**
• Ask students to complete Activity 4, question 6 by underlining three to five words in their writing that they feel could be improved. • Ask students to note two or three synonyms that could replace each word they have underlined, and then to tick the one option they feel is most effective. • Take feedback, asking volunteers to share sample sentences and to justify their vocabulary choices.	Recognise and validate any effective vocabulary choices. **Deepen** Challenge students to review every word in their writing and identify as many alternatives as possible.

Set workbook activities 5 minutes

- Point students towards the activities on pp. 180–181 of the Workbook.
- Check understanding and answer any questions.
- These activities focus on using a thesaurus and choosing vocabulary.

<table>
<tr><td>Year 8</td><td colspan="3">Unit 5: A Moment in Time</td></tr>
<tr><td colspan="2">Section 5 Assessment: Lesson 9</td><td>Skills focus: Writing to explain and describe</td><td>Student Book pp. 194–195
Workbook pp. 182–183</td></tr>
<tr><td rowspan="2">Main Curriculum Objectives</td><td>R8.2A Explore a writer's or speaker's intention and viewpoint.</td><td>R8.2B Express a critical response to a text through writing, discussion or presentation, by considering the text's features and their effects.</td><td>W8.1A Gather and structure a range of relevant ideas before writing.</td></tr>
<tr><td>R8.4B Explore the impact of some of the writer's or speaker's significant vocabulary choices.</td><td>W8.2C Use the organisational conventions of a range of forms, for a range of purposes and audiences, with confidence and understanding, including spoken-language forms such as presentations.</td><td>W8.3G Select vocabulary in text and spoken language with growing precision.</td></tr>
<tr><td>Secondary Curriculum Objectives</td><td colspan="3"></td></tr>
</table>

Introduction **10 minutes**

- Ask students to read the newspaper article, and check their understanding of any unfamiliar vocabulary.
- Check students' understanding of the context of the article: it is a newspaper article recounting the writer's experience of a childhood visit to a safari park.
- Explain to students that they will have 25 minutes to complete the reading section of the assessment, and a further 25 minutes to complete the writing section.

Assessment task **50 minutes**

- Ask students to complete the reading section of the assessment. Any students finishing sooner can begin the writing task.
- After 25 minutes, ask students to move on to complete the writing section of the assessment.
- Point out that they should plan their writing, and that you will assess their plans as well as their finished pieces of writing.
- You may wish to give students further guidance on how much they should write, and the amounts of time they should use for planning, writing and checking their responses.

Workbook assessment task

- Point students towards the extract and activities on pp. 182–183 of the Workbook.
- Give students the opportunity to read the extract. Briefly discuss it with them and answer any questions.
- Students should read the extract again carefully before answering the questions that follow it.
- Make clear your expectations of when this task will be completed. For example, it may be a homework, or students may be given time during an additional lesson.

Year 8	Unit 5: A Moment in Time		
Section 6 Expressing feelings: Lesson 10		Skills focus: Writing to explain and describe	Student Book pp. 196–197 Workbook pp. 184–185
Main Curriculum Objectives	**R8.1E** Make inferences from specific evidence found in a text or in spoken language, including specific vocabulary choices.	**R8.2A** Explore a writer's or speaker's intention and viewpoint.	**R8.2B** Express a critical response to a text through writing, discussion or presentation, by considering the text's features and their effects.
Secondary Curriculum Objectives			

Introduction 10 minutes • Ask students to imagine a scene: a stadium in which the crowd wait for runners in a marathon to arrive and complete the race. • Ask students to note verbs, nouns, adjectives and adverbs they might use to describe the runners and the crowd in their imagined scene. • Take feedback, recognising the range and effectiveness of students' choices.	**Support** Prompt students to consider specifically what they might see, hear, and feel if they were in the crowd. **Deepen** Suggest that students consider all five senses as well as emotions, and encourage them to note as wide a variety of vocabulary as possible.
First phase 15 minutes • Read the extract and take students' initial responses both to the situation described and to Pietri. • Ask a volunteer to recap the difference between stated and implied information. • Ask students to complete Activity 1. • Take feedback to check understanding.	**Support** Complete Activity 1, question 1 as a whole class or in supported groups, to check and consolidate inference skills. **Deepen** Encourage students to note as many different responses to each question as possible.
Second phase 20 minutes • Read through Activity 2 and summarise its focus: exploring how the reader is encouraged to respond to different figures in the extract. • Ask: Which person described in the extract causes the strongest response? • Discuss the reasons for students' responses. • Ask students to complete Activity 2.	**Support** Complete Activity 2, question 1 as a whole class or in supported groups, to ensure understanding of the difference between stated and implied information. **Deepen** Encourage students to support their ideas with quotations.
Plenary 10 minutes • Take feedback on Activity 2, focusing on how the writer has manipulated the reader's response to each person mentioned. • Ask: How could the writer have created even more sympathy for Pietri, for example in his presentation of Johnny Hayes?	**Support** Recognise and validate any relevant responses. **Deepen** Challenge students to describe Hayes and Pietri as though they were characters in a story.

Set workbook activities
- Point students towards the activities on pp. 184–185 of the Workbook.
- Check understanding and answer any questions.
- These activities focus on inferring ideas and responding to people.

Year 8	Unit 5: A Moment in Time		
Section 6 Expressing feelings: Lesson 11	Skills focus: Writing to explain and describe		Student Book pp. 198–199 Workbook pp. 186–187
Main Curriculum Objectives	**W8.1A** Gather and structure a range of relevant ideas before writing.	**W8.2C** Use the organisational conventions of a range of forms, for a range of purposes and audiences, with confidence and understanding, including spoken-language forms such as presentations.	**W8.3G** Select vocabulary in text and spoken language with growing precision.
Secondary Curriculum Objectives	**W8.3I** Use upper-case letters, end punctuation, commas, speech marks and apostrophes correctly, with accuracy and consistency.		

Introduction **10 minutes** • Introduce or recap the concept of symptoms by asking students to complete the following sentences with as many details as possible. *You know you have a cold when …* *You know you are feeling miserable when …* *You know you are happy when …* • Discuss suggestions, reinforcing the concept by referring to the 'symptoms' of misery and happiness.	**Support** Complete the first example as a whole class before asking students to complete the task in pairs. **Deepen** Challenge students to identify at least five symptoms for each example.
First phase **15 minutes** • Read through Activity 3, question 1 and discuss the question as a whole class. Look for recognition that describing a feeling requires readers to use their skills of inference. • Ask students to complete Activity 3. • Take feedback, gathering as wide a range of responses as possible. • Read the introduction to the Skills Boost activity, and ensure understanding of the rules of speech punctuation. • Ask students to complete the Skills Boost activity. • Take feedback to check understanding and accuracy.	**Support** In Activity 3, use examples from the extract to model responses to question 2. **Deepen** In Activity 3, challenge students to identify the symptoms of one more feeling, and then to share these with the class. Ask the class to identify the feeling from its symptoms.
Second phase **20 minutes** • Read the introduction to Activity 4. Give students two minutes to note down two or three possible ideas. Take feedback to share and develop thinking. • Ask students to complete question 1. • Look at the opening paragraph of the extract. Note how the writer sets the scene in the description of the stadium and crowd. • Ask students to complete questions 2 and 3.	**Support** Take feedback after each step in the process to monitor progress and understanding. **Deepen** Encourage students to make vivid, descriptive vocabulary choices to add to their accounts.
Plenary **10 minutes** • Take feedback from a variety of volunteers in the class, focusing on each section of their texts in turn: expositions, conflicts, climaxes and then resolutions. • Ask the class to evaluate the effectiveness of the techniques used in each case.	**Support** Recognise and validate any effective choices. **Deepen** Encourage students to make constructive suggestions for improvements to each other's work.

Set workbook activities **5 minutes**

- Point students towards the activities on pp. 186–187 of the Workbook.
- Check understanding and answer any questions.
- These activities focus on direct and reported speech, and planning an account.

Year 8	Unit 5: A Moment in Time		
Section 7 Structuring paragraphs: Lesson 12	Skills focus: Writing to explain and describe		Student Book pp. 200–201 Workbook pp. 188–189
Main Curriculum Objectives	**R8.2A** Explore a writer's or speaker's intention and viewpoint.	**R8.2B** Express a critical response to a text through writing, discussion or presentation, by considering the text's features and their effects.	**R8.3A** Explore the impact of some of the writer's key structural or organisational choices.
Secondary Curriculum Objectives			

Lesson	Support / Deepen
Introduction — 10 minutes • Ask students to imagine that you are planning a text about the school. • Explain that you have identified three key topics to include: its location, its aims and how successful it is. Display these three key topics for reference. • Ask students to suggest two or three pieces of information that could be included in the text for each of the topics. • After suggestions have been collated, ask students to identify what they consider the most important information for each topic.	**Support** Provide prompts for each topic, such as details about the school's surrounding countryside or town, curriculum, extra-curricular activities and exam results. **Deepen** Ask students to suggest their own ideas for three key topics.
First phase — 15 minutes • Read the extract and take students' initial responses. • Ask students to summarise what they have learned about the Tunguska event in just one or two sentences. • Ask students to complete Activity 1. • Take feedback, gathering as wide a range of responses as possible.	**Support** Focus on paragraph 1 as a whole class or in supported groups, and then ask students to complete Activity 1 with respect to paragraphs 2 and 3 independently. **Deepen** Ask students to identify all the details and vocabulary choices that show dramatic impact in each paragraph.
Second phase — 20 minutes • Ask students to complete Activity 2, questions 1a and 1b. • Take feedback, checking students' understanding and maths skills. • Ask students to complete Activity 2, questions 1c and 2.	**Support** Complete Activity 2, questions 1a and 1b verbally as a class, before asking students to complete the rest of the activity independently. **Deepen** Ask: Is there only one possible answer to Activity 2, question 1c?
Plenary — 10 minutes • Take feedback on Activity 2. • Ask students to justify their responses to question 2, clearly identifying the key information and supporting detail in each paragraph they have identified.	**Support** Look at each paragraph's first sentence in turn. Ask: Is this key information? Do all of the other sentences in this paragraph add supporting detail to it? **Deepen** Ask: Can you identify elements of different structures in the extract? Does it have any features of narrative structure?

Set workbook activities — 5 minutes

- Point students towards the activities on pp. 188–189 of the Workbook.
- Check understanding and answer any questions.
- These activities focus on exploring structure.

Year 8	Unit 5: A Moment in Time		
Section 7 Structuring paragraphs: Lesson 13	Skills focus: Writing to explain and describe		Student Book pp. 202–203 Workbook pp. 190–191
Main Curriculum Objectives	**W8.2C** Use the organisational conventions of a range of forms, for a range of purposes and audiences, with confidence and understanding, including spoken-language forms such as presentations.	**W8.3B** Divide text into paragraphs with accuracy and consistency.	
Secondary Curriculum Objectives			

Introduction **10 minutes** • Display the following sentences, explaining that each is the first sentence of a paragraph from a story. o *Three weeks later, there was a knock at the door.* o *Meanwhile, in London, a phone was ringing.* o *"I can't hear you!" she shouted.* o *Dev was afraid of just two things: spiders and vegetables.* • Ask students to note possible reasons why the writer decided to start a new paragraph when they wrote these sentences.	**Support** Reveal that a writer may choose to start a new paragraph when there is a change of topic, time, setting or speaker, and then ask students to pair each example sentence with a probable reason. **Deepen** Establish the four reasons for starting a new paragraph and challenge students to write their own four example sentences, one for each reason.
First phase **15 minutes** • Ask students to complete question 1 of the Skills Boost activity. • Take feedback, comparing students' answers and their justifications. • Ask students to complete question 2. • Take feedback to check understanding and accuracy. • Read through Activity 3, checking students' understanding of the task. • Ask students to complete Activity 3. • Take feedback, recognising as wide a variety of valid responses as possible.	**Support** In the Skills Boost activity, advise students that the first three sentences may be grouped into one introductory paragraph. Reveal that they should identify three further paragraphs. **Deepen** In Activity 3, challenge students to organise all the given facts into paragraphs, noting which would provide the key information in each.
Second phase **20 minutes** • Ask students to complete Activity 4, question 1. • Take feedback to share and develop ideas. • Ask students to complete questions 2–4. • Take feedback on students' planning. Ask the class to evaluate the effectiveness of each other's ideas. • Ask students to complete question 5.	**Support** Take feedback after each step in the planning and writing process to monitor progress and understanding. **Deepen** Remind students to consider the effectiveness of their vocabulary choices as they write.
Plenary **10 minutes** • Ask partners to check the structure of each other's paragraphs. • Suggest that they ask: Is all the information on the same topic? Does the first sentence give key information? Do the other sentences add supporting detail/information? • Ask volunteers to share their writing with the class.	**Support** Recognise and validate any effective elements of students' writing. **Deepen** Ask students to write the next paragraphs of their articles.

Set workbook activities **5 minutes**
- Point students towards the activities on pp. 190–191 of the Workbook.
- Check understanding and answer any questions.
- These activities focus on paragraph breaks and paragraph planning.

Year 8	Unit 5: A Moment in Time		
Section 8 Experimenting with sentences: Lesson 14	Skills focus: Writing to explain and describe		Student Book pp. 204–205 Workbook pp. 192–193
Main Curriculum Objectives	**R8.1B** Identify and retrieve a range of key information in a text or in spoken language.	**R8.2A** Explore a writer's or speaker's intention and viewpoint.	**R8.4A** Explore the impact of some of a writer's or speaker's choices of grammatical features and sentence structure.
Secondary Curriculum Objectives	**R8.2B** Express a critical response to a text through writing, discussion or presentation, by considering the text's features and their effects.		

Introduction — 10 minutes	Support
• Verbally introduce key vocabulary from the article extract you are going to read: 'science', 'scientist', 'laboratory', 'lightbulb', 'experiment', 'discovery' and 'invention'. • Ask a volunteer from the class to define the meaning of each word. • Ask students to comment on the spellings of 'science', 'scientist' and 'lightbulb', drawing out awareness of their 'silent' letters. • Ask students to note how to create plurals of the words 'laboratory' and 'discovery', drawing out understanding of the change from 'y' to 'ie' in each.	**Support** Prompt students by asking them to look specifically for 'silent' letters and then for changes in spelling at the ends of the words. **Deepen** Challenge students to list other words featuring the same 'silent' letters.
First phase — 15 minutes • Read the article extract. • Take students' initial responses. Ask: Are you surprised by any of the information included, or the viewpoint expressed? • Ask students to complete Activity 1, question 1a. • Take feedback to check and develop understanding. • Ask students to complete questions 1b and 2. • Take feedback on question 2.	**Support** Complete Activity 1, question 1a verbally as a whole class to ensure literal comprehension, before asking students to complete the rest of the activity independently. **Deepen** Encourage students to identify a range of responses to Activity 1, question 1b, including their own ideas.
Second phase — 20 minutes • Read the introduction to Activity 2 aloud. Use tone of voice to highlight the emphasis of the short sentences in the original version, and the length of the single sentence in the rewritten version. • Ask students to complete Activity 2, question 1. • Take feedback to check understanding. • Ask students to complete questions 2 and 3.	**Support** Prompt students to consider differences and similarities in both the information given and in the structuring of the sentences. **Deepen** Challenge students to experiment with producing yet another version, using a variety of sentence structures.
Plenary — 10 minutes • Take feedback. Ask: How is the sound, rhythm, clarity and impact of the sentences altered in the second version of the passage? • Check understanding that the writer has used short sentences to emphasise his key focus: the frustration and determination of inventors. • Discuss responses to Activity 2, question 3.	**Support** Recognise and validate any relevant responses. **Deepen** Encourage students to be as precise and detailed as possible in justifying their responses.

Set workbook activities

- Point students towards the activities on pp. 192–193 of the Workbook.
- Check understanding and answer any questions.
- These activities focus on identifying information and sentence structure.

Year 8	Unit 5: A Moment in Time		
Section 8 Experimenting with sentences: Lesson 15	Skills focus: Writing to explain and describe		Student Book pp. 206–207 Workbook pp. 194–195
Main Curriculum Objectives	**W8.1A** Gather and structure a range of relevant ideas before writing.	**W8.3C** Use a balance of single-clause sentences, coordinate and subordinate clauses with confidence.	**W8.3E** Make deliberate choices of sentence length to achieve clarity.
Secondary Curriculum Objectives	**W8.2C** Use the organisational conventions of a range of forms, for a range of purposes and audiences, with confidence and understanding, including spoken-language forms such as presentations.		

Introduction 10 minutes • Display the following three sentences. *John Logie Baird invented the television. He invented it in the 1920s. Although broadcasters began broadcasting soon afterwards, television did not become popular until the 1950s.* • Ask students to identify the 'odd one out'. • Look for responses that show awareness of sentence length and of clauses.	**Support** Prompt students to focus on the structure of the three sentences rather than their content. **Deepen** Challenge students to combine or link these sentences in as many ways as they can.
First phase 15 minutes • Read through the introduction to the Grammar Boost activity. Check students' understanding of clauses. • Ask students to complete the Grammar Boost activity. • Take feedback to check clarity and understanding. • Note that clauses beginning with these subordinating conjunctions form adverbial clauses. • Read through the introduction to Activity 3. • Model linking all the sentences in the given section of the article extract, to create one long sentence. Compare its clarity with that of the original version. • Ask students to complete Activity 3. • Take feedback, focusing on clarity of expression.	**Support** In the Grammar Boost activity, allow students to omit question 1d. In Activity 3, question 2, suggest that students write five sentences, combining only two of the points into a multi-clause sentence. **Deepen** In the Grammar Boost activity, challenge students to join all the sentences in questions 1a–1d to form a very long, multi-clause sentence. In Activity 3, challenge students to review and revise their sentence structures for added impact.
Second phase 20 minutes • Read through the introduction and question 1 of Activity 4. Check students' understanding of the task, and of first-person narration. • Ask students to complete question 1. • Take feedback to share and develop thinking. • Ask students to complete questions 2 and 3.	**Support** In Activity 4, question 1, encourage students to make full use of the given suggestions. **Deepen** In Activity 4, question 1, encourage students to use mainly their own ideas.
Plenary 10 minutes • Ask partners to complete Activity 4, question 4 verbally, and to review the clarity of their responses. • Ask volunteers to share one or two particularly effective and/or clearly expressed sentences with the whole class. • Ask students to complete question 5.	**Support** Recognise and validate any effective writing, emphasising variety and clarity. **Deepen** Encourage partners to analyse whether and how they have lost any clarity.

Set workbook activities 5 minutes
- Point students towards the activities on pp. 194–195 of the Workbook.
- Check understanding and answer any questions.
- These activities focus on restructuring sentences and structuring sentences for clarity.

Year 8	**Unit 5: A Moment in Time**		
Section 9 Experimenting with openings: Lesson 16	**Skills focus: Writing to explain and describe**		**Student Book pp. 208–209 Workbook pp. 196–197**
Main Curriculum Objectives	**R8.2A** Explore a writer's or speaker's intention and viewpoint.	**R8.2B** Express a critical response to a text through writing, discussion or presentation, by considering the text's features and their effects.	**R8.3A** Explore the impact of some of the writer's key structural or organisational choices.
Secondary Curriculum Objectives			

Introduction **10 minutes** • Discuss the sport of skeleton with the class, referring to the image on page 210 in the Student Book. If possible, watch online footage of the sport. • Ask students to note down vocabulary they might use to describe this experience. • Take feedback to share and develop ideas, noting students' choices for reference in the next lesson.	**Support** Suggest that students focus on key areas to describe, such as the emotional and physical feelings of the athlete, and the sport's setting. **Deepen** Challenge students to note vocabulary related to all five of the senses: sight, sound, touch, smell and taste.
First phase **15 minutes** • Read the article extract. • Take students' initial responses. Ask: Does the article extract capture and convey the experience you imagined? • Ask students to complete Activity 1. • Take feedback on Activity 1, focusing on the intended impact created by the details and vocabulary the writer has chosen.	**Support** Complete Activity 1, question 1 as a whole class or in supported groups to model an approach. **Deepen** Encourage students to find as many relevant details as possible and to comment on each one fully.
Second phase **20 minutes** • Recap the terms 'chronological' and 'non-chronological'. • Discuss the concept of a text that begins non-chronologically, to engage the reader, before resuming a chronological structure. • Ask students to complete Activity 2.	**Support** Begin Activity 2 by discussing as a whole class which of the key topics, if any, would *not* make an effective opening. **Deepen** Ask students to consider and note the likely impact(s) of each topic as a possible opening.
Plenary **10 minutes** • Take feedback on Activity 2. Explore whether or not students are able to reach a class consensus about what topic would make the most gripping opening. • Ask: What advice would you give the writer of the extract about his article? Would you suggest a different opening, and so a non-chronological structure?	**Support** Recognise and validate any relevant responses. **Deepen** Referring to Activity 2, question 2, challenge students to suggest ways in which the writer's fifth attempt could be the focus of an effective opening.

Set workbook activities **5 minutes**
- Point students towards the activities on pp. 196–197 of the Workbook.
- Check understanding and answer any questions.
- These activities focus on exploring openings.

Year 8	Unit 5: A Moment in Time		
Section 9 Experimenting with openings: Lesson 17	Skills focus: Writing to explain and describe		Student Book pp. 210–211 Workbook pp. 198–199
Main Curriculum Objectives	**W8.1A** Gather and structure a range of relevant ideas before writing.	**W8.2C** Use the organisational conventions of a range of forms, for a range of purposes and audiences, with confidence and understanding, including spoken-language forms such as presentations.	**W8.2D** Link paragraphs in text and spoken language, using adverbials to signal the development of ideas.
Secondary Curriculum Objectives			

Introduction **10 minutes** • Ask students to explain how to complete a familiar task, such as finding their seat in the classroom or making a simple snack. • Each time a student uses an adverbial of time, note and display it. • Ask: What do the displayed words and/or phrases have in common?	**Support** Display a selection of adverbials of time to support students' explanations. **Deepen** Ask students to list other adverbials of time that perform similar roles to those displayed.
First phase **15 minutes** • Read through the Grammar Boost activity and clarify the purpose of adverbials of time. • Ask students to complete the Grammar Boost activity. • Take feedback to check understanding and accuracy. • Recap your exploration of effective openings in the previous lesson, and then read through Activity 3. • Ask students to complete Activity 3. • Take feedback. Discuss the impact of various suggestions on the reader.	**Support** In Activity 3, discuss as a whole class which of the key topics would *not* make an effective opening. **Deepen** In question 2 of the Grammar Boost activity, ask students to explain how the use of the noun 'writer' and pronoun 'he' give clues to the correct sequence.
Second phase **20 minutes** • Read through Activity 4 to clarify the task. • Ask students to complete question 1. • Take feedback to share and develop ideas. • Ask students to complete questions 2–4.	**Support** Take feedback after each step in the planning process to ensure understanding and progress. **Deepen** If time allows, ask students to write a second paragraph using a different topic.
Plenary **10 minutes** • Ask volunteers from the class to share their openings with their classmates. • Ask the class to evaluate how effective each opening is. Ask: Does this opening make you want to read the remainder of the article? • Discuss and formulate supportive and constructive guidelines for creating engaging openings.	**Support** Recognise and validate any effective elements in students' openings. **Deepen** Encourage students to review and revise their opening sentences to make them as engaging as possible.

Set workbook activities **5 minutes**
- Point students towards the activities on pp. 198–199 of the Workbook.
- Check understanding and answer any questions.
- These activities focus on adverbials of time and selecting an opening.

Year 8	Unit 5: A Moment in Time		
Section 10 Experimenting with endings: Lesson 18	Skills focus: Writing to explain and describe		Student Book pp. 212–213 Workbook pp. 200–201
Main Curriculum Objectives	**R8.2A** Explore a writer's or speaker's intention and viewpoint.	**R8.2B** Express a critical response to a text through writing, discussion or presentation, by considering the text's features and their effects.	**R8.3A** Explore the impact of some of the writer's key structural or organisational choices.
Secondary Curriculum Objectives			

Introduction 10 minutes	
• Ask students to suggest and discuss stories that have great endings, and one or two examples of endings they found disappointing. • Ask: Can you identify what makes an effective ending? What should be avoided if a writer or film-maker wants to create a satisfying ending?	**Support** Refer to recent stories read in class, or popular films or television dramas, to prompt ideas. **Deepen** Ask students to devise a list of three 'Dos' and three 'Don'ts' for creating a satisfying ending.
First phase 15 minutes	
• Read the newspaper article. • Take students' initial responses. Ask: Does the article create a vivid impression of the writer's experience? • Ask students to complete Activity 1. • Take feedback on Activity 1, focusing on the details and vocabulary identified as contributing to the impressions created.	**Support** For Activity 1, questions 1, 2b and 4b, find one detail or vocabulary choice as a whole class before asking students to find another independently. **Deepen** Encourage students to find as many relevant details as possible, and to comment on each one.
Second phase 20 minutes	
• Read through Activity 2. Clarify the premise of the activity: selecting the best point at which to bring the article to a close in a satisfying way. • Draw an analogy between reading and eating: you do not want to end a meal or text feeling you have been given too little or too much. • Ask students to complete Activity 2.	**Support** Take feedback after Activity 2, question 1 to check and develop understanding. **Deepen** Ask students to imagine other ways in which the article could have ended.
Plenary 10 minutes	
• Take feedback on Activity 2. • Explore whether or not students are able to reach a class consensus about what topic would make the most satisfying ending. • Ask: Imagine that the article had ended with the writer dreaming about the mountains. Would it have been necessary to include all the topics given before this in question 2? Why is that? • Consider whether the discussed endings tally with the ideas the class considered during the introduction to the lesson.	**Support** Recognise and validate any justified responses. **Deepen** Ask students to rate each suggested ending from 'not at all satisfying' to 'extremely satisfying' and to justify their ratings.

Set workbook activities 5 minutes

- Point students towards the activities on pp. 200–201 of the Workbook.
- Check understanding and answer any questions.
- These activities focus on exploring endings.

Year 8	Unit 5: A Moment in Time		
Section 10 Experimenting with endings: Lesson 19	Skills focus: Writing to explain and describe		Student Book pp. 214–215 Workbook pp. 202–203
Main Curriculum Objectives	**W8.1A** Gather and structure a range of relevant ideas before writing.	**W8.1B** Correct a range of errors in spelling, punctuation and grammar independently after writing, beginning to develop strategies for proofreading.	**W8.2C** Use the organisational conventions of a range of forms, for a range of purposes and audiences, with confidence and understanding, including spoken-language forms such as presentations.
Secondary Curriculum Objectives			

Introduction 10 minutes	**Support**
• Explain the meaning of the term 'digraph': a pair of letters that, combined, create a single sound. • Ask students to note down at least one example of a word that includes each of the following letters and digraphs. • hard 'c' • soft 'c' • 'k' • 'ck' • 'ph' • Take feedback, asking students to spell each word aloud to check accuracy.	Provide an example for each letter and digraph. For example: *The word 'car' includes a hard 'c'.* *The word 'face' includes a soft 'c'.* **Deepen** For each letter and digraph, allow 20 seconds for students to note down as many examples as they can.
First phase 15 minutes • Ask students to complete the Skills Boost activity. • Take feedback to check accuracy. • Read through Activity 3 to ensure understanding of the task. • Ask students to complete Activity 3. • Take feedback, comparing different endings and discussing how they relate to the openings and middles chosen.	**Support** Complete Activity 3 as a whole class or in supported groups, discussing and agreeing each step that the text should take. **Deepen** In Activity 3, ask students to create two plans: one to create a dramatic narrative and the other to create a descriptive travelogue.
Second phase 20 minutes • Read through Activity 4 to clarify the task. • Ask students to complete question 1. • Take feedback to share and develop ideas. • Ask students to complete Activity 4. Encourage them to note as many ideas as possible in question 2, to provide the greatest range of options for question 3.	**Support** Encourage partners to share their planning periodically, to prompt and develop ideas. **Deepen** Encourage students to develop two or three possible endings.
Plenary 10 minutes • Ask partners to review each other's planning. Ask them to consider how satisfying the ending is, and whether it should have stopped sooner or later. • Ask volunteers to share their summaries with the class. • Ask the class to evaluate each ending's effectiveness, making positive, constructive suggestions.	**Support** Recognise and validate any effective choices. **Deepen** Ask students to write and share the final sentence of the text they have planned.

Set workbook activities **5 minutes**

- Point students towards the activities on pp. 202–203 of the Workbook.
- Check understanding and answer any questions.
- These activities focus on beginning, middle and end.

<table>
<tr><td>Year 8</td><td colspan="3">Unit 5: A Moment in Time</td></tr>
<tr><td colspan="2">Section 11 Assessment: Lesson 20</td><td>Skills focus: Writing to explain and describe</td><td>Student Book pp. 216–217
Workbook pp. 204–205</td></tr>
<tr><td rowspan="2">Main Curriculum Objectives</td><td>W8.1A Gather and structure a range of relevant ideas before writing.</td><td>W8.2C Use the organisational conventions of a range of forms, for a range of purposes and audiences, with confidence and understanding, including spoken-language forms such as presentations.</td><td>W8.3B Divide text into paragraphs with accuracy and consistency.</td></tr>
<tr><td>W8.3C Use a balance of single-clause sentences, coordinate and subordinate clauses with confidence.</td><td>W8.3E Make deliberate choices of sentence length to achieve clarity.</td><td>W8.3G Select vocabulary in text and spoken language with growing precision.</td></tr>
<tr><td>Secondary Curriculum Objectives</td><td colspan="3"></td></tr>
</table>

Introduction **10 minutes**

- Ask students to read Activity 1. Point out that they should plan their writing, and that you will assess their plans as well as their finished pieces of writing.
- Explain to students that they will have 15 minutes to complete the planning section of the assessment, a further 25 minutes to complete the writing section and a further 10 minutes to review, revise and proofread their writing.

Assessment task **50 minutes**

- Ask students to complete the planning section of the assessment.
- After 15 minutes, ask students to move on to complete the writing section of the assessment.
- After a further 25 minutes, ask students to move on to complete the reviewing and revising section of the assessment.
- You may wish to give students further guidance on how much they should write, and the amounts of time they should use for planning, writing and checking their responses.

Workbook assessment task **5 minutes**

- Point students towards the task and sample student response on pp. 204 of the Workbook.
- Give students the opportunity to read the task and sample response. Briefly discuss these with them and answer any questions.
- Students should identify the errors in the sample response before planning how they will improve it. They should then write an improved version, adding one or two paragraphs of text.
- Make clear your expectations of when this task will be completed. For example, it may be a homework, or students may be given time during an additional lesson.

Year 8	Unit 6: Dramatic!		
Section 1 Curtain up: Lesson 1		Skills focus: Reading: Drama	Student Book pp. 220–221 Workbook pp. 206–207
Main Curriculum Objectives	**R8.1E** Make inferences from specific evidence found in a text or in spoken language, including specific vocabulary choices.	**R8.2A** Explore a writer's or speaker's intention and viewpoint.	**R8.2B** Express a critical response to a text through writing, discussion or presentation, by considering the text's features and their effects.
Secondary Curriculum Objectives	**R8.1B** Identify and retrieve a range of key information in a text or in spoken language.		

Lesson	Support / Deepen
Introduction **10 minutes** • Display the key terms 'script', 'scene', 'line', 'stage direction', 'character' and 'setting'. • Looking at the extract, ask students to give an example for each term. • Note and fill any gaps in understanding.	**Support** Highlight the differences in the terms' meanings in the context of drama and in other contexts (for example, a line in a script, in a poem and in prose). **Deepen** Ask students to suggest and define other relevant vocabulary, such as 'audience', 'theatre' and 'curtain'.
First phase **15 minutes** • Ask five volunteers to read the extract, each taking the lines of one character. • Take students' initial responses. Ask: How do you respond to characters? What do you think will happen next? • Ask students to complete Activity 1. • Take feedback on Activity 1, gathering as wide a range of different responses as possible.	**Support** Complete Activity 1, question 1 as a whole class, discussing the depiction of character in the stage direction and throughout the extract. **Deepen** Encourage students to develop their comments on character, using evidence from the extract.
Second phase **20 minutes** • Read through Activity 2, emphasising the difference between impressions of a character (as explored in Activity 1) and a reader's or audience's response (caused by those impressions). • Ask students to complete Activity 2.	**Support** For each given character, ask students to note just one word of response and to identify a quotation that supports it. **Deepen** Encourage students to develop their comments on character as fully as possible, using evidence from the extract.
Plenary **10 minutes** • Take feedback on Activity 2, again noting as wide a range of different responses as possible. Focus in particular on responses to Sammy. • Ask: Did the writer intend to create a mixed response to the character of Sammy? Why do you think that may be? • Discuss how quickly and clearly the playwright has established character and relationships in the opening lines of the play, and why this is important.	**Support** Prompt students to recognise ambiguity in the character of Sammy. Ask: What should Sammy have done? **Deepen** Ask students to suggest ways in which the play might develop and end, based on this opening and these characters.

Set workbook activities **5 minutes**

- Point students towards the activities on pp. 206–207 of the Workbook.
- Check understanding and answer any questions.
- These activities focus on reading between the lines.

Year 8	**Unit 6: Dramatic!**		
Section 1 Curtain up: Lesson 2	**Skills focus: Reading: Drama**	**Student Book pp. 222–223** **Workbook pp. 208–209**	
Main Curriculum Objectives	**R8.3A** Explore the impact of some of the writer's key structural or organisational choices.	**W8.1A** Gather and structure a range of relevant ideas before writing.	**W8.2A** Use the presentational conventions of a range of forms, for a range of purposes and audiences (e.g. academic essays, stories, scripts and notes for talks and presentations), with confidence and understanding
	W8.2C Use the organisational conventions of a range of forms, for a range of purposes and audiences, with confidence and understanding.		
Secondary Curriculum Objectives			

Introduction **10 minutes** • Read or display a short synopsis of a locally familiar traditional tale. • Remind students of what a non-chronological narrative structure is: a structure that begins somewhere in the middle or at the end of a story, before recalling what happened beforehand. • Ask students to suggest different points at which the chosen tale could begin, and why each might make an effective story opening.	**Support** Prompt students with given points in the chosen tale, discussing each as effective or ineffective. **Deepen** Ask students to create their own four- or five-point synopsis of a familiar tale.
First phase **15 minutes** • Ask students to recap the extract. • Read through Activity 3, noting the point in the synopsis from which the opening is taken (point E). • Ask students to complete Activity 3. • Take feedback, encouraging as wide a range of responses as possible. • Ask students to complete the Skills Boost activity, taking feedback after each question to check accuracy and understanding.	**Support** In Activity 3, question 2, select a point as a whole class or in supported groups. Discuss and develop ideas about what would make this an effective opening. **Deepen** Ask students to suggest ways in which each point in the synopsis could be an effective opening scene.
Second phase **20 minutes** • Read through Activity 4, clarifying the aim: to produce a short extract from the opening of a play. • Ask students to complete questions 1 and 2. • Take feedback to share and develop ideas. • Ask students to complete questions 3–6.	**Support** Take feedback after each step in the writing and planning process to monitor progress and understanding. **Deepen** Challenge students to develop two initial ideas and select the most promising.
Plenary **10 minutes** • Ask partners to discuss what they can infer about the characters and relationships in each other's scripts. • Ask partners or groups to read, and perhaps perform, short extracts from their scripts. Ask the class to identify their most effective lines.	**Support** Recognise and validate any effective choices of action, character, dialogue or stage direction. **Deepen** Challenge students to suggest how the plot might develop in their or their partner's script.

Set workbook activities
- Point students towards the activities on pp. 208–209 of the Workbook.
- Check understanding and answer any questions.
- These activities focus on beginnings.

Year 8	Unit 6: Dramatic!		
Section 2 Setting the scene: Lesson 3		Skills focus: Reading: Drama	Student Book pp. 224–225 Workbook pp. 210–211
Main Curriculum Objectives	**R8.2B** Express a critical response to a text through writing, discussion or presentation, by considering the text's features and their effects.	**R8.3A** Explore the impact of some of the writer's key structural or organisational choices.	
Secondary Curriculum Objectives	**R8.1B** Identify and retrieve a range of key information in a text or in spoken language.		

Introduction **10 minutes** • Ask students to note some ideas for a description of the last five minutes, for example the five minutes before the start of the lesson. Ask: What did you see, hear and feel? What words could you use to describe those things? • Compile responses for display. • Ask students to evaluate the compiled ideas. Ask: Do they accurately convey your experience of those five minutes?	**Support** Complete the activity verbally as a whole class. Prompt students to consider details of place, people and events. **Deepen** Challenge students to describe a similar five minutes in a different time or place, for example at the beginning of a lesson 200 years ago.
First phase **15 minutes** • Read the extract and take students' initial responses. • Ask students to complete Activity 1. • Take feedback, focusing on how quickly and clearly a performance of the play could establish its setting.	**Support** Complete Activity 1, question 2 as a whole class or in supported groups, debating which methods of conveying information are most and least effective. **Deepen** In Activity 1, question 1, ask students to note everything that reveals each idea, not just the first thing.
Second phase **20 minutes** • Read through Activity 2, checking familiarity with the vocabulary suggested in question 2. • Ask students to complete Activity 2.	**Support** Work with the class to complete Activity 2, question 1a, identifying the undeveloped characters before focusing on the others. **Deepen** Encourage students to select short, focused quotations to support their ideas.
Plenary **10 minutes** • Take feedback on Activity 2, focusing on the writer's choices for building character and mood. • Ask students to suggest how they might be portrayed if they were characters in this play. Ask: What might you do during this registration scene to convey your character?	**Support** Recognise and validate all relevant responses. **Deepen** Ask: Why might the writer have decided not to include the teacher on stage in this opening scene?

Set workbook activities **5 minutes**

- Point students towards the activities on pp. 210–211 of the Workbook.
- Check understanding and answer any questions.
- These activities focus on building a picture, and creating mood and character.

Year 8	Unit 6: Dramatic!		
Section 2 Setting the scene: Lesson 4	Skills focus: Reading: Drama		Student Book pp. 226–227 Workbook pp. 212–213
Main Curriculum Objectives	**R8.2A** Explore a writer's or speaker's intention and viewpoint.	**W8.1A** Gather and structure a range of relevant ideas before writing.	**W8.3H** Spell homophones, words with single/double letters and 'silent' letters with some accuracy.
Secondary Curriculum Objectives			

Lesson	Differentiation
Introduction **10 minutes** • Hold a spelling test of the following terms (from the introduction to the Spelling Boost activity): 'audience'; 'character'; 'dialogue'; 'playwright'; 'rehearse'; 'rehearsal'; 'scene'; 'scenery'; 'stage directions'; 'theatre'. • Ask students to mark each other's tests. • Discuss which spellings proved challenging. • Discuss and then clarify the meanings of the terms. • Explain that the suffix '–wright' indicates a maker (for example, a wheelwright makes wheels). Ask: What is a shipwright? Note that, other than 'playwright', words with these suffixes are rarely used today.	**Support** Provide students with definitions to match with the given terms. **Deepen** Challenge students to identify other words that include the following spelling patterns in the given terms: 'au'; 'ch'; 'gue'; 'wr'; 'sc'.
First phase **20 minutes** • Ask students to complete the Spelling Boost activity. • Take feedback to check accuracy and understanding. • Ask students to complete Activity 3. • Take feedback to check and develop understanding.	**Support** In the Spelling Boost activity, provide examples of other familiar words featuring the same spelling patterns, such as 'wrong' and 'earth'. **Deepen** Following the Spelling Boost activity, retest students on the key words' spellings to monitor improvement.
Second phase **20 minutes** • Ask students to begin Activity 4. • Ask them to focus on their planning, but aim to write at least the first two or three lines of their scripts.	**Support** Take feedback after each step in the process to monitor understanding and progress. **Deepen** Ask students to review their planning and produce a short written evaluation of it. Ask: Will your script achieve your intended response?
Plenary **10 minutes** • Ask volunteer pairs to perform the opening lines of their scripts. • Ask the class to identify how, and how effectively, the scenes have been set.	**Support** Recognise and validate any effective planning choices. **Deepen** Encourage students to consider how characters speak, as well as what they say.

Set workbook activities **5 minutes**

- Point students towards the activities on pp. 212–213 of the Workbook.
- Check understanding and answer any questions.
- These activities focus on drama terminology, exploring the playwright's intentions and writing a scene.

Year 8	Unit 6: Dramatic!		
Section 3 From page to stage: Lesson 5		Skills focus: Reading: Drama	Student Book pp. 228–229 Workbook pp. 214–215
Main Curriculum Objectives	**R8.1B** Identify and retrieve a range of key information in a text or in spoken language.	**R8.1E** Make inferences from specific evidence found in a text or in spoken language, including specific vocabulary choices.	
Secondary Curriculum Objectives	**R8.2A** Explore a writer's or speaker's intention and viewpoint.	**R8.3A** Explore the impact of some of the writer's key structural or organisational choices.	**R8.4B** Explore the impact of some of the writer's or speaker's significant vocabulary choices.

Lesson	Support / Deepen
Introduction **10 minutes** • Display the following lines. (They each stand alone; they aren't consecutive from one script.) *Dad* *It's the best present I've ever been given. Thank you!* *Jai* *Help! Please! Somebody! Anybody?* *Ayo* *No, I won't! And you can't make me!* • Ask students to note what they can infer from these lines about character, setting and action. • Take feedback, ensuring students justify their inferences.	**Support** Discuss the lines as a whole class, encouraging volunteers to perform them aloud. Ask: How should each line be delivered? What does that performance imply? **Deepen** Challenge students to write their own single line from which character and/or situation can be inferred.
First phase **15 minutes** • If possible, watch the opening of one of the many film adaptations of *Great Expectations*. • Read Extract A on page 228 of the Student Book: a stage adaptation of the opening of the novel. Take students' initial responses to the characters. • Ask students to complete Activity 1. • Take feedback, compiling responses for display in the next lesson.	**Support** Complete Activity 1 as a class or in supported groups. For questions 2 and 3, focus first on Pip and then on the Man. **Deepen** Challenge students to compile a set of director's notes giving suggestions on setting, costume and performance.
Second phase **20 minutes** • Read Extract B on page 229 of the Student Book: an extract from the novel *Great Expectations* that details the same events as the script does. • Ask: How similar do you think the script and this extract from the novel are? • Explain that Activity 2 will help students to develop their response by comparing the two extracts more closely. • Ask students to complete Activity 2.	**Support** Work as a class or in supported groups to compare the first two paragraphs of the novel extract with the script, before asking students to continue independently. **Deepen** Ask students to identify details in the story that have been altered or omitted in the script, and consider why this may have been done.
Plenary **10 minutes** • Take feedback on Activity 2. Ask students to justify their responses with examples from the script extract and the novel extract. • Challenge students to guess what will happen next in the story, based on their knowledge of the two characters featured.	**Support** Validate any accurate responses. **Deepen** Discuss any examples of films based on books that students have seen and read. Ask: How faithfully does the film follow the novel?

Set workbook activities **5 minutes**
- Point students towards the activities on pp. 214–215 of the Workbook.
- Check understanding and answer any questions.
- These activities focus on key information, inference and exploring differences between extracts.

Year 8	Unit 6: Dramatic!		
Section 3 From page to stage: Lesson 6	Skills focus: Reading: Drama		Student Book pp. 230–231 Workbook pp. 216–217
Main Curriculum Objectives	**R8.2B** Express a critical response to a text through writing, discussion or presentation, by considering the text's features and their effects.	**W8.1A** Gather and structure a range of relevant ideas before writing.	**W8.2C** Use the organisational conventions of a range of forms, for a range of purposes and audiences, with confidence and understanding, including spoken-language forms such as presentations.
Secondary Curriculum Objectives			

Lesson	
Introduction 10 minutes • Ask students to suggest how different settings (such as a busy city, the Amazon rainforest, the North Pole) could be conveyed to an audience in a theatre using costume, scenery, sound effects and performance. • Discuss which methods would be most and least effective.	**Support** Model examples of how the different methods could be used to convey a rainforest setting. **Deepen** Ask students to suggest ways in which they could convey more-challenging settings, such as the surface of the moon or prehistoric Earth.
First phase 15 minutes • Recap the comparison of prose and a script that students explored in the previous lesson. • Ask students to complete Activity 3, question 1. • Take feedback to compare suggestions. • Display the responses to Activity 1 compiled in the previous lesson. • Ask students to complete Activity 3, question 2. • Take feedback, guiding discussion towards the understanding that description in fiction does the same job as performance, scenery, costume and sound in theatre. • Ask students to complete Activity 4. • Take feedback to share and develop understanding.	**Support** Complete Activity 4 verbally as a whole class, exploring responses to the two characters briefly (but fully enough to inform the scriptwriting task that follows in Activity 5). **Deepen** Ask students to identify specific evidence in both the script and the novel extract to support their responses. They should consider the use of vocabulary and sentence structures as well as the selection of ideas.
Second phase 20 minutes • Read Extract C on page 231 of the Student Book, at the start of Activity 5. • Ask students to complete Activity 5, question 1. • Take feedback to ensure understanding of both key information and the more-important details. • Ask students to begin work on question 2.	**Support** Complete Activity 5, question 1 verbally, as a whole class or in supported groups. **Deepen** Challenge students to maintain the impressions of Pip and the Man that they identified in Activity 4.
Plenary 10 minutes • Ask partners to prepare a reading of one of their scripts. • Ask volunteer pairs to share their reading with the class. • Discuss whether each script includes the information necessary to tell the story, and how whether it includes an effective amount of detail.	**Support** Recognise and validate any effective choices in students' scripts. **Deepen** Challenge students to review every line of their scripts, removing anything that does not develop character, action or mood.

Set workbook activities 5 minutes
- Point students towards the activities on pp. 216–217 of the Workbook.
- Check understanding and answer any questions.
- These activities focus on comparing the script and the novel.

Year 8	Unit 6: Dramatic!		
Section 4 Creating conflict: Lesson 7	Skills focus: Reading: Drama		Student Book pp. 232–233 Workbook pp. 218–219
Main Curriculum Objectives	**R8.1B** Identify and retrieve a range of key information in a text or in spoken language.	**R8.2B** Express a critical response to a text through writing, discussion or presentation, by considering the text's features and their effects.	**R8.2C** Select relevant, focused evidence to support ideas.
Secondary Curriculum Objectives	**R8.2A** Explore a writer's or speaker's intention and viewpoint.	**R8.4B** Explore the impact of some of the writer's or speaker's significant vocabulary choices.	

Introduction **10 minutes** • Ask students to describe their relationship with any siblings they have. Ask: Do you sometimes experience conflict? What causes the conflict? • Ask: What advice would you give to your sibling(s) to reduce conflict? • Remind students of the meaning of 'conflict' in the context of narrative structure: a problem or challenge that characters face, and that causes events that are central to the story.	**Support** Suggest scenarios that could be causes of conflict, for example being asked to share or borrowing without permission. **Deepen** Ask students to identify the conflict in extracts already explored in this unit.
First phase **15 minutes** • Ask nine volunteers to read and/or perform the extract. • Take students' initial responses. • Ask students to complete Activity 1. Point out that the words selected as evidence in questions 2 and 3b need not be consecutive. • Take feedback to check understanding. • Note the difference in the father's and the writer's motivations for asking characters to make a choice.	**Support** Discuss the characters and the situation more fully, in order to clarify understanding, before asking students to complete the activity. **Deepen** Encourage students to develop their responses to the characters as fully as possible, selecting precise vocabulary as relevant evidence.
Second phase **20 minutes** • Read though the introduction to Activity 2. Ask students to suggest stories, novels, films or television dramas in which each example type of conflict is seen. • Ask students to complete Activity 2.	**Support** Complete the activity in discussion as a whole class. **Deepen** Challenge students to suggest types of conflict different from those suggested, and examples of them in stories, novels, films or television dramas.
Plenary **10 minutes** • Take feedback on Activity 2, focusing on the roles of the father and the brother in creating conflict. Ask: Why would the writer not want the characters to resolve their differences at this point? • Ask students to suggest how the play might develop from this point onwards.	**Support** Point out different ways in which the brother could have acted, and ask students to consider the impact of these possibilities on the story. **Deepen** Ask students to suggest different ways in which the brother could have acted, and the impact these possibilities would have on the story.

Set workbook activities **5 minutes**

- Point students towards the activities on pp. 218–219 of the Workbook.
- Check understanding and answer any questions.
- These activities focus on creating conflict.

Year 8	Unit 6: Dramatic!		
Section 4 Creating conflict: Lesson 8	Skills focus: Reading: Drama		Student Book pp. 234–235 Workbook pp. 220–221
Main Curriculum Objectives	**R8.3A** Explore the impact of some of the writer's key structural or organisational choices.	**W8.2C** Use the organisational conventions of a range of forms, for a range of purposes and audiences, with confidence and understanding, including spoken-language forms such as presentations.	**W8.3J** Use grammatical terminology for parts of speech with some accuracy.
Secondary Curriculum Objectives			

Introduction **10 minutes** • Discuss the concept of justice. Ask: What does 'justice' mean? How might it be applied at school, for example in a case of bad or very good behaviour? • Ask: How do you expect justice to affect good characters and bad characters in stories?	**Support** Focus initially on the most familiar formal application of justice: the criminal justice system. **Deepen** Ask students to suggest examples of stories in which justice is done.
First phase **15 minutes** • Ask volunteers to recap the extract. • Ask students to complete Activity 3, question 1. Take feedback, validating any plausible responses. • Ask students to complete Activity 3, question 2, emphasising that they should select elements that they feel would make an engaging story. • Take feedback. • Ask students to complete the Grammar Boost activity. • Take feedback to check accuracy and understanding.	**Support** Discuss and complete Activity 3 as a whole class or in supported groups. **Deepen** In Activity 3, question 2, challenge students to use as many of the given elements as possible, and add their own, to create a credible and engaging plot.
Second phase **20 minutes** • Ask students to complete Activity 4, questions 1 and 2. Take feedback to share and develop ideas. • Ask students to complete Activity 4, question 3.	**Support** Take feedback after each step to monitor progress. Suggest that students can, if necessary, refer to the list of conflicts in Activity 2 to support their planning. **Deepen** Encourage students to develop their own ideas rather than relying on the suggestions provided.
Plenary **10 minutes** • Ask partners to rehearse readings of short sections of their scripts. • Ask volunteers to share their readings with the class. • For each reading, ask: has the writer created an engaging conflict? • Ask the class to guess what characteristics the writers chose when planning their characters. Ask: Are those characteristics made apparent in the script?	**Support** Recognise and validate any effective elements in students' scripts. **Deepen** Challenge students to write (a short section of) the final scene of the play they have planned.

Set workbook activities **5 minutes** • Point students towards the activities on pp. 220–221 of the Workbook. • Check understanding and answer any questions. • These activities focus on building a story.

Year 8	Unit 6: Dramatic!		
Section 5 Crafting characters: Lesson 9	Skills focus: Reading: Drama		Student Book pp. 236–237 Workbook pp. 222–223
Main Curriculum Objectives	**R8.1E** Make inferences from specific evidence found in a text or in spoken language, including specific vocabulary choices.	**R8.2B** Express a critical response to a text through writing, discussion or presentation, by considering the text's features and their effects.	**R8.4B** Explore the impact of some of the writer's or speaker's significant vocabulary choices.
Secondary Curriculum Objectives	**R8.2A** Explore a writer's or speaker's intention and viewpoint.	**W8.1A** Gather and structure a range of relevant ideas before writing.	

Introduction 10 minutes • Introduce or recap the concept of stereotypes: ideas about a type of person or thing that are widely believed but often inaccurate. • Ask students to note ideas about the stereotype of a businessman or woman. • Take feedback.	**Support** Prompt students to think about appearance, attitudes and abilities. **Deepen** Challenge students to create dialogue for the businessperson consisting of stereotypical things they might be expected to say.
First phase 15 minutes • Read the extract. • Take students' initial responses. Ask: Is Max a stereotypical businessman? • Ask students to complete Activity 1. • Take feedback. • Discuss students' responses to the two characters – in particular, the impressions left at the end of the extract.	**Support** Discuss Activity 1, questions 1 and 2 as a whole class or in supported groups. Prompt students to identify parts of the extract that helped them to form their impressions. **Deepen** Refer back to the concept of justice, explored in the previous section. Ask: Do you think justice has been done in this play?
Second phase 20 minutes • Point out to students that directors and actors often have nothing more than the script to guide their productions of a play. Note that this makes the writer's language choices vital. • Ask students to complete Activity 2.	**Support** To support Activity 2, questions 1 and 2, read some of Flora's lines aloud and exaggerate her annoyance. **Deepen** Challenge students to identify all of the persuasive language that Max uses.
Plenary 10 minutes • Take feedback on Activity 2, focusing on the ways in which language choice reflects attitude, thoughts and feelings. • Ask students to suggest other situations in which a character's silence could be revealing.	**Support** Recognise and validate any relevant responses. **Deepen** Ask: In how many of Flora's lines does she actually respond to what Max has said? What does this suggest?

Set workbook activities 5 minutes

- Point students towards the activities on pp. 222–223 of the Workbook.
- Check understanding and answer any questions.
- These activities focus on exploring character through language.

Year 8	Unit 6: Dramatic!		
Section 5 Crafting characters: Lesson 10	Skills focus: Reading: Drama		Student Book pp. 238–239 Workbook pp. 224–225
Main Curriculum Objectives	**R8.2B** Express a critical response to a text through writing, discussion or presentation, by considering the text's features and their effects.	**R8.2C** Select relevant, focused evidence to support ideas.	**W8.3F** Use determiners to achieve cohesion and clarity.
Secondary Curriculum Objectives			

Introduction 10 minutes	**Support**
• Display the words 'this' and 'that'. Ask students to write a sentence featuring one of them. • Take feedback. Ask students to explain how the words 'this' and 'that' can be used. • Clarify that both words can operate as determiners, preceding a noun (for example, 'read this book'), and as pronouns, replacing a noun (for example, 'read this').	Model example sentences to prompt students. For example: *Sit on this chair.* *Do not go that way; go this way.* *I wouldn't do that if I were you.* **Deepen** Include the pronoun/determiner 'both' when students are confident in their understanding of 'this' and 'that'.
First phase 15 minutes	**Support** Work with students to complete the Skills Boost activity and question 1 of Activity 3, to develop and support understanding.
• Read the introduction to the Skills Boost activity. • Ask students to complete the Skills Boost activity. • Take feedback to check understanding and accuracy. • Recall the discussion of stereotypes in the previous lesson. • Ask students to complete Activity 3, pointing out that question 2 gives an opportunity to develop responses to question 1 in the more formal context of a critical response. • Ask partners to ensure that each other's responses to question 2 feature the key elements of critical response: a key point, evidence and an explanation.	**Deepen** After the Skills Boost activity, ask: When might overusing pronouns and determiners lead to confusion and ambiguity?
Second phase 20 minutes	**Support** Take feedback after each step of the planning process to ensure understanding.
• Take feedback on Activity 3, checking students' understanding of the concept of a stereotype. • Ask students to complete Activity 4. Note that characters need not have more than two or three lines each, depending on the time available.	**Deepen** Encourage students to develop characters that are not simply the direct opposite of the stereotypes, but are more nuanced.
Plenary 10 minutes	**Support** Recognise and validate any effective responses or writing choices.
• Ask partners to prepare readings of their scripts. • Ask volunteer pairs to perform their scripts. • Ask the class to deduce the writer's responses to Activity 4, questions 2a and 2c: the three words chosen to describe each character. Ask: Has the writer created the impressions they intended?	**Deepen** Challenge students to add stage directions to their scripts, and to consider how actions could contribute to their characterisations.

Set workbook activities 5 minutes

- Point students towards the activities on pp. 224–225 of the Workbook.
- Check understanding and answer any questions.
- These activities focus on referring back using pronouns and writing a response to characters.

Year 8	Unit 6: Dramatic!		
Section 6 Assessment: Lesson 11		Skills focus: Reading: Drama	Student Book pp. 240–241 Workbook pp. 226–227
Main Curriculum Objectives	**R8.1B** Identify and retrieve a range of key information in a text or in spoken language.	**R8.1E** Make inferences from specific evidence found in a text or in spoken language, including specific vocabulary choices.	**R8.2A** Explore a writer's or speaker's intention and viewpoint.
	R8.2B Express a critical response to a text through writing, discussion or presentation, by considering the text's features and their effects.	**R8.2C** Select relevant, focused evidence to support ideas.	**R8.4B** Explore the impact of some of the writer's or speaker's significant vocabulary choices.
Secondary Curriculum Objectives			

Introduction **10 minutes**

- Ask students to read the extract, and check their understanding of the context of the extract.
- Explain to students that they will have 25 minutes to complete the reading section of the assessment, and a further 25 minutes to complete the writing section.

Assessment task **50 minutes**

- Ask students to complete the reading section of the assessment. Any students finishing sooner can begin the writing task.
- After 25 minutes, ask students to move on to complete the writing section of the assessment.
- Point out that they should plan their writing, and that you will assess their plans as well as their finished pieces of writing.
- You may wish to give students further guidance on how much they should write, and the amounts of time they should use for planning, writing and checking their responses.

Workbook assessment task

- Point students towards the extract and activities on pp. 226–227 of the Workbook.
- Give students the opportunity to read the extract. Briefly discuss it with them and answer any questions.
- Students should read the extract again carefully before answering the questions that follow it.
- Make clear your expectations of when this task will be completed. For example, it may be a homework, or students may be given time during an additional lesson.

Year 8	Unit 6: Dramatic!		
Section 7 Shakespearean speech: Lesson 12	Skills focus: Reading: Drama		Student Book pp. 242–243 Workbook pp. 228–229
Main Curriculum Objectives	**R8.1A** Read largely accurately and with understanding.	**R8.1E** Make inferences from specific evidence found in a text or in spoken language, including specific vocabulary choices.	**R8.2B** Express a critical response to a text through writing, discussion or presentation, by considering the text's features and their effects.
Secondary Curriculum Objectives	**R8.2C** Select relevant, focused evidence to support ideas.		

Introduction — 10 minutes	Support / Deepen
• Ask students to discuss and note what they know about Shakespeare. • If any of his work is familiar, ask students what difficulties they have in understanding his language, and any methods they have used to decipher it. • Allow students' familiarity with Shakespeare to guide your delivery of the lesson.	**Support** Focus discussion on Shakespeare's plays and reputation. **Deepen** Ask students to describe experiences of Shakespeare that they have found helpful and engaging.
First phase — 15 minutes • Read the extract. • Gauge students' level of understanding by asking them to summarise the conversation. • Take students' responses to the events and characters depicted. • Ask students to complete Activity 1. • Take feedback to check and share understanding, and to develop responses.	**Support** Ask students to identify specific words, phrases, lines or speeches that they do not understand. **Deepen** Challenge students to write stage directions for the scene, considering how each character should act and react to the dialogue.
Second phase — 20 minutes • Read through Activity 2 to check understanding of the task and the concept of scoring the characters. • Ask students to complete Activity 2, question 1. • Take feedback on question 1 to share and develop ideas. • Ask students to complete Activity 2, question 2.	**Support** Suggest that students work in pairs to complete Activity 2, question 1. **Deepen** In Activity 2, question 1, ask students to use adverbials rather than numbers to indicate their ideas about each character (for example 'quite' or 'not at all'). In question 2, encourage them to develop detailed explanations supported with evidence.
Plenary — 10 minutes • Take feedback on Activity 2, question 2, and compare ideas. • Encourage disagreement and debate, ensuring that opinions are based on close reference to the text. • Discuss whether or not the class can reach a consensus about each character.	**Support** Recognise and validate any relevant responses. **Deepen** Encourage students to suggest other adjectives that could be used on a scale to score the characters.

Set workbook activities — 5 minutes
• Point students towards the activities on pp. 228–229 of the Workbook. • Check understanding and answer any questions. • These activities focus on checking understanding and responding to dialogue.

Year 8	Unit 6: Dramatic!		
Section 7 Shakespearean speech: Lesson 13	Skills focus: Reading: Drama		Student Book pp. 244–245 Workbook pp. 230–231
Main Curriculum Objectives	**R8.2A** Explore a writer's or speaker's intention and viewpoint.	**R8.4A** Explore the impact of some of a writer's or speaker's choices of grammatical features and sentence structure.	**R8.4B** Explore the impact of some of the writer's or speaker's significant vocabulary choices.
	W8.3H Spell homophones, words with single/double letters and 'silent' letters with some accuracy.		
Secondary Curriculum Objectives	**W8.1A** Gather and structure a range of relevant ideas before writing.	**W8.3C** Use a balance of single-clause sentences, coordinate and subordinate clauses with confidence.	**W8.3E** Make deliberate choices of sentence length to achieve clarity.
	W8.3G Select vocabulary in text and spoken language with growing precision.		

Introduction **10 minutes** • Ask a volunteer to recap the conversation conducted in the extract. • As a class, recap responses to the three central characters. • Ask: What advice would you give King Lear, if you were his special advisor? Allow two or three minutes for students to discuss their answers in pairs or small groups. • Take feedback to share ideas.	**Support** Prompt students with appropriate sentence starts. For example: • *If I were you, I would …* • *It may be a good idea to …* **Deepen** Ask students to suggest advice that ranges from polite and respectful to brutally honest. Ask: How would the king react to each piece of advice?
First phase **15 minutes** • Ask students to complete the Spelling Boost activity. • Take feedback to check accurate usage. • Introduce Activity 3, explaining that it focuses on how sentence length and vocabulary choice can influence responses to dialogue. • Ask students to complete Activity 3. Suggest that they could reuse some of the vocabulary given in the Spelling Boost activity. • Take feedback to share and develop understanding.	**Support** In Activity 3, take feedback after question 1d. Complete question 1e verbally, in supported groups. **Deepen** Encourage students to explore Shakespeare's language choices in more depth, for example looking at Goneril's repeated use of lists and comparisons.
Second phase **20 minutes** • Read the introduction to Activity 4. Note the parallels with the extract: a figure of authority who may be deceived by one character, and then may be surprised by the blunt honesty of the other. • Ask students to complete the activity, encouraging them to focus on creating detailed plans before starting to write.	**Support** Take feedback after each stage of the writing process to ensure progress. **Deepen** Encourage students to make use of language features they identified in Activity 3, for example Goneril's repeated lists and comparisons.
Plenary **10 minutes** • Ask partners to share their scripts, and to identify effective choices of vocabulary and/or sentence structure in each other's work. • Ask volunteer pairs to share parts of their scripts. • Ask the class to evaluate their effectiveness.	**Support** Recognise and validate any effective elements of students' scripts. **Deepen** Ask students to write a brief response to their own or a partner's script, exploring the impact of its language.

Set workbook activities **5 minutes** • Point students towards the activities on pp. 230–231 of the Workbook. • Check understanding and answer any questions. • These activities focus on exploring dialogue and planning a script.

Year 8	Unit 6: Dramatic!		
Section 8 Performing: Lesson 14		Skills focus: Reading: Drama	Student Book pp. 246–247 Workbook pp. 232–233
Main Curriculum Objectives	**R8.1A** Read largely accurately and with understanding.	**R8.1E** Make inferences from specific evidence found in a text or in spoken language, including specific vocabulary choices.	
Secondary Curriculum Objectives			

Introduction 10 minutes	Support
• Display the following short script. A *Thou art a knave!* B *Dost thou dare to call me a knave?* A *I do.* B *I will fight thee!* • Explain to students that these sentences are examples of the English language as it was written in Shakespeare's time. • Challenge students to work out the meaning of the unfamiliar words.	If students struggle, discuss and then reveal the meanings of the unfamiliar words one by one, using context to aid deductions. **Deepen** Encourage students to explain how they deduced the meanings of the unfamiliar words.
First phase 15 minutes • Read the extract, discussing unfamiliar vocabulary using the definitions provided. You may find it helpful to read the extract again afterwards. • Take students' responses to the extract's events. • Ask: Do you find this extract easier or harder to understand than the extract from *King Lear* (explored in the previous lessons)? Why is that? • Ask students to complete Activity 1. • Take feedback to check understanding.	**Support** Provide an additional pre-prepared glossary for terms that may be unfamiliar but that are not defined in the extract (for example 'nay', 'budge', 'inmost'). In Activity 1, take feedback after each question to monitor understanding. **Deepen** Challenge students to write their own sentences (or short scripts) using the unfamiliar words encountered.
Second phase 20 minutes • Read through the Skills Boost activity, clarifying the roles of subject and object pronouns. • Ask students to identify the words 'thee' and 'thy' in the extract. • Ask students to complete the Skills Boost activity. • Take feedback to check accuracy. • If time allows, ask partners to prepare a reading of the script. • Ask volunteer pairs to share one or two lines from their reading.	**Support** Complete the Skills Boost activity through discussion as a whole class or in supported groups. **Deepen** Challenge students to write stage directions for the scene in the extract, considering how Hamlet and Queen Gertrude might move or stand as they talk.
Plenary 10 minutes • Discuss the relationship between Hamlet and his mother. • Ask: What does this scene suggest about the impact that his mother's second marriage had upon Hamlet? How do you think this marriage may have changed his feelings towards his mother?	**Support** Encourage students to compare this relationship with other examples of parent–child relationships in fiction. **Deepen** Ask students to suggest how the plot of the play relationship might develop from this point on.

Set workbook activities 5 minutes
• Point students towards the activities on pp. 232–233 of the Workbook. • Check understanding and answer any questions. • These activities focus on understanding the text and Shakespeare's language.

Year 8	Unit 6: Dramatic!		
Section 8 Performing: Lesson 15	Skills focus: Reading: Drama		Student Book pp. 248–249 Workbook pp. 234–235
Main Curriculum Objectives	**R8.2B** Express a critical response to a text through writing, discussion or presentation, by considering the text's features and their effects.	**W8.1C** Review and revise vocabulary choice after writing.	**W8.2C** Use the organisational conventions of a range of forms, for a range of purposes and audiences, with confidence and understanding.
Secondary Curriculum Objectives	**R8.2A** Explore a writer's or speaker's intention and viewpoint.	**R8.2C** Select relevant, focused evidence to support ideas.	**W8.1A** Gather and structure a range of relevant ideas before writing.

Introduction **10 minutes** • Display the following short script. *(A young man knocks on an elderly man's front door.)* *Old Man* *Yes?* *Young Man* *I wonder if you could help me?* *Old Man* *Do come in.* • Challenge volunteers to read the script in two different ways, one presenting the young man as a threat, and then one presenting the elderly man as a threat. • Discuss how performance can alter the effect of a script.	**Support** Perform the two readings yourself, each time asking students to identify which character is in danger. **Deepen** Ask students to add more stage directions to the script to guide the actor in the delivery of each line.
First phase **15 minutes** • Read through Activity 2, question 1. Ask four volunteers to suggest at least two different ways in which each line could be delivered, and to perform them. Discuss the impact of each performance. • Ask students to complete Activity 2. • Take feedback to compare ideas and responses. • Ask students to complete the Skills Boost activity. • Take feedback to compare ideas.	**Support** In Activity 2, take feedback after question 1 to ensure understanding before students complete question 2. **Deepen** In Activity 2, encourage students to add their own vocabulary suggestions to those provided.
Second phase **20 minutes** • Read through Activity 3, clarifying that its focus is on exploring different interpretations of the chosen character's lines. • Ask students to complete Activity 3, suggesting that they could refer to their responses to Activity 2 when considering performance suggestions.	**Support** Take feedback on questions 1–4 in Activity 3 before asking students to complete question 5. **Deepen** Ask students to write two paragraphs: one about each character.
Plenary **10 minutes** • Give students three to five minutes to review and revise their vocabulary choices. Ask them to consider whether any vocabulary could be made more precise. • Take feedback, asking volunteers to read extracts from their paragraphs. Focus on the range and precision of responses expressed. • Discuss the effective use of the elements of a critical response paragraph.	**Support** Recognise and validate any effective elements of critical response and/or vocabulary choices. **Deepen** Ask students to share improvements they made to the precision of their vocabulary, and the reasons for them.

Set workbook activities **5 minutes**
- Point students towards the activities on pp. 234–235 of the Workbook.
- Check understanding and answer any questions.
- These activities focus on writing a response.

Year 8	Unit 6: Dramatic!		
Section 9 Exploring themes: Lesson 16	Skills focus: Reading: Drama		Student Book pp. 250–251 Workbook pp. 236–237
Main Curriculum Objectives	**R8.1A** Read largely accurately and with understanding.	**R8.2B** Express a critical response to a text through writing, discussion or presentation, by considering the text's features and their effects.	**R8.2C** Select relevant, focused evidence to support ideas.
Secondary Curriculum Objectives			

Introduction **10 minutes** • Display the following examples of responses to King Lear (studied in Section 7). o *King Lear is disappointed with Cordelia's answer: 'Nothing will come of nothing: speak again.'* o *King Lear is disappointed with Cordelia's answer and orders her to 'speak again'.* • Ask students to note the different ways in which the quotations are presented. • Clarify that a short quotation can be positioned inside a sentence: it can be 'embedded'. • Ask students to rewrite the following sentence using an embedded quotation. *Ayo was angry: 'I've never been so embarrassed!'*	**Support** Suggest that students focus on embedding the single-word quotation 'embarrassed' in their new sentences. **Deepen** Ask students to write their own imaginary comments on imaginary lines from an imaginary playscript, and then to rewrite their sentences to include embedded quotations.
First phase **15 minutes** • Read the extract, cautioning students that it is likely to be challenging. Note that they may be unable to understand some lines, but should focus on the ones they find more accessible. • Discuss the unfamiliar vocabulary and turns of phrase using the definitions provided, and then the extract's metaphors. You may find it helpful to read the extract again afterwards. • Work with students to summarise the content of the extract broadly and briefly. • Ask students to complete Activity 1. • Take feedback to check and develop understanding.	**Support** Complete Activity 1 orally as a whole class or in supported groups. **Deepen** Ask: How persuasive do you find Lady Macbeth?
Second phase **20 minutes** • Remind students of the key features of a successful quotation: it should be short, focused and relevant. • Read through Activity 2 and check students' understanding of the terms 'ruthless' and 'manipulative'. • Ask students to complete Activity 2.	**Support** Work with students to create a shortlist of possible responses to Activity 2, question 2 from which they can select the most relevant. **Deepen** Challenge students to shorten their selected quotations to be yet more focused.
Plenary **10 minutes** • Take feedback on Activity 2. Use any differing answers to encourage discussion and debate. • Challenge students to write sentences in which they embed the quotations they selected in answer to question 2.	**Support** Recognise and validate all arguable responses. **Deepen** Challenge students to identify other quotations that back up the views expressed in each of their sentences.

Set workbook activities **5 minutes**
- Point students towards the activities on pp. 236–237 of the Workbook.
- Check understanding and answer any questions.
- These activities focus on understanding, and selecting evidence.

Year 8	Unit 6: Dramatic!		
Section 9 Exploring themes: Lesson 17	Skills focus: Reading: Drama		Student Book pp. 252–253 Workbook pp. 238–239
Main Curriculum Objectives	**R8.2A** Explore a writer's or speaker's intention and viewpoint.	**R8.2B** Express a critical response to a text through writing, discussion or presentation, by considering the text's features and their effects.	**W8.3E** Make deliberate choices of sentence length to achieve clarity.
Secondary Curriculum Objectives	**R8.4B** Explore the impact of some of the writer's or speaker's significant vocabulary choices.	**W8.1A** Gather and structure a range of relevant ideas before writing.	**W8.2C** Use the organisational conventions of a range of forms, for a range of purposes and audiences, with confidence and understanding, including spoken-language forms such as presentations.

Introduction 5 minutes • Discuss the concept of a theme: an idea that runs through a text, which is usually explored in different characters and scenarios. • Ask students to suggest one or two key themes explored in locally familiar folk tales, recent films and/or novels you have read as a class.	**Support** Suggest a familiar story, and give students three options for a theme it contains. Ask: Which idea is an important theme in this story? **Deepen** Suggest possible themes (such as growing up, ambition or money), and ask students to suggest stories that could explore them.
First phase 20 minutes • Ask volunteers to recap the extract, and refer to the definitions alongside it to refresh understanding. • Ask students to complete Activity 3. • Take feedback, exploring students' reasoning. • Ask students to complete the Skills Boost activity. • Ask volunteers to share their rewritten responses, and ask the class to comment on each one's clarity.	**Support** Complete Activity 3 through discussion, as a whole class or in supported groups. **Deepen** Ask students to use their answers to Activity 3, questions 1–4 to discuss the balance or imbalance of power in the extract.
Second phase 20 minutes • Ask students to complete Activity 4, encouraging them to focus on creating detailed plans before starting to write.	**Support** Take feedback after Activity 4, questions 1 and 2 to ensure understanding. **Deepen** Challenge students to use only short, focused and relevant embedded quotations in their response.
Plenary 10 minutes • Ask students to review their sentence structures in their response to Activity 4. • Ask volunteers to share example sentences, including the evidence they have chosen. • Ask: How does Shakespeare's presentation of these two characters highlight and explore the theme of power?	**Support** Recognise and validate any effective elements of students' responses. **Deepen** Challenge students to write a third paragraph, exploring Shakespeare's presentation of the theme of power.

Set workbook activities 5 minutes
- Point students towards the activities on pp. 238–239 of the Workbook.
- Check understanding and answer any questions.
- These activities focus on exploring the theme of power and reviewing sentence structure.

Year 8	Unit 6: Dramatic!		
Section 10 Introductions and conclusions: Lesson 18	Skills focus: Reading: Drama		Student Book pp. 254–255 Workbook pp. 240–241
Main Curriculum Objectives	**R8.1A** Read largely accurately and with understanding.	**R8.2B** Express a critical response to a text through writing, discussion or presentation, by considering the text's features and their effects.	**W8.1A** Gather and structure a range of relevant ideas before writing.
Secondary Curriculum Objectives			

Introduction 10 minutes • Ask students to explain the meaning of 'regret'. • Ask students to suggest real or imaginary situations or circumstances that could lead to feelings of regret. • Ask students to describe the thoughts, and the physical and emotional feelings, they associate with regret.	**Support** Suggest example situations to students, such as upsetting someone or carelessly breaking something. **Deepen** Ask students to write a short monologue showing the thoughts of someone experiencing regret.
First phase 15 minutes • Read the extract. • Discuss the unfamiliar vocabulary and turns of phrase using the definitions provided, and then the extract's metaphors. You may find it helpful to read the extract again afterwards. • Take students' initial responses, focusing on the idea of regret. • Ask: Are you surprised by the characters' responses to their murder of King Duncan? • Ask students to complete Activity 1. • Take feedback to check and develop understanding.	**Support** Reread the relevant section of the extract aloud before asking students to complete each question. **Deepen** In Activity 1, question 4, encourage students to use their own ideas rather than the vocabulary suggested. Then ask them to allocate all of the suggested words to one character or the other. Ask: Which one word does not apply to either character?
Second phase 20 minutes • Introduce Activity 2, and place it in context with Activities 3 and 4: students will plan a response and then, in the next lesson, write an introduction and conclusion to that response. • Ask students to complete Activity 2.	**Support** Complete Activity 2, question 1a as a whole class before asking students to complete question 1b and the rest of the activity independently. **Deepen** Ask students to note two points for each character in Activity 2, question 1, and then, in question 2, to identify a quotation for each of the four points.
Plenary 10 minutes • Take feedback, focusing on students' responses to Activity 2, question 3. • Ask: Are these responses consistent with Shakespeare's presentation of the characters in the previous session's extract, from earlier in the play? • Aim to develop a sense of each extract in the context of the other, and the consistency of characterisation.	**Support** Briefly recap or reread the extract from Section 9, focusing on the presentation of the characters and their relationship. **Deepen** Ask students to predict how the characters may behave later during the play, and to justify those predictions. Ask: What do you think they will do in the end?

Set workbook activities 5 minutes
- Point students towards the activities on pp. 240–241 of the Workbook.
- Check understanding and answer any questions.
- These activities focus on understanding, and planning a response.

Year 8	Unit 6: Dramatic!		
Section 10 Introductions and conclusions: Lesson 19		Skills focus: Reading: Drama	Student Book pp. 256–257 Workbook pp. 242–243
Main Curriculum Objectives	**W8.2C** Use the organisational conventions of a range of forms, for a range of purposes and audiences, with confidence and understanding, including spoken-language forms such as presentations.	**W8.1B** Correct a range of errors in spelling, punctuation and grammar independently after writing, beginning to develop strategies for proofreading.	
Secondary Curriculum Objectives			

Introduction **10 minutes** • Display the following: an introduction to the lesson. *We have been exploring Macbeth and developing our critical writing skills. Today, we will explore how to write an introduction to a critical response.* • Ask: Is this an effective introduction to the lesson? Why is that? • Look for responses recognising that the introduction places the lesson in context, and then provides a very brief overview that indicates today's topic. • Ensure students have access to the planning work they completed in the previous lesson.	**Support** Before displaying the introduction, provide criteria for effectiveness: placing a subject in context and indicating its content. Then ask students to evaluate the displayed introduction against these criteria. **Deepen** Challenge students to write an effective introduction for another subject, for example their next lesson or a sports match.
First phase **15 minutes** • Ask volunteers to recap the extract and their plans from the previous lesson. • Ask students to complete Activity 3. • Take feedback, checking students' responses against the given criteria. • Ask students to complete the Skills Boost activity. • Take feedback to check accuracy. • Ask students to proofread their responses to Activity 3.	**Support** In Activity 3, suggest students refer to your displayed introduction to the lesson, and to the introduction to the extract, for support. **Deepen** Ask students to write a further sentence for their introductions that summarises their impressions of both characters in just a few words.
Second phase **20 minutes** • Read the introduction to Activity 4. Emphasise that a conclusion should not repeat the introduction or key points, but summarise them. • Ask students to complete Activity 4, question 1. • Take feedback to ensure students have summarised their ideas appropriately. • Ask students to complete question 2. • Take feedback to share and develop ideas.	**Support** Complete Activity 4, question 2a verbally, as a whole class or in supported groups, before students complete question 2b independently. **Deepen** Encourage students to summarise a response to the characters' relationship in their conclusion.
Plenary **10 minutes** • Ask partners to evaluate their own and each other's conclusions against the criteria given in the introduction to Activity 4. • Ask volunteers to share (sentences from) their conclusions with the class. • Ask students to summarise the key elements of an effective critical response: its introduction; its paragraphs of key points, evidence and explanations; and its conclusion.	**Support** Recognise and validate any effective elements of conclusions. **Deepen** Challenge students to shorten their conclusions to two sentences, each with ten words or fewer. Ask: Do they still achieve the given criteria?

Set workbook activities **5 minutes**
- Point students towards the activities on pp. 242–243 of the Workbook.
- Check understanding and answer any questions.
- These activities focus on introductions, proofreading and conclusions.

Year 8	Unit 6: Dramatic!		
Section 11 Assessment: Lesson 20		Skills focus: Reading: Drama	Student Book pp. 258–259 Workbook pp. 244–245
Main Curriculum Objectives	**R8.1A** Read largely accurately and with understanding.	**R8.2A** Explore a writer's or speaker's intention and viewpoint.	**R8.2B** Express a critical response to a text through writing, discussion or presentation, by considering the text's features and their effects.
	R8.2C Select relevant, focused evidence to support ideas.	**R8.4B** Explore the impact of some of the writer's or speaker's significant vocabulary choices.	**W8.2C** Use the organisational conventions of a range of forms, for a range of purposes and audiences, e.g. to explain, to describe or to persuade, with confidence and understanding.
Secondary Curriculum Objectives			

Introduction **10 minutes**

- Read the extract as a whole class. Discuss the unfamiliar vocabulary and turns of phrase using the definitions provided. You may find it helpful to read the extract again afterwards.
- Check students' broad understanding of the events depicted and their context: this extract, from the end of the play, describes the eventual effect on Lady Macbeth of her and her husband's actions.
- Explain to students that they will have 25 minutes to complete the reading section of the assessment, and a further 25 minutes to complete the writing section.

Assessment task **50 minutes**

- Ask students to complete the reading section of the assessment. Any students finishing sooner can begin the writing task.
- After 25 minutes, ask students to move on to complete the writing section of the assessment.
- Point out that they should plan their writing, and that you will assess their plans as well as their finished pieces of writing.
- You may wish to give students further guidance on how much they should write, and the amounts of time they should use for planning, writing and checking their responses.

Workbook assessment task

- Point students towards the extract, question and sample student response on pp. 244 of the Workbook.
- Give students the opportunity to read the extract, question and sample response. Briefly discuss these with them and answer any questions.
- Students should identify the errors in the sample response before planning how they will improve it. They should then write an improved version, adding one or two paragraphs of text.
- Make clear your expectations of when this task will be completed. For example, it may be a homework, or students may be given time during an additional lesson.

GLOSSARY

abbreviation - shortened **word** or **phrase** (e.g. Doctor becomes Dr; Susan becomes Sue; telephone becomes phone)

abstract noun - **noun** that names ideas you cannot see, hear, smell, taste or touch (e.g. 'happiness'; 'idea')

account - telling or retelling of factual or fictional events (e.g. an account of the football match, or an account of an adventure)

active voice - form in which the thing that is performing the action of a **verb** is the grammatical **subject** of a **sentence**

adjective - **word** that adds information to a **noun**

adverb - single-word **adverbial**

adverbial - **words** (adverbs), **phrases** or **clauses** that add information to a **verb**, **adjective** or other adverbial

alliteration - use of one sound to begin two or more **words**

analyse - examine carefully, to improve understanding

analysis - careful examination that improves understanding

antonyms - **words** with opposite meanings

argument - explanation of an idea with the purpose of changing or guiding someone's **opinions** and/or actions

argument text - text that presents and explains an idea with the purpose of changing or guiding someone's **opinions** and/or actions

article (text type) - usually factual piece of writing about a given topic (e.g. news / magazine / internet article)

autobiography - **biography** someone writes about their own life

biography - **account** of someone's life

bullet point - the symbol '•', used to organise a vertical **list** by introducing each new item

capital letter - upper-case version of a letter, commonly used at the start of **sentences** and for proper **nouns**

character - fictional person in a **story**, play or film

chronological - in a manner showing the order in which events happen or happened

clause - group of more than one **word**, including a **verb**

cliché - **phrase** or idea that is overused and so has lost its impact

climax (in a story) - moment of greatest **conflict**

comma splice - incorrect use of a comma to link two **main clauses**

comparison - looking at similarities and differences between two or more things

conclusion (of a text) - last part, often a result or summary

concrete noun - **noun** that names a physical thing you can see, hear, smell, taste or touch (e.g. 'cat'; 'tree')

conflict (in a story) - challenge or opposition

conjunction - **word** used to connect **clauses**, or before the final item in a **list**

connotation - connected idea

consonant - letter of the alphabet that is not a **vowel**

context - situation or **setting** for a **word** or event that helps to explain it

contraction - shortened form of two or more **words**, using an apostrophe to show where letters have been missed out

coordinating conjunction - **conjunction** used to link two **clauses** with equal importance

counter-argument - **argument** against a first argument, presenting an objection and/or opposing views

description / descriptive writing - writing that aims to create a vivid image in the reader's mind

determiner - **word** (such as 'the' and 'a') that begins a **noun** or **noun phrase**, indicating whether the noun names something general or specific, and **plural** or **singular**

diagram - simple picture used to illustrate a point or idea, usually in **non-fiction**

dialogue - speech between people or fictional **characters**

direct address - method of speaking directly to the reader or listener

direct speech - **words** exactly as they are spoken, usually given within **speech marks** and with an **identifier**

embedded quotation - **quotation** positioned inside a **sentence** and that functions as a part of the sentence

emotive language - **words** and **phrases** that stir readers' emotions

emphasis - forcefulness of expression that suggests importance

evidence - supporting **facts** or information

example - something with characteristics typical of its type

explanation text - text that makes information and ideas clear and easy to understand

exposition (in a story) - early part of a **story** that introduces the situation, **characters** and/or **setting**

extract - short passage taken from a text or other source

fact - true and proveable idea

fiction - imagined idea, often a **story**

figurative language - **words** and **phrases** with meanings different from but related to their usual ones, based on their **connotations** (e.g. **similes** and **metaphors**)

finite verb - **verb** that shows **tense** and **person** (e.g. I saw, he made)

first person - storytelling **viewpoint** where the person doing the action is the writer, **speaker** or **narrator**, using the **pronouns** 'I' and 'me'

flashback - scene that shows events from the past

form (of a text) - shape and **structure**

formal (language) - suitable for an audience that is important, in authority or not known

fronted - positioned at the start of a **sentence**

future - **verb tense** indicating that actions or events will happen but have not happened yet

heading - main title

homophones - **words** that sound alike but have different spellings and different meanings

identifier - **phrase** that tells the reader who is speaking (e.g. 'he said'; 'they shouted')

imperative verb - **verb** that gives a command or instruction (e.g. 'go'; 'come')

impression - idea or **opinion** (about something or someone)

inference - use of clues to work something out

infinitive - root form of a **verb**, preceded by 'to'

informal (language) - casual; suitable for peers

information text - see **explanation text**

instruction text - text that tells readers how to do something

intention - desired effect

introduction (of a text) - beginning, often establishing **context**

key points - most-important ideas in a text

leaflet - sheet or sheets of paper, sometimes folded, including key information on a topic (often used in advertising)

letter (text type) - written way of communicating with a person or organisation, usually sent using a postal service

line (in a play) - single line of text, or one instance of **words** spoken by a **character**

line (in a poem) - **sentence** or part of a sentence that finishes at the end of a line

list - **sequence** of connected items written one after another

main body (of a text) - majority of the writing in a text (as opposed to, for example, an **introduction** and/or **conclusion**)

main clause - **clause** that makes a main point in a **sentence**, and that could stand alone

metaphor - description of something as though it is something else

modal verb - auxiliary **verb** that expresses possibility or importance

modify (a word) - make small alterations to, by adding to or changing meaning (e.g. with an **adjective** or **adverb**)

multi-clause sentence - **sentence** composed of more than one **clause**

myth - traditional **story**, often about early history or explaining natural events

narration - description by a **story**'s **narrator**

narrative - **account** of connected events, often **fiction**

narrator - **character** who is telling the **story**

non-fiction - factual writing; representing truth

non-finite clause - **clause** that contains a **non-finite verb**

non-finite verb - **verb** that does not show **tense**, such as an **infinitive verb** or **present participle**, meaning it does not indicate when something happened

noun - **word** that names a person, place, object or idea

noun phrase - group of **words** containing a **noun** that name a single person, place, object or ideas

object (of a sentence) - thing that is being acted on by a **verb** or **preposition**

onomatopoeia - technique of using a **word** that sounds like its meaning

opinion - personal ideas that may or may not be based on **facts**

paragraph - group of related **sentences** that develop an idea, presented as a block of text

passive voice - form in which the thing that is being acted on by a **verb** or **preposition** is the grammatical **subject**, rather than **object**, of a **sentence**

past continuous - **verb tense** indicating that events or actions in the past were still happening when something else happened (e.g. The sun was shining when the elephant came out of the jungle)

past participle - **verb** form indicating completed events or action (e.g. walked)

past perfect - **verb tense** indicating events or actions in the past that happened before something else (e.g. Jan looked for Ben but he had already left)

past tense - **verb tense** indicating that events or actions happened in the past

person (of a verb) - manner in which **verb** forms change depending on the person doing the action

personification - **metaphor** that uses human qualities to describe something non-human

persuasive text - text designed to change or guide someone's **opinions** and/or actions

phrase - group of more than one **word**, without a **verb**

plural - indicating more than one

poetry - stylised text structured by the **rhythm** of language, often used to express ideas or feelings

point of view - **opinion**, or manner in which events are experienced

preposition - **word** that expresses how things are connected, for example by place or time (e.g. 'in'; 'with'; 'before')

prepositional phrase - group of **words** that begins with a **preposition**

present continuous - **verb tense** indicating that events or actions are happening now (e.g. I am walking)

present participle - **verb** form indicating continuous events or action (e.g. walking)

present perfect - **verb tense** indicating that events or actions that happened in the past are still having an effect (e.g. I have left: I left in the past, but am still absent)

present tense - **verb tense** indicating events or actions that are currently happening

presentational features - features used to organise content visually, such as **headings** and **subheadings**

pronoun - **word** that replaces or stands in for a **noun** or **noun phrase**

proofread - check writing for errors

prose - written or spoken language in its ordinary form - such as in stories or explanations - as opposed to **poetry**

punctuate - give **punctuation** (to)

punctuation - symbols used to assist and alter meaning (e.g. full stops, question marks, exclamation marks, dashes, commas and apostrophes)

quotation - words taken from a text or speech and repeated

quotation marks - see **speech marks**

reasoning - clear, logical explanation or **argument**

register - tone and style of language (see **formal** and **informal**)

relative clause - **clause** that adds information to a **noun** or **noun phrase**, beginning with a **relative pronoun**

relative pronoun - **word** that indicates information related to a **noun** or **noun phrase**

repetition - technique of doing or saying something more than once

reported speech - **summary** or paraphrasing of speech that is included in a writer's or **narrator**'s description

resolution (in a story) - settling and/ or explanation of **conflict**

response - reaction; reply

review - evaluate critically

revise - make changes, or recap learning

rhetorical device - language technique that a writer or speaker uses to present ideas persuasively

rhetorical question - question asked when an answer is not expected

rhyme (noun) - similar sounds at the end of two or more **words** or **lines**

rhythm - beat or pulse

scan - look through (a text) for something specific

scene (of a play) - continuous piece of action within a play, often based in a particular **setting**

script - written text of a play or film

second person - storytelling **viewpoint** where the person doing the action is the reader or listener, using the **pronoun** 'you'

sentence - group of **words** that is complete in itself, including a **verb** and a **subject** (sometimes implied): a statement, question, exclamation or command

sequence (verb) - arrange things in a particular order

setting - location

'silent' letters - letters that are not sounded independently when a **word** is spoken aloudsimile - comparison made by using the **words** 'like' or 'as'

simple past - **verb tense** (see **past tense**)

simple present - **verb tense** (see **present tense**)

single-clause sentence - **sentence** composed of only one **clause**

singular - indicating only one

skim-read / skim - look very quickly (at a text) for an idea of its content

slang - informal **words** or **phrases**, often used amongst friends

speaker (in a poem) - see **narrator**

speech marks - **punctuation** marks indicating **direct speech**

stage direction - instruction to people acting in or producing a play, for example about where to stand or what to do

Standard English - English that is grammatically correct

stanza - group of **lines** in a poem (sometimes referred to as a 'verse')

statistic - **fact** relating to numerical information

story - retelling of events, either real or fictional

structure (noun) - manner in which parts of something are organised, arranged and related

subheading - smaller **heading** that appears below a main title, used to signal different topics within a longer piece of writing

subject (of a sentence) - **noun** that is the focus of a **sentence**, usually representing what or who is doing the action described by the **verb**

subordinate clause - **clause** that adds information to a **main clause** (for example about cause, effect, time, condition or concession)

subordinating conjunction - **conjunction** used to link a **subordinate clause** to a **main clause**

summary - brief description of the main points

superlative - **adjective** that shows the highest level of the quality described (e.g. 'biggest'; 'most hungry')

syllable - part of a **word** that makes a single sound

synonyms - **words** with the same or very similar meanings

synopsis - see **summary**

tense (of a verb) - manner in which **verb** forms change depending on when the action happens

terminology - technical and/or specialised **vocabulary**

theme - overall subject or idea

third person - storytelling **viewpoint** where the person or thing doing the action is not the writer, speaker or **narrator**, using the **pronouns** 'he', 'him', 'she', 'her', 'it', 'they' and 'them'

topic sentence - **sentence** that clearly states the topic of a **paragraph**

triple structure - persuasive pattern of three ideas

verb - **word** that names an action or state of being

viewpoint - perspective when telling a **story**

vocabulary - **words** used

vowel - A, E, I, O or U (letter of the alphabet that is not a **consonant**)

word - arrangement of letters that has one unit of meaning

word class - group of **words** that have similar roles in **sentences**

Published by Pearson Education Limited, 80 Strand, London, WC2R 0RL.
www.pearsonglobalschools.com

Text © Pearson Education Limited 2020
Designed by Pearson Education Limited 2020
Typeset by PDQ Digital Media Solutions Ltd
Project managed by Just Content Ltd
Produced by Just Content Ltd and Danielle Whisker
Edited by Hannah Hirst-Dunton, Liliane Nénot and Judith Shaw
Cover design © Pearson Education Limited 2020
With thanks to Sarah Ryan

Cover images: Shutterstock/Song_about_summer

First published 2020

Second impression 2020

British Library Cataloguing in Publication Data
A catalogue record for this book is available from the British Library

ISBN 978 0 435 20075 6

Printed in the UK by Ashford Colour Press Ltd